MONKEY
BUSINESS

MARVIN OLASKY & JOHN PERRY

THE TRUE STORY OF THE SCOPES TRIAL

MONKEY BUSINESS

Nashville, Tennessee

Printed in the United States of America

Ten-Number ISBN: 0805431578
Thirteen-Digit ISBN: 978085431575

Published by Broadman & Holman Publishers
Nashville, Tennessee

Dewey Decimal Classification: 973.91
Subject Heading: SCOPES TRIAL / EVOLUTION / CREATIONISM

1 2 3 4 5 6 7 8 9 10 10 09 08 07 06 05

To all those over the past eighty years who have shown courage in the face of ridicule by stating, "In the beginning God created the heavens and the earth."

This world, after all our science and sciences,
is still a miracle.

—Thomas Carlyle

Contents

Introduction

WHY DOES THE TRIAL of a small-town Tennessee schoolteacher eighty years ago still stir such passionate debate? Why have so many myths attached themselves to the historical account of a dozen July days in 1925? Like barnacles on a ship, a thick layer of Hollywood fiction, junk science, and political spin covers what truly happened at the Scopes trial in Dayton, Tennessee.

The creation debate is as intense as ever because it's as important as ever: what we believe about where we came from determines what we believe about everything else.

Scientists and academics now close ranks to declare evolution an accomplished fact, bristling at any suggestion otherwise. The title of the *National Geographic* cover feature for November 2004 states it plainly enough: "Was Darwin Wrong? NO. The Evidence for Evolution is Overwhelming." The article describes evolution as "a theory you can take to the bank . . . the supporting evidence is abundant, various, ever increasing, solidly interconnected, and easily available in museums, popular books, textbooks, and a mountainous accumulation of peer-reviewed scientific studies. No one needs to, and no one should, accept evolution merely as a matter of faith."

Yet later in the same article, writer David Quammen admits that "the fossil record is like a film of evolution from which 999 of every 1,000 frames have been lost on the cutting room floor." Herein lies the mystery: how can we take a theory to the bank if 99.9 percent of its proof is missing? The same scientific establishment—the Mandarins of Science, Phillip Johnson calls them—that insists we accept evolution as an accomplished fact relies on filling in a great many theoretical blanks with hypotheses. William Jennings Bryan dismissed these scientific suppositions as "a bunch of guesses strung together." Then and now, the evolutionist position teeters not because its ideas aren't true, but because they've never won a fair fight.

Twenty-first century Americans, many of them, are astounded to learn that Bryan prevailed in Tennessee and that John Scopes was convicted despite the fact that he almost certainly never taught evolution. Mistaken assumptions and oversimplifications concerning the Scopes trial still abound, and the results of the 2004 election brought many of them back into the public eye. Historian Robert Dallek wrote that "Somewhat like the 2000 and 2004 elections, Scopes was a clash of the coasts and big cities in the upper Midwest on one hand, and the millions of generally less educated, white Protestants in the South and prairie states, on the other." But is that all it was?

New York Times columnist Maureen Dowd, while praising William Jennings Bryan because he was economically on the left, went on a rampage against the cultural position which she saw Bryan and President Bush sharing: "W.'s presidency rushes backward, stifling possibilities, stirring intolerance, confusing church with state, blowing off the world, replacing science with religion, and facts with faith. We're entering another dark age, more creationist than cutting edge . . . the Bushies cocoon in a scary, paranoid, regressive reality. Their new health care plan will probably be a return to leeches." But is that what Bryan and those on his side in the Scopes trial wanted?

Was the Scopes trial nothing but a clash between educated urbanites and the great unwashed? Did believers in creation want to turn back the clock to a dark age of superstition and fear? The truth doesn't end with the answers to these questions, it begins with them. In Darwin's time as in 1925, intelligent people on both sides had spiritual reasons for coming down as they did in the evolution debate. In 1925 as in 2005, scientists' beliefs about God generally determined what they discovered about the universe.

Bryan's modern counterparts aren't railing against contemporary science and free intellectual inquiry: they invite it. No, they demand it. And so should everybody. Even scientists and intellectuals.

CHAPTER 1

Desperate Dayton

IT ALL STARTED with a big bang. Actually there were three of them.

The first stirring of events leading up to the "Trial of the Century" took place just after seven o'clock on Friday morning, December 20, 1895, almost thirty years before the trial and nearly five years before its famous defendant, John Thomas Scopes, was born.

An explosion in a mine owned by the Dayton Coal and Iron Company ripped through an entrance tunnel for more than a mile, burning some miners beyond recognition and crushing others in a hail of slate from the tunnel roof and walls. A miner's lamp had touched off a pocket of gas, possibly due to someone carrying an open flame beyond a warning mark placed by an inspector less than thirty minutes before.

Twenty-nine miners died, including a father and son and several boys; the youngest was fourteen. The *Nashville Banner* proclaimed it the "most appalling catastrophe in the history of East Tennessee. . . . The tragic event came so suddenly and is so horrible in its details that the people are dazed and wander aimlessly about, crying." The *Chattanooga News* declared, "In years to come, mothers will tell their children of the awful calamity which occurred . . . and for generations the people of Dayton will revere the dark days of the city." Those rescued alive were treated at the scene and carried to their homes to recover; the dead were brought home to be prepared for burial. It was the greatest disaster and the worst loss of life in the history of Dayton, Tennessee.

The explosion signaled the beginning of the end for the Dayton Coal and Iron Company and the start of a long and agonizing decline in the fortunes of Dayton, a picturesque county seat on the west bank of the Tennessee River that had grown prosperous on the labor of its men and the capital of its far-off benefactors.

Dayton Coal and Iron was wholly owned by Titis Salt and Sons, Ltd., of Saltaire, England, founded by Sir Titis Salt, MP, a wealthy textile manufacturer who wanted to branch out into other operations. Low-grade iron smelters had been operating in Rhea County for more than sixty years by the time Sir Titis's son and heir, also named Titis, began buying up land and primitive equipment in the area in 1879. Soon Salt and Sons owned almost twenty-four thousand acres in the county plus the mineral rights to nearly four thousand more.

The planned operation combined iron ore mining, coal mining, and coking, the process of converting coal into coke by heating it under controlled conditions. Coke was then used as furnace fuel to refine the iron ore. In fulfilling Salt's dream, Dayton found itself prospering beyond anything imaginable only a year or two before. Twenty carloads of railroad rails arrived from England. Local workers set out to prepare a right-of-way and lay miles of track. Salt ordered two hundred coke ovens and wanted them fast. Tennesseans flocked to the work and built three kilns to supply fifty thousand bricks at a time for oven construction. They assembled two giant blast furnaces, along with an engine house, crating house, a store, and other structures. The company built more than two hundred houses for miners and their families, and spent $15,000 on an especially handsome home for the general manager, J. A. Ferguson. It was a Victorian masterpiece with ten bedrooms and the finest furnishings available. Salt and his associates also used it on their annual visits to the premises.

By the time the first mine opened in September 1885, land prices within two miles of the city had tripled to $200 an acre, and an estimated two thousand people were employed by Dayton Coal and Iron. Rhea County had a population of fewer than five thousand, so men and boys from surrounding counties found plenty of work as well. On February 8, 1889, according to the *Chattanooga Times,* the company paymasters handed out $20,000. Miners' wages were only seventy-five cents a day, paid in company scrip, but the total effect of all the jobs in construction, manufacturing, transportation, management, accounting, and other areas gave Dayton and Rhea County a boomtown atmosphere. The smelting furnaces glowed day and night as smoke roiled from stacks more than a hundred feet above the town.

Successful as it all was, this massive undertaking by 1884 stood on financial underpinnings as fragile and unpredictable as a mine tunnel roof. Titis Salt and Sons secretly reorganized that year to gain access to new capital from James Watson & Company, iron merchants of Glasgow, Scotland. The next year a British member of the board of directors replaced Mr. Ferguson as general manager; the new boss ran the company from Cincinnati.

Tariffs enacted in 1890 to protect America's textile industry from foreign competition began hurting the company's core textile business. Accidents, strikes, and lawsuits so dampened the spirits of investors and directors that in the summer of 1892 directors sold the Dayton operation to Watson & Company. The nationwide depression of 1893 led to more losses and the decision to cut wages by 10 percent. Many employees walked out, and the giant furnaces went dark for more than three months, giving local bankers and businesses an abrupt taste of what life in Dayton would be like without the money that coal and iron operations brought in.

The company shook off another strike in January 1894. Two mines were now operating, and the company continued to invest in equipment, building sixty more coke ovens and a steam-powered conveyer system, and installing $20,000 worth of electrical pumping gear. On October 28, 1895, Dayton Coal and Iron was again secretly reorganized in Britain with a capitalization of £50,000. Shareholders and directors seemed intent on protecting their investment in Tennessee. Unlike many iron works the Dayton facilities had the great advantage of ore, coal, coking ovens, limestone (used in the coking process), and furnaces all in one area, keeping costs low and productivity high. With the company newly capitalized and world markets improving, the owners had every reason to be optimistic.

Then came the big bang of December 20. Fearing lawsuits, Watson & Company deeded the property of Dayton Coal & Iron to individual directors and reorganized again under a new charter to shield their assets. After settling the last death claim—the highest individual payout was only $400—Watson & Company reclaimed the property in 1898. Given Dayton's workers, coal, and ore, the company seemed ready to thrive. But then a second mine explosion shook both the hills along Richland Creek and the financial bedrock of the town's economy.

On May 27, 1901, a stick of dynamite set to loosen a coal seam by exploding inside a small cavity instead ignited a layer of coal dust, causing a blast so violent that it destroyed the iron rail carts used to transport coal to the mouth of the mine. Twenty men died instantly, simultaneously incinerated and thrown violently against the tunnel wall, leaving thirteen widows and forty-six fatherless children. Several other workers died within the week. Nashville papers reported that the "mine horror of 1895" was "almost equaled" on this tragic spring day. Mining stopped for weeks so fallen rock could be cleared out and the tunnel and cart rails repaired.

Another disaster—the last of the three big bangs—came only ten months later, on March 31, 1902, when a dynamite explosion once more set off a concentration of coal dust, this time killing twenty-five miners. Watson & Company's troubles mounted. The Dayton furnaces, once described by Titis Salt Jr. as "the two finest furnaces on the American continent," had become inefficient and expensive compared with newer designs. Attempts to modernize the Dayton works failed to make them competitive. Finally in 1913 Watson & Company went bankrupt, and Dayton Coal and Iron sank along with it. In one final tragedy Peter Donaldson, a Scotsman who was president and managing director of both companies, committed suicide in London by chaining himself inside his motorcar and driving into the River Thames.

Desperate to salvage something of the operation that had fueled their economy for a generation, local leaders and businessmen considered what they might do with the company's considerable assets in the county, including six coal mines, an iron ore mine, more than thirty thousand acres of land, and a large number of mules and livestock. Out of the ashes of bankruptcy, the Dayton Iron Co. was incorporated on November 28, 1916, but it survived less than a year. A group of former employees tried to take it over; their effort came to nothing.

Others also failed to revive the once-great company. The last attempt was the formation of the Cumberland Coal & Iron Company in about 1925. By this time the huge furnaces that loomed over the town had been cold for years and the coal mines abandoned and flooded with creek water, their entrances covered with barbed wire. Iron ore mining was the one activity that had survived the original bankruptcy, and portions of the railroad network built over the years to serve the ore operation were still in service. The company also owned vast tracts of timber and farmland.

Dayton's economy was still poor, though. Nationwide the Roaring Twenties lifted the stock market, automobile ownership skyrocketed, and Rudolph Valentino and Mary Pickford became movie millionaires, but Dayton struggled for financial security and self-respect. Furniture factories, textile mills, and commercial strawberry growers provided some employment, but population in the area fell by more than half as laborers, office workers, and managers moved on in search of jobs.

Few people were in a better position to see how far Dayton had fallen than George Washington Rappleyea, a metallurgical engineer and manager of Cumberland Coal & Iron. From his office he could look out and see the abandoned equipment and wire-covered mine entrances that recalled the company's glory days. Rappleyea was thirty-one in 1925, a transplanted New Yorker who met his future wife, Ova, when she was a nurse in Chattanooga and he was her patient in the hospital. (Depending on the source, he arrived either via snakebite or a pick-up football injury.) Rappleyea, a short, energetic man, was a snappy dresser with tousled hair under his straw boater. He loved dancing and tennis and always seemed to be in motion.

On May 4, 1925, George Rappleyea read a notice in the *Chattanooga Daily Times* placed by the American Civil Liberties

Union of New York. It concerned a Tennessee state law passed two months previously that made it a misdemeanor for any teacher in a school supported by public funds "to teach any theory that denies the story of the Divine Creation of man as taught in the Bible, and to teach instead that man has descended from a lower order of animals."

The ACLU press release said: "We are looking for a Tennessee teacher who is willing to accept our services in testing this law in the courts. Our lawyers think a friendly test case can be arranged without costing a teacher his or her job. Distinguished counsel have volunteered their services. All we need now is a willing client."

Though only two states, Oklahoma and Florida, had previously banned the teaching of evolution, several others had tried: a ban in the Kentucky legislature failed by one vote, and the debate was high-profile national news, as the ACLU's attention indicated. In 1923 the Southern Baptist Convention, the country's largest Protestant denomination, had declared the Bible and evolution incompatible. The Anti-evolution League of America was mounting a nationwide campaign to drive Darwinism from public education. The director of the American Museum of Natural History, Henry Fairfield Osborn, felt compelled to issue a statement reconciling science with religion. Walter Lippmann, influential columnist for the *New York World*, considered the rising tide of anti-Darwinism a threat to education. An ACLU survey released in April 1925 claimed more restrictions on school curriculum had been enacted in the previous six months than at any other time in American history.

Rappleyea attended the Methodist church in Dayton and personally believed that evolution and Christianity were not mutually exclusive. He had written a letter to the Chattanooga paper opposing the anti-evolution law, claiming that "John Wesley, the founder of Methodism, . . . advanced the theory of evolution of man 100 years before Darwin."

But in the ACLU newspaper announcement that spring afternoon, George Rappleyea saw something beyond a law or an argument. He saw a national cause in search of a focal point, a national stage casting for a willing star. Surrounded by the rusted relics of Dayton's prosperous past, he saw in the ACLU appeal a chance to put his struggling community in the national spotlight. Big news would generate big crowds, and that meant big business—maybe even a return to the glory years.

Here was a unique and awesome opportunity. The energetic young mining engineer had no intention of letting it slip away.

CHAPTER 2
A City's Opportunity

THE NATIONAL CIVIL LIBERTIES BUREAU, founded in 1917 as a "bureau for advice and help to conscientious objectors" to keep them from being drafted during World War I, was rechartered as the American Civil Liberties Union in 1920. Its founder, Roger Nash Baldwin, spent nine months in prison for refusing to report for his draft physical.

After the war and the draft ended, the ACLU cast about in several directions for causes to support: unions, socialists, and at least initially, Russian Communism. Many prominent and talented lawyers volunteered their time to defend cases the ACLU deemed unconstitutional intrusions into the public rights of "free press, free speech, peaceable assembly, liberty of conscience, and freedom from unlawful search and seizure," as an early pamphlet explained.

The organization had a steady flow of money from wealthy sympathizers, and Baldwin's legendary frugality made balancing the books even easier. What the ACLU needed more than cash was publicity: to that end Baldwin and the rest of the leadership constantly scanned the political and social landscape for government actions they could challenge or laws they could test. With their original rationale gone,

ACLU leaders moved from one cause to another in defense of free speech and free thought.

Executive committee meetings at the ACLU opened with a "Report on the Civil Liberty Situation for the Week," in which Baldwin went down his list of newsworthy events and reported on anything the group might be interested or involved in. One source of information for these meetings was the stack of newspaper clippings collected by Lucille B. Milner, indefatigable secretary of the ACLU and Baldwin's part-time lover. Thumbing through a paper in spring 1925 she noticed a story, "Tennessee Bars the Teaching of Evolution," about Tennessee Governor Austin Peay signing the Butler Act on March 21, making it illegal to teach any theory in opposition to divine creation and teach instead that man descended from "a lower order of animals."

Rather than adding the Tennessee item to her stack, Milner showed it to Baldwin immediately. According to a later account by Baldwin, he was already familiar with the issue, but he and Milner agreed on the spot that enactment of the law signaled an important opportunity to promote the ACLU and its liberal agenda. The evolution/creation debate had simmered and spewed all over the country; here was a clear-cut law to attack.

At the next executive committee meeting, Milner presented the Butler Act story. The committee agreed as one to challenge it immediately, thinking the case might eventually come before the U.S. Supreme Court. All the ACLU needed was a client willing to violate the law. The committee issued a press release to run in Tennessee newspapers soliciting teachers to participate in a "friendly test case."

Along with the ACLU notice in the May 4 *Chattanooga Daily Times,* a front-page story read, "There is little likelihood that the test case proposed by a Northern organization will be staged here." Superintendent Ziegler of the Chattanooga schools insisted his district had no interest in the offer. Darwinian theory, he explained, "is recognized by all our teachers . . . as a debatable theory and, as such, has no place in our curriculum." The superintendent in Knoxville, seventy or so miles up the Tennessee River, also declined, saying,

"Our teachers have a hard enough time teaching the children how to distinguish between plant and animal life."

As George Rappleyea read these accounts of the ACLU's offer and the two largest cities in eastern Tennessee turning them down, his big, round eyes may have grown wider still behind his thick glasses. Dayton could gain national, even worldwide attention: Rappleyea quickly contacted Frank E. "Doc" Robinson, chairman of the Rhea County School Board and owner of Robinson's Drug Store in Dayton.

According to Robinson, Rappleyea said, "Mr. Robinson, you and [local attorney] John Godsey are always looking for something that will get Dayton a little publicity. I wonder if you have seen the morning paper." The druggist had seen the paper but missed the ACLU notice. Rappleyea excitedly told him about the challenge to the Butler Act and what it could mean for the local economy. With his New York background, Rappleyea thought he might have some connections that could help secure the deal.

The next day, May 5, Rappleyea and Robinson met at the drug store where—this being the Prohibition era—townspeople of every age gathered throughout the day for refreshment, gossip, and informal business. They brought a few other men into the conversation. Staged reenactment photos of the meeting show a crowd of ten men sitting and standing around a tiny round soda fountain table, with drugstore shelves in the background and empty Coca-Cola glasses on a nearby counter. According to one eyewitness, though, the men talking as plans took shape were Rappleyea; Robinson; Mr. Brady, who ran the town's other drugstore; Sue Hicks, identified as the town's leading lawyer, who had been arguing for the Butler Act; Wallace Haggard, another attorney, whose father owned the leading bank and was "Mr. Dayton"; and a fellow who worked at the post office.

This account was given by John Thomas Scopes, who, until late in the meeting, was playing tennis down the street and had no inkling of the ACLU appeal or George Rappleyea's publicity plans.

The exact order of events that followed over the next few days, and even details of the events themselves, have been retold, reinterpreted, and spun to the point where no definitive account clearly emerges from the historical mist. At some point early on, the superintendent of schools in Rhea County, Walter White, endorsed Rappleyea's plan as a way to boost the local economy, even though he personally supported the antievolution legislation. Sue K. Hicks—a man named in honor of his mother, who died giving him birth—and his brother Herbert E. Hicks, Dayton's city attorneys, said they would prosecute the case if Rappleyea could find a volunteer who had taught evolution between March 21 when the Butler Act became law and May 1 when the school year ended at Central High School in Dayton.

The plan still lacked that crucial component: a teacher who had broken the law and was willing to be arrested for it. The logical man for the job was the school principal, W. F. Ferguson, who was also the biology teacher. Rappleyea called him on the telephone and explained the plan. Ferguson, a career educator with a wife and children, refused outright. This "friendly test case" could cost him his job, and he wanted no part of it.

Then someone (possibly Ferguson) suggested the name of Scopes, a young Kentucky native who had just finished his first year of teaching. Late the previous summer the high school football coach had unexpectedly resigned, and Scopes was hired on short notice to fill the vacancy. Recently graduated from the University of Kentucky, Scopes wanted to go on to law school but had to work a year or two first to save enough money.

Coach Scopes, one of the most popular teachers in school, also taught algebra, physics, and chemistry. Being single and younger than the other faculty, Scopes socialized more with the students and recent graduates than with his colleagues. The reason he might possibly fit into Rappleyea's plan was that at the end of the school year, when Mr. Ferguson was out sick, Scopes had taught a biology class for him that included a review of the textbook, which had been in Tennessee classrooms since 1909 and officially sanctioned by the state since 1919. The book included references to Darwin and evolution.

The drugstore caucus sent a boy to find Scopes. The boy spotted him playing doubles tennis with three members of his football team: Crawford Purser and C. L. Lott, who had just graduated, and Ross Cunningham, a younger student who lived on the corner by the school. The young messenger stood patiently by the clay court, watching until the two sides finished their point. Then he told Coach Scopes that Mr. Robinson wanted to see him down at the drugstore. The players finished the game but agreed to postpone the rest of their match until the coach found out what Mr. Robinson wanted. Scopes excused himself and walked the several blocks to Robinson's store.

Years later Scopes noted wryly that under normal circumstances he would have been home in Paducah after graduation on May 1. "If I hadn't lingered in Dayton," he mused, "there wouldn't have been any evolution trial there." He stayed on for two reasons: because of a car crash that injured two of his students the last week of school and because of a girl, "a beautiful blonde I had somehow previously overlooked," who had promised to let Scopes escort her to an upcoming church social. With that date to look forward to, "there was no chance of my leaving town prematurely," he admitted.

Inside the drugstore Scopes found Robinson, Rappleyea, and others waiting for him. Robinson had the soda jerk serve him a Coca-Cola, and Rappleyea began explaining their plan. Scopes liked the fast-talking mining engineer and had been a party guest in his home. Rappleyea started by asking Scopes if he agreed that no one could teach biology without teaching evolution.

"That's right," Scopes replied. Then he pulled a copy of the text off a nearby shelf—Robinson's sold school books—and showed it to the men. The over four hundred pages of *A Civic Biology*, by George William Hunter, Ph.D., included a five-page section on evolution, including a chart labeled "The Evolutionary Tree."

The accompanying lesson explained:

> Animal forms may be arranged so as to begin with very simple one-celled forms and culminate with a group which contains man himself. This arrangement is called the *evolutionary series*. Evolution means change, and these groups are believed by scientists to represent stages in complexity of development of life on earth. . . . The great English scientist, Charles Darwin, from this and other evidence, explained the theory of evolution. This is the belief that simple forms of life on earth slowly and gradually gave rise to those more complex.

Specifically concerning the final evolution of man, the text affirmed: "Undoubtedly there once lived upon the earth races of men who were much lower in their mental organization than the present inhabitants. If we follow the early history of man upon the earth, we find that at first he must have been little better than one of the lower animals. . . . At the present time there exist upon the earth five races or varieties of man . . . including . . . finally, the highest type of all, the Caucasians, represented by the civilized white inhabitants of Europe and America."

According to Hunter, this "wonderful discovery of the doctrine of evolution" came about in large part because of Darwin's "iron determination and undaunted energy."

Rappleyea asked Scopes if he had taught from the book. Scopes explained that yes, he had taken a copy from the stockroom at school and used it to prepare his review for Mr. Ferguson's class. "Then you've broken the law," Scopes later recalled Mr. Robinson saying. "So has every other teacher then," Scopes answered.

Robinson handed Scopes the Chattanooga paper and pointed out the ACLU article. "John," he asked, according to Scopes's account, "would you be willing to stand for a test case? Would you be willing to let your name be used?"

Though Scopes evidently didn't care much one way or another about the law and had made no public statement on it, he thought it was impossible to teach biology without teaching evolution and believed the Butler Act was a mistake. Years later he would explain his position in detail: "The Fundamentalists had an inalienable right to believe what they did, but when they insisted that others hold those beliefs too, they were violating other people's rights. They missed the spirit of Christ's teachings by clinging desperately to literal, narrow interpretations of the Bible. . . . Instead of growing with the advance of science and knowledge, they wanted everybody to get That Old Time Religion."

The fact was that Scopes had no specific recollection of teaching evolution during the few days he conducted the biology review on Mr. Ferguson's behalf. This detail seemed not to bother Robinson and Rappleyea. Scopes talked it over with Sue Hicks, a close friend who would be one of the prosecutors in any legal action. Hicks said he wouldn't mind prosecuting if Scopes would agree to the plan.

After some more talk John Scopes said, according to Hicks, "I'll be glad to do it!" (In his autobiography, Scopes recorded a less dramatic and more cagey reply: "If you can prove that I've taught evolution, and that I can qualify as a defendant, then I'll be willing to stand trial.")

Elated, the group went out to spread the news. Robinson called the newspapers in Chattanooga and Nashville while Rappleyea sent a telegram to the ACLU in New York. Rhea County school superintendent Walter White rounded up a local news stringer to give him a usable quotation: "Something has happened that's going to put Dayton on the map!"

The next day a front-page article in the *Nashville Banner* exclaimed:

> J. T. Scopes, head of the science department of the Rhea County high school, was . . . charged with violating the recently enacted law prohibiting the teaching of evolution in the public schools of Tennessee. Prof. Scopes is being prosecuted by George W. Rappleyea, manager of the Cumberland Coal and Iron Co., who is represented in the prosecution by S. K. Hicks. . . . The case is brought as a test of the new law. The prosecution is acting under the auspices of the American Civil Liberties Association [sic] of New York, which, it is said, has offered to defray the expenses of such litigation.

The Associated Press picked up the story, and by the time a panel of three justices of the peace formally charged Scopes on May 9, the young Kentucky schoolteacher was already a national celebrity.

Commenting on his decision to sign the Butler Act into law, Governor Austin Peay had told the state legislature, "I can find nothing of consequence in the books now being taught in our schools with which this bill will interfere in the slightest manner. . . . Nobody believes that it is going to be an active statute." If the governor sincerely expected that was the case, he underestimated both the passion and commitment of its proponents and the irresistible appeal of the notoriety that violating it would bring.

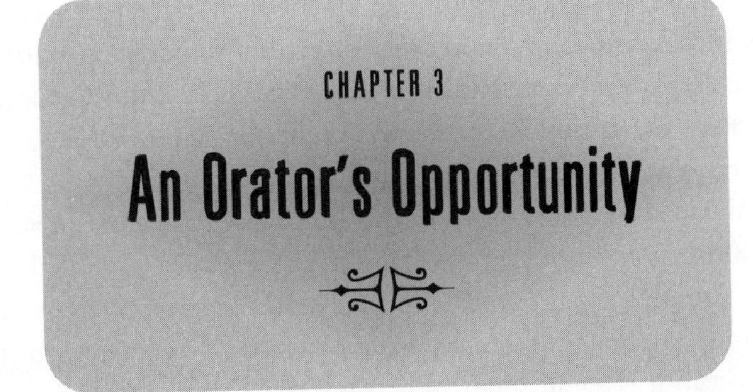

CHAPTER 3

An Orator's Opportunity

OTHER TENNESSEE TOWNS lost no time condemning Dayton's acceptance of the ACLU proposal as a cheap publicity stunt. In Nashville, the state capital, The *Tennessean* declared, "Apparently the 'booster' element in Dayton have with questionable wisdom and taste, seized on this as an opportunity to get widespread publicity for their city, evidently proceeding on the doubtful theory that it is good advertising to have people talking about you, regardless of what they are saying." The *Knoxville Journal* claimed, "The major actors on the Dayton stage [are] there for publicity and don't care three straws for what may be decided in the court." The *Chattanooga Times* condemned the whole business as "humiliating." The *Nashville Banner* wryly admitted, "Dayton could not have overlooked such an opportunity to secure front page advertising space throughout the civilized world."

Within a day or two of the first wire service news release, John Scopes was walking downtown when someone told him a man at the Hotel Aqua wanted to meet him. As he went through the front door, he heard someone say, "Mr. Neal, that is John Scopes now."

The stranger approached Scopes, stuck out his hand, and said, "Boy, I'm interested in your case, and whether you want me or not, I'm going to be here. I'll be available twenty-four hours a day." He was a disheveled-looking figure in need of a shave, with rumpled clothes and hair sticking out in every direction. But as Scopes was soon to learn, John Randolph Neal had earned a Ph.D. from Columbia at twenty-four and taught law at the University of Tennessee in Knoxville for fifteen years.

Neal had served two terms in the Tennessee legislature in addition to teaching law school and also taught in Colorado part of the year. But he crossed swords with university administrators over his lax appearance, frequent absences from class, and tendency to grade papers without reading them. When his contract was not renewed in 1924, he ran for governor but lost to Austin Peay and so opened his own private law academy in Knoxville.

The ACLU's newly appointed general counsel in New York, Arthur Garfield Hays, knew the wisdom of having for the Scopes case someone who knew the local people and local traditions and who would be somewhat familiar to the members of the jury. John Scopes took an immediate liking to the odd but brilliant Neal, and after discussions with the ACLU, the former law professor became chief counsel for the defense.

Meanwhile in Memphis, legendary orator William Jennings Bryan, three-time candidate for president of the United States and fiery apologist for fundamentalism, was speaking at the World's Christian Fundamentals Association annual meeting when the news broke of Scopes's arrest. Adapting his speech to the event, Bryan thundered, "People who hold the Bible dear should make themselves heard." He noted the challenge to Tennessee's new antievolution law and hoped it would be upheld.

WCFA leaders, remaining behind in Memphis for an unrelated meeting of the Southern Baptist Convention, believed the ACLU and the merchants of Dayton were staging the Scopes trial for their own benefit. They warned that a shoddy trial would derail their goal of affirming the truth of biblical creation and halting the teaching of evolution in public schools as a scientific fact. On May 13, with his proclamations on divine creation still ringing in their ears, the WCFA sent Bryan a telegram inviting him to appear on its behalf at the Scopes trial. Picking up the story, the *Memphis Press* telegrammed the Dayton team, "Will you be willing for William Jennings Bryan to aid the state in prosecution of J. T. Scopes?" Sue Hicks answered in the affirmative, then became the first of the prosecutors to contact Bryan directly, writing, "We will consider it a great honor to have you with us in the prosecution."

By the time Hicks's letter reached Bryan, he had already publicly accepted the WCFA offer, declaring, "We cannot afford to have a system of education that destroys the religious faith of our children. . . . There are about 5,000 scientists, and probably half of them are atheists, in the United States. Are we going to allow them to run our schools? We are not!" Bryan dashed off a quick note to Hicks: "I appreciate your invitation [and] shall be pleased to be associated with your forces in the case." He added in the margin, "I shall, of course, serve without compensation."

Bryan, through most of his career, had been compensated largely with fame and adulation. When he first commented for the record on the subject of Darwinism, he was already one of the most famous public figures in America. Born in Salem, Illinois, in 1860, he moved to Nebraska in 1887 to continue his law practice, then gained election to the U.S. House of Representatives in 1890 and 1892. In 1896 he ran for president against the Republican candidate, former Ohio Governor William McKinley, after giving an incendiary speech at the Democratic National Convention in Chicago on July 9, 1896. The speech attacked the U.S. gold standard, which meant that all the paper currency in America was backed by gold. A gold standard limited the amount of money in circulation and kept inflation down, but Bryan thought inflation would help farmers, debtors, small-town businessmen, and others on the lower end of the economic scale. He wanted a "bimetalism" or "free silver" standard using both metals.

In his speech Bryan insisted that only bankers and the wealthy benefited from the gold standard. Gold proponents could find "where the holders of fixed investments have declared for a gold standard, but not where the masses have." He roared, "The sympathies of the

Democratic party . . . are on the side of the struggling masses who have ever been the foundation of the Democratic party. . . . You come to us and tell us that the great cities are in favor of the gold standard; we reply that the great cities rest upon our broad and fertile prairies. Burn down your cities and leave your farms, and your cities will spring up again as if by magic; but destroy our farms and the grass will grow in the streets of every city in the country."

News accounts described twenty thousand delegates listening intently as Bryan concluded, "Having behind us the producing masses of this nation and the world, supported by the commercial interests, the laboring interests, and the toilers everywhere, we will answer their demand for a gold standard by saying to them: You shall not press down upon the brow of labor this crown of thorns,"—here he pantomimed placing a crown of thorns on his head—"you shall not crucify mankind upon a cross of gold!" On the last phrase he extended his arms to form a cross. He stood for a long moment in absolute silence, arms out, staring at his shoes. The hall was stifling. The hint of a breeze from Lake Michigan drifted through the windows.

The room erupted in wild shouts and deafening applause that turned into a forty-seven-minute demonstration. Bryan, the Great Commoner, received the party's nomination and launched his campaign against big-city interests and in favor of those "struggling masses." Positioning himself against business during the campaign, he said, "No one can earn a million dollars honestly." Bryan logged eighteen thousand railroad miles making speeches across the country, but McKinley played on concerns that a Bryan presidency would be bad for the economy and won both the popular vote and the electoral college.

Though Bryan ran twice more as the Democratic candidate, he never came so close to victory, losing again to McKinley in 1900 and to William Howard Taft in 1908. After Bryan helped to elect Woodrow Wilson in 1912, Wilson appointed him secretary of state, but Bryan resigned in 1915 when he opposed Wilson's policies that were likely to lead to war with Germany. After leaving Washington, Bryan became less involved in government and law and gave more speeches about topics at the intersection of politics, religion, and culture.

Bryan in the early 1920s was one of the most popular figures and greatest draws on the stages of church conventions, political and fraternal organizations, and Chatauqua events. He supported Prohibition, women's suffrage, world peace and disarmament, and a host of other popular causes. His voice was legendary: somehow, without seeming to strain or shout, he could be heard plainly by every member of a crowd of twenty thousand or more. He had never been a wealthy man, but in 1921 he moved to Florida and according to some accounts became a millionaire through successful land speculation. His Sunday school class there had an attendance of five thousand; his weekly Bible lesson was syndicated in one hundred newspapers with a readership totaling 15,000,000. Bryan was hot during what could have been a political winter.

He had long complained about evolution. His mention of it in 1904 came during a low point in his political career, when the Democrats had taken a conservative tack to try and regain the White House (their candidate that year, Alton B. Parker, lost to Theodore Roosevelt). Bryan's stump speech, "The Prince of Peace," covered a wide range of related topics including the person of Christ, the concept of peace, materialism, salvation, immortality, forgiveness, and others. "I offer no apology for writing upon a religious theme," he said, "for it is the most universal of all themes." It became his most popular address, delivered hundreds of times from coast to coast as well as in Egypt, India, Japan, and elsewhere.

The way the speech touched on evolution anticipated his later orations: he offered up the subject more as a conversation piece than a point of argument, and he disparaged it with the humor his audiences loved:

> I do not mean to find fault with you if you want to accept the theory [of Darwinian evolution]; all I mean to say is that while you may trace your ancestry back to the monkey if you find pleasure or pride in doing so, you shall not connect me with your family tree without more evidence than has yet been produced. . . . It is a dangerous theory. If a man links himself in generations with the monkey, then it becomes an important

> question whether he is going towards him or coming from him—and I have seen them going in both directions.

Light as the speech was in some places, it also made unequivocal distinctions:

> The ape, according to [Darwinian] theory, is older than man and yet the ape is still an ape while man is the author of the marvelous civilization which we see around us. . . . [The theory] does not explain the origin of life. . . . Go back as far as we may, we cannot escape from the creative act, and it is just as easy for me to believe that God created man as he is as to believe that, millions of years ago, He created a germ of life. . . .
>
> I object to the Darwinian theory, until more conclusive proof is produced, because I fear we shall lose the consciousness of God's presence in our daily life. . . . I fear that some have accepted it in the hope of escaping from the miracle [of Divine creation], but why should the miracle frighten us?

Audiences around the world ate it up, and as the years passed Bryan became increasingly strident in his views on evolution. Looking at the growing challenge to traditional standards in fashion, literature, music, and public behavior in the 1920s, he became convinced that the nation was losing its historic moral compass based on Christian precepts. He forecast a devastating moral decline unless trends changed: "There is no hope unless we can get back to a religion that makes men believe in God and a future life and give them a sense of responsibility. The world needs Christ." State legislatures began hotly debating a raft of laws aimed at curtailing the teaching of Darwinian theory or banning it altogether. Some thought evolution could be eliminated as a threat to national morality the same way alcohol had been purportedly eliminated by Prohibition in 1920.

At noon on January 24, 1924, Bryan delivered a speech in Nashville's Ryman Auditorium titled "Is the Bible True?" It was an unapologetic manifesto against evolution, delivered to an eager audience including Governor Peay and other important civic, political, and religious figures. "Evolution is an hypothesis," he stated. "What does hypothesis mean? . . . It means guess—GUESS. . . . If Darwin had called it a guess, it would not have lived a year; but 'guess' is too small a word for a scientist, so he blew into it and inflated it until it had four syllables in it—'hypothesis'—and then because it was empty it would float on the surface of public opinion."

Bryan was interrupted by hearty applause, then quickly resumed the hunt:

> What was Darwin's guess? That about two hundred millions of years ago, one of a few germs appeared on this planet . . . and then, according to Darwin, they immediately went to work reproducing. Not quite according to kind, but with just enough variation to give us finally between two and three millions of species. . . .
>
> This is the guess: A little animal that did not have any legs was just wriggling along on its belly one day, when all at once, without any notice in advance and without any premonitory symptom, a wart appeared on the belly—if that wart had appeared on the back, the whole history of the world would have been different, but luckily that wart appeared on the belly—and the little animal found it could use that little wart to work itself along a little and it worked itself along until it came to depend on that wart, and that developed the wart into a leg. People can believe this who cannot believe the Bible!

Loose interpretation of Darwinian theory though it was, Bryan's speech held the crowd spellbound. After it was over an ad hoc group called Friends of the Bible, the Friends of William Jennings Bryan, printed up thousands of copies and sent them all over the state. A year later, when the Tennessee legislature was debating state representative John Washington Butler's antievolution bill at the state capitol a few blocks down the street, W. B. Marr, the attorney who had invited Bryan to speak, sent five hundred copies of the speech to the legislators. State representatives approved Butler's bill 71 to 5; the state senate passed it 24 to 6. The bill became law, with Bryan's oration receiving some credit.

That Bryan believed in the creationist cause is clear. That he used his anti-Darwinism as a crowd pleaser is also clear. He garnered applause, but the sympathetic audiences that cheered him did not challenge him to delve into the nuances or to prepare for what a hostile questioner might throw at him.

"When I am defending a thing," Bryan declared, "I do not wait for the enemy to come and attack." In the matter of John Thomas Scopes of Dayton, Tennessee, the Great Commoner would be true to his word.

CHAPTER 4
Anticipation

THE NEXT STEP in the legal process was for a grand jury to indict John Scopes for violating the Butler Act. However, no jury was impounded and the next one would not be called until August. Within days of Scopes's arrest, Chattanooga boosters, seeing the whirlwind of publicity the story was generating, had a change of heart and began angling to have the trial there. Knoxville was a candidate too, as was larger and more politically liberal Nashville. The *Chattanooga Daily Times* offered John R. Neal the city's Memorial Auditorium, suggesting it might be better to have the trial in a bigger, more accessible place than Dayton. When that failed, the paper ran a story about the teaching of evolution in Chattanooga schools. The *St. Louis Post-Dispatch* published an editorial asking, "Why Dayton, of all places?"

Doc Robinson and W. E. Morgan answered with a booklet that replied, "Of all places, why not Dayton?" The Progressive Dayton Club had formed the Scopes Trial Entertainment Committee and was already preparing for the expected onslaught of visitors. Rappleyea, Neal, and the other chief instigators were adamant. No one would steal the spotlight from them if they could help it.

That spotlight grew far hotter the day Neal received a telegram from Clarence Darrow, perhaps the most famous and successful defense lawyer of the time and certainly one of the most flamboyant, offering to assist in defending Scopes. Darrow had most recently been in the national limelight as defense counsel for Nathan Leopold Jr. and Richard Loeb, Chicago-area teenagers who killed a thirteen-year-old acquaintance with a hammer, then demanded a $10,000 ransom from the boy's father. Though evidence against them was overwhelming, Darrow saved the defendants from the electric chair. (They received life imprisonment.)

Noted journalist H. L. Mencken, covering a convention in Richmond, Virginia, where Darrow was speaking, first proposed Darrow's involvement in the Scopes case. "Nobody gives a damn about that yap schoolteacher," Mencken said with trademark irascibility: "The thing to do is to make a fool out of Bryan." Though Darrow, at sixty-eight, had been talking of retirement, he couldn't resist such an enormous target. He wired Neal from New York, where he was consulting with a high-society divorce lawyer named Dudley Field Malone. Darrow worked with Malone, who had an office in Paris, to secure expensive but discreet French divorces for wealthy American clients. Darrow said he and Malone were "willing, without fees or expenses, to help the defense of Professor Scopes in any way you may suggest or direct."

Neal quickly accepted the offer, and the next day Darrow went on the attack: "Had Mr. Bryan's ideas of what a man may do towards free thinking existing throughout history, we would still be hanging and burning witches and punishing persons who thought the world was round." The ACLU, fearing Darrow was too much of a headline hunter and that the trial would become a circus, appealed directly to Darrow and Malone to step aside. But the two stood firm, insisting they would counterbalance Bryan's celebrity and oratorical skills.

Scopes himself eventually got his two cents' worth in and backed Darrow completely. "It was going to be a down-in-the-mud fight," he later wrote, "and I felt that situation demanded an Indian fighter rather than someone who graduated from the proper military academy." Meanwhile the people of Dayton, seeing their town could be replaced as the trial venue if the indictment waited until August, went into action. John T. Raulston, judge of the eighteenth judicial circuit, which covered seven east Tennessee counties and included Dayton, convened a special (and legally suspect) grand jury on May 25 to hear evidence against Scopes. Though he arrived late for the proceedings, the judge took time to pose for photographs and speak to reporters.

Thomas Stewart, attorney general for the eighteenth judicial district, presented the evidence. Stewart lived in Winchester, Tennessee, seventy air miles southwest across the Cumberland Plateau near the district border, and had moved temporarily to Dayton to prosecute the case. His straightforward approach was to introduce *A Civic Biology* into evidence, read passages from it to the jury, and call on several students to testify that Scopes used the book to teach them in the classroom. None of them knew anything significant about evolutionary theory, but according to a widely accepted account, Scopes himself secretly coached the boys in the back of a taxi to make sure their testimony produced the desired results. (Many years later Scopes wrote, "If the boys had got their review of evolution from me, I was unaware of it. I didn't remember teaching it. . . . Yet I am sure they had not perjured themselves.") One student said later that Scopes had definitely talked in class about Tarzan the Ape Man.

After Stewart was through, Judge Raulston read the Butler Act aloud, followed by the entire first chapter of Genesis. Charging the jury, he said in part, "If you find that the statute has thus been violated you should indict the guilty party promptly. . . . I make no reference to the policy or constitutionality of the statute, but to the evil example of the teacher disregarding constituted authority in the presence of those whose thought and morals he is to direct."

The jury returned an indictment before noon, affirming that John Thomas Scopes "did unlawfully and wilfully teach in the public schools . . . certain theory and theories that deny the divine story of the Bible, and did teach instead thereof that man has descended from a lower order of animals . . . against the peace and dignity of the state." Judge Raulston set the trial for July 10, "when all universities and schools will be through their terms of school in order that scientists, theologians and other school men will be able to act as expert witnesses." He suggested preparing a trial venue that would seat twenty thousand spectators.

When news of the indictment was released, reporters asked Scopes for a comment. "I am ready to go through with it," he replied simply. One reporter wrote that when pressed, Scopes started to explain his view that "Darwinian evolution is not incompatible with the idea of an ever-present, loving father of the universe." Neal quickly shut him up and hustled him down the street.

Over the next several weeks, the ACLU tried valiantly to regain control of the snowball it had rolled down the slope. Scopes and Neal went to New York to consult with a raft of high-profile lawyers including Bainbridge Colby, secretary of state under Wilson in 1920–21; Charles Evans Hughes, later chief justice of the U.S. Supreme Court, who resigned as an associate justice to run for president in 1916 against Wilson and who would presumably one day argue the Scopes case before the Supreme Court; and Felix Frankfurter, Harvard law professor, longtime ACLU supporter, and future Supreme Court justice.

Of all those who participated in the discussions, only Arthur Garfield Hays supported Darrow as defense counsel. (Scopes later wrote that Roger Nash Baldwin also supported Darrow in the meetings; Baldwin's biographer says he "opposed Darrow's appointment" because Baldwin "wanted to emphasize the issue of academic freedom" and because he wanted a more "respectable" figure such as Hughes.) When Baldwin finally asked Scopes who he wanted, the young teacher replied, "I want Darrow."

There would be still more jockeying behind the scenes, but in the end Scopes's defense team in court consisted of chief counsel John R. Neal "assisted" by Clarence Darrow, Dudley Field Malone, and Arthur Garfield Hays. On the prosecution side George Rappleyea had yielded his position as plaintiff to county school superintendent Walter White. (Among the several unproven theories for the change: Rappleyea had no strong personal objection to evolution whereas White did; White was more conservative in general; Rappleyea made too many enemies in town in the course of stage-managing his scheme.) The prosecution was directed by Attorney General Tom Stewart "assisted" by William Jennings Bryan, Sue and Herbert Hicks, local attorney Wallace Haggard, county judge Gordon McKenzie, and Gordon's heavyset and jovial father, Ben, a courthouse fixture for more than thirty years.

On his second trip to New York, John Scopes made the front page of the June 13 *New York Times*: "Scopes Refuses $50,000 Movie Offer Here; Stunned, He Pays $7.70 for a Show Ticket." The movie offer was news to him, though no one seemed to believe it. The price of a New York show was no doubt truly stunning to anyone earning Scopes's salary of $150 a month. Returning south, Scopes went home to his parents in Paducah to escape the hubbub for a while.

His father, Thomas Scopes, was born in the slums of London in 1860, trained as a marine machinist, and emigrated to America in 1885. Forty years later he retained hints of his Cockney accent and his love of a good cup of tea. He married Mary Alva Brown, a brown-eyed Kentucky native whose father was a Cumberland Presbyterian minister. Thomas was a successful railroad machinist who got involved in union politics after being fired for refusing to work as a strikebreaker.

The strike, in Chicago in 1894, affected two other men who would play important roles in John Scopes's story. The leader of the American Railway Union, Socialist activist Eugene V. Debs, was instrumental in starting the American Civil Liberties Union. When Debs faced conspiracy charges for destroying Chicago and Northwestern Railway equipment, the general counsel for the railroad, Clarence Darrow, resigned his job to defend him. It was Darrow's first taste of national acclaim.

As unlikely as the coming of the trial to Dayton had seemed, residents wanted to make the most of it. They cleaned and painted the big courtroom on the second floor of the Rhea County Courthouse and the halls leading to it. They rearranged seating to increase its capacity from six hundred to a widely reported one thousand—though standing in the room today it seems impossible that eight hundred could squeeze in, much less a thousand—and installed new telephone and telegraph lines. They built new public restrooms and replaced the water pump on the lawn with four modern push-button drinking fountains. The post office hired extra messengers and clerks. Refreshment and souvenir stands sprouted in empty fields and on sidewalks. Merchants planned to turn six blocks around the courthouse into a pedestrian mall to make room for even more hawkers and spectators.

Daytonites were shocked, then, to learn that Scopes, Neal, Hays, and Darrow had met in Cookeville, Tennessee, to argue that the case should be moved from the state circuit court to the federal court in Nashville, Knoxville, or Chattanooga. On July 4, the Associated Press reported from Chattanooga that the defense team was "in a quandary among themselves and that a split in the ranks threatens," and that "it is understood that it was Darrow's idea to ask for a federal court of injunction, and take the case away from Dayton altogether."

Scopes agreed that a federal trial would be cheaper and more likely to offer "a sedate educational approach," but federal judge John Gore in Cookeville rejected his plea and dashed the last hope for moving the trial out of Dayton. On July 7, the Associated Press reported from Dayton, where two telegraph lines would be manned day and night during the trial: "Tourists arriving, newspaper correspondents streaming into town on every incoming train, merchants, hotelkeepers, garage men, vendors and plain citizens point forward to Friday [July 10] as the beginning of things."

It seemed everybody had something to say about the upcoming trial. Interviewed before stepping aboard a Europe-bound liner, Dr. Grier Hibben, president of Princeton University, called the Butler Act "an outrageous law and nothing else. . . . Tennessee has been stampeded by William Jennings Bryan. He has swept the people of that state off their feet. Enforcement of such a law would end freedom of education in the United States." Bryan himself claimed that the real issue was "not what can be taught in schools, but who shall control the education system. . . . The case may be determined without any discussion whatsoever of the merit of evolution."

John Washington Butler originally had no plans to attend the trial but changed his mind when a wire service offered to pay him for his commentary. He explained to the Associated Press his rationale for the law: "The Bible is the foundation upon which rests the structure of our American government . . . [threatening the Bible threatens] the foundation of our government and even civilization itself." He knew personally of students whose faith had been weakened by teaching in the public schools. Since his constituents were paying for that teaching, they had the right to determine what was taught, and what they wanted was the Bible.

From his office in Chicago, Clarence Darrow fired a pretrial salvo:

> The man in the street is rising to the realization that his sacred rights are menaced. When that sort of realization crystalizes, it can raise more hell than red fire and mob excitement.
>
> Those who are behind the prosecution are honest. They believe with the zeal of the crusader and have no doubt they are right. The less men know, the fewer doubts they have. They are opening the doors for a reign of bigotry and heresy equal to anything in the Middle Ages. No man's belief will be safe if they win. They will not be satisfied with even a belief in Christ and Christianity, but will enforce their own sort of belief in them.

In Miami, Bryan honed his argument at a meeting of the Kiwanis Club on July 3. A week before the trial, his public statements still focused at least in part on the issue of who should decide what was taught in public schools. It was, he said, "absurd" to teach a subject as important as the origin of man "according to the teacher's own ideas." If evolution was right, Bryan told his audience, it would triumph. If facts proved it to be "a dangerous thing," then "the American people will find methods of enforcing their will."

Up the Atlantic coast in Jacksonville, Major Edward James Monroe agreed. The 109-year-old son of President James Monroe told an inquiring reporter, "I believe Adam was the first man, not the first monkey." Evolution was "bunk" he added, and "anyone who teaches it should go to jail!"

The citizens of Dayton threw themselves into their role. They may have opposed teaching evolution in school, but they saw nothing wrong with plastering monkeys everywhere. Signs welcomed visitors to "Monkeyville." A motorcycle policeman put "Monkeyville Police" across the front of his handlebars. Robinson's Drug Store advertised a Monkey Fizz. Robinson's became the local news clearinghouse, where reporters met, the public congregated, and the latest news was taped to the store windows for all to read. Hotel rooms went from $2.75 to $8.00 a night as their managers set up cots in the hallways.

The morning of July 7, William Jennings Bryan stepped off the Southern Railway *Royal Palm Limited* to great a throng of Dayton well-wishers. That was when, according to Scopes, "the monkey signs went down and the religious posters started going up."

The Progressive Dayton Club held a banquet in Bryan's honor that night at the Hotel Aqua that was by popular agreement the biggest social event in the town's history. Oddly enough Scopes was invited too. He was, after all, the one who had made the whole adventure possible. Scopes and Bryan sat across from each other at the head table and talked agreeably. Bryan reminded Scopes that they had met once before, when Bryan delivered the graduation address to Scopes's high school class in 1919 in Salem, Illinois; it was Bryan's hometown, and Scopes lived there several years as a teenager. Scopes and some friends had gotten the giggles and interrupted the speech when Bryan whistled his *s* sounds at the beginning of the address.

Mention of it made Scopes blush, but Bryan made light of the story. At the end of the meal, he asked Scopes for his uneaten corn and potatoes, which Scopes gave him, marveling at the older man's appetite.

Wednesday, July 8, Thomas Stewart drove in from his home in Winchester virtually unnoticed. Clarence Darrow arrived from Chicago the next day (his wife, Ruby, followed soon after) and met his colleagues Dudley Field Malone and Arthur Garfield Hays. Though no one had planned a welcoming banquet for Darrow, city leaders hastily set one up in order to give both sides equal treatment.

Darrow had arranged to bring a number of expert witnesses to Dayton to testify about evolution and the Bible, including the dean of the divinity school, the dean of the college of science, and the professor of anthropology at the University of Chicago. To give them a place to stay and the defense team a place to meet out of the public eye, the resourceful George Rappleyea fixed up the old Victorian mansion built for the original mine superintendent and the comfort of the well-heeled Scottish investors on their annual inspections. That became the defense headquarters.

At the courthouse officials installed telegraph keys, muffled so as not to disturb the proceedings, and a bank of telephone booths downstairs for the reporters. Preachers of every stripe and persuasion were streaming into town hoping to make their opinions known to the trial participants and perhaps save a few souls among the crowd; in some places a listener could hear three or four sermonettes at once. Some preached from a large platform outside along the north wall of the courthouse set up for Independence Day festivities. Vendors hawked food and souvenirs, including a monkey-shaped key fob for sixty-five cents. A truck fitted with electric loudspeakers, the first of its kind most townspeople had ever seen, cruised up and down the street promoting Bryan's Florida real estate developments.

Mountain folk came to see all the commotion shouldering their rifles as they always did, to the shock of outsiders. The story spread of a shoot-out in the local barbershop supposedly sparked by an argument over the trial; most sources agree that the argument was a publicity stunt staged by Rappleyea and that the gunman was firing blanks.

The only thing missing from the Scopes trial was Scopes. Some said he was home in Paducah resting or visiting his sick mother. But nearly eighty years later, Attorney General Tom Stewart's son, Tom Jr., who was eleven in the summer of 1925, provides a new twist on the story. He says Scopes was simply scared to death. What started out scarcely two months before as a discussion at Robinson's and a plan to garner a little publicity for the town had become a worldwide event. John Scopes was on the front page of the *New York Times,* and his name was known around the world. A newspaper in Japan was preparing to print the trial testimony every day. Radio station WGN was setting up a live radio feed via telephone line all the way to Chicago at the cost of $1,000 a day. Twenty-two Western Union telegraph operators set up a command post in a room off a grocery store. Reporters who couldn't find any other place to sleep lived in a big room over the hardware store: there they typed their dispatches. Scopes wanted to get away.

Rappleyea called Scopes at his parents' home and, according to the younger Stewart, ran up a huge long-distance bill trying to convince the skittish teacher to return to Dayton and finish what the two of them had started. Scopes was ready to call the whole thing off. But somehow Rappleyea persuaded him to return to Dayton and to what Scopes called, "one of the rarest collection of screwballs I have seen in my life."

At 9:00 AM on Friday, July 10, 1925, John T. Raulston of Gizzards Cove, Tennessee, judge of the eighteenth judicial district, entered the second-floor courtroom of the Rhea County Courthouse. The freshly painted room was packed to the walls, with people standing on tables and sitting in the windowsills to hear the case pitting a three-time presidential candidate against a trio of the most famous and successful defense lawyers in American history.

At the request of photographers, the judge remained standing while Scopes, Bryan, Darrow, and the other principal players on both sides posed around the bench. When the cameramen were finished, the judge took his seat, and the two groups returned to their tables.

Judge Raulston rapped his gavel. The din in the room softened but never stopped.

"The court will come to order. The Reverend Cartwright will open court with a prayer."

The reverend stood. "Oh God, our Divine Father, we recognize Thee as the Supreme Ruler of the universe. . . ."

CHAPTER 5

The Circus Begins

AS SOON AS Reverend Cartwright finished his lengthy prayer, John R. Neal suggested the court take a moment to introduce the visiting counsel on both sides. Tom Stewart stood and presented Bryan and his son, William Jr., "both of whom need no introduction," as the only two outside lawyers for the state. Neal rose in turn and introduced Darrow, Hays, Malone, and Darrow's law partner W. O. Thompson.

After exchanging pleasantries, Judge Raulston addressed Stewart's request for a new grand jury indictment. Stewart was worried that the jury that had indicted Scopes, convened on the fly in order to beat Chattanooga to the punch in responding to the ACLU, could be challenged later on. Another jury was impaneled, and the court recessed for a little over an hour, until eleven, for them to deliberate. At the appointed time court reconvened, the new jury reindicted Scopes, and Judge Raulston approved Stewart's motion to quash the old indictment.

The judge dismissed the grand jury, and the court prepared to choose the trial jurors. When the judge asked Stewart how long he thought it would take to interview and select twelve men, the attorney general said he thought about half a day. Though he took Stewart's answer with apparent ease, Darrow must have been flabbergasted at the thought. He often spent weeks interviewing prospective jurors—*veniremen,* as they were called in the courtroom—and considered the process an essential step in the success of the defense.

Aware of Judge Raulston's public relations concerns (he was up for reelection next year) and eager not to offend, Darrow asked as deferentially as possible whether that might not be enough time:

"Your honor, this case has had a great deal of publicity, as the court knows, and in any case of this sort . . . it is very hard to get impartial juries that the law prescribes. We may get it quickly, but we feel we ought to have a reasonable liberty of examination to see that we do get as impartial a jury as is possible. As people generally have some general opinions on such subjects and I apprehend it might take some little time to get a jury."

When the judge agreed to extend "any reasonable courtesy we can" in examining veniremen, Darrow asked about the distinguished scholars he had summoned from New York, Chicago, and elsewhere to supply expert testimony on evolution: the old Ferguson mansion was filled with them at that very moment. Darrow wanted them to testify as soon as possible since they were all appearing without compensation and at their own expense. He didn't want them to sit around Dayton for a week or two only to have the judge rule their evidence and testimony inadmissible.

Darrow and Stewart talked informally for a moment, then Stewart addressed the bench: "As Mr. Darrow stated, the defense is going to insist on introducing scientists and Bible students to give their ideas of certain views of this law, and that, I am frank to state, will be resisted by the state as vigorously as we know how to resist it. We have had a conference or two about that matter, and we think that it isn't competent as evidence."

In keeping with numerous earlier statements by the prosecutors and their supporters, Stewart insisted that the question of law had nothing to do with whether evolution was true, compatible with the Bible, dangerously restrictive to science, unfair to taxpayers, or anything else. The only question before the court, Stewart believed, was whether John Scopes had taught material in the public school that denied the biblical story of divine creation and promoted the theory that man was descended from a lower order of animals. A definition or defense of evolution was immaterial. In fact, the word *evolution* did not appear either in the Butler Act or in the indictment.

Stewart proposed to the court that, as soon as the jury was selected, the judge rule on whether the expert witnesses could testify. He told Judge Raulston that he and Darrow had agreed to adjourn until Monday, when they could interview veniremen first thing in the morning and then consider the expert witnesses.

But the judge wanted to get to work. Skipping over the matter of expert testimony for the time being, Raulston told Darrow that if he was concerned about finding twelve unbiased men out of the small pool of sixteen prospects, the sheriff could round up a hundred qualified men by the end of the lunch hour.

"I want to show all the courtesy I can to these visiting lawyers," Stewart replied, still hoping for an early adjournment. "These gentlemen have come in here on trains from a long distance last night and they are tired and not feeling very well."

"Well, it wouldn't require any great amount of energy to select a jury, would it?" the judge shot back. In the end the court reconvened at 1:30 PM, and jury selection began.

Men were interviewed one at a time, first briefly by the judge, then by the attorney general, and last of all by Darrow, whose questions sometimes took ten or fifteen minutes. Darrow was friendly, respectful, and asked questions that suggested he had a genuine interest in the lives and experiences of these rural Tennesseeans. The questions also gave him the only indications he would have whether a man could make an unbiased decision as a juror.

He asked them what they did for a living; almost all were farmers. Many had lived in Tennessee all their lives, though one man had traveled widely during a tour of duty in the army. Most of them testified that they had no opinion about Scopes's guilt and knew little if anything about evolution.

When one man, J. P. Massingill, said he was a preacher, Darrow asked, "Ever preach on evolution?"

The man gave an indirect answer, and Darrow repeated the question.

"Yes," the preacher admitted. "I haven't as a subject, just taken that up in connection with other subjects. I have referred to it."

"Against it or for it?" Darrow asked. Massingill gave another roundabout answer, and the attorney again repeated his question.

The preacher looked at Judge Raulston. "Is that a fair question, judge?"

"Yes, answer the question," Raulston replied.

"Well, I preached against it, of course!"

The courtroom broke out in applause. The judge rapped for order, and Darrow insisted anyone who applauded leave the courtroom. Raulston agreed. Reverend Massingill was excused. Like all the other men examined, he had wanted to be chosen regardless of his opinions or preconceptions. A spot on the jury meant not only a little cash for serving but, potential jurors believed, also a front-row seat for the courtroom circus.

Stewart continued to resist Darrow's efforts to introduce evolutionary theory into the proceedings. When Darrow asked one venireman whether evolution "is a true doctrine or a false one," Stewart appealed to the judge: "I submit that is not a proper interrogation, whether evolution is true or not. The correct test is whether or not he has an opinion that the defendant is guilty or not guilty." Judge Raulston allowed Darrow to continue. After a few more minutes, the man was seated in the jury box, which had been moved to the corner of the room from its usual place in the center to make room for microphones feeding loudspeakers out on the courthouse lawn and elsewhere in town.

The issue came up again later when Darrow wanted to excuse a man who admitted he thought the Bible and evolution conflicted with each other. Stewart appealed to the judge: "The result is, the defense will challenge every man who does not believe in evolution. . . . That would give the state the right to challenge every man who does believe in the theory of evolution. . . . The result is, everybody who was capable of having an opinion at all would be subject to challenge by one side or the other."

Darrow, easygoing and pleasant, joked, "I think, your honor, that statement is hardly correct. If you can find one that believes in [evolution] we will promptly challenge him."

Once the jurors were all chosen, Tom Stewart returned to the matter of the defense's expert witnesses; again the judge declined to rule or even comment. Darrow requested, and Stewart agreed, not to hold court the next day, Saturday, so the defense could confer. Declaring he would swear in the jury on Monday, Raulston adjourned the proceedings until then.

The big double doors on the side of the courtroom opened, and a thousand people, some of whom had been crowding into hallways or on the steps, rushed down the broad staircase and outside to get what little relief they could from the stifling heat of the chamber. It was over ninety degrees outside, hotter than usual even for July, but it had been worse inside, where the still, stale air grew steadily more moist and fetid as the day wore on. Only the judge had any relief at all, in the form of a small electric fan aimed at him behind the bench.

Reporters ran to their typewriters in their makeshift headquarters over the hardware store or to the new public phones. Others joined the lines in front of the new public toilets in the courthouse, so hastily built that ditches for some of the water lines remained uncovered on the square. Lay preachers and souvenir vendors shouted into the shimmering summer air as the crowd invaded the lemonade, Coca-Cola, and hot dog stands that stretched out in ramshackle lines in every direction.

John Scopes returned to Bailey's Boarding House just up Market Street, where he had lived during the school year and stayed during the trial. In their makeshift headquarters next to the grocery store, twenty-two Western Union operators worked into the late hours filing stories for reporters around the world, despite the fact that nothing directly related to the charges against Scopes had happened.

The many well-known reporters, including representatives of the New York *Herald Tribune,* the *Nation,* the *Philadelphia Inquirer,* and the London *Times,* scattered around the hotels, boarding houses, private homes, and makeshift dormitories of Rhea County. John Scopes took note of "Adolph Shelby Ochs of the *Chattanooga Times*" in town for the trial, who was in fact Adolph Simon Ochs, who had built the Tennessee paper into one of the best in the state before buying control of the *New York Times* in 1896, the same year he began his forty-year run as its publisher.

The most famous, admired, and feared reporter in Dayton that July week was a round-faced, cigar-chomping man with brilliant blue eyes that missed nothing and a razor-sharp wit that showed no mercy. Henry Louis Mencken of the *Baltimore Sun* was forty-four that summer and at the height of his power and popularity. In his daily columns, books, essays, and contributions to the *American Mercury* magazine (which he also edited), H. L. Mencken took aim at politicians, businessmen, foreigners, country folk, the poor, minorities, preachers, and anybody else he could find to take down a notch for the amusement of his adoring readers.

It would be difficult for a later generation to imagine the power and sway such widely read newspapermen as Mencken and Walter Lippman of the *New York World* (later and most famously of the *Herald Tribune*) held over public opinion. When Mencken declared something to be so, millions believed it. It was Mencken who first suggested to Clarence Darrow that he rise in opposition to Bryan in the Scopes trial. It was Mencken who early on christened the whole business the Monkey Trial. And it was Mencken who, before he ever arrived in Dayton, Tennessee, decided what the world would believe about the proceedings if he had anything to say about it. And he had plenty.

In his column for the *Sun* on June 29, 1925, Mencken proposed that the whole campaign to outlaw the teaching of evolution in Tennessee was "nothing more, at bottom, than the conspiracies of the inferior man against his betters." The problem, as he saw it, was that Tennesseans and their ilk were too dull witted to understand the complexities of science and so retreated to the comfortable simplicity of biblical creationism:

> The inferior man's reasons for hating knowledge are not hard to discern. He hates it because it is complex—because it puts an unbearable burden upon his meager capacity for taking in ideas. Thus his search is always for short cuts. All superstitions are such short cuts. . . . The popularity of Fundamentalism among the inferior orders of men is explicable in exactly the same way. The cosmologies that educated men toy with are all inordinately complex. To comprehend

> their veriest outlines requires an immense stock of knowledge, and a habit of thought. It would be as vain to try to teach to peasants or to the city proletariat as it would be to try to teach them to streptococci. But the cosmogony of Genesis is so simple that even a yokel can grasp it. It is set forth in a few phrases. It offers, to an ignorant man, the irresistible reasonableness of the nonsensical. So he accepts it with loud hosannas, and has one more excuse for hating his betters.

Far more people would read and remember Mencken's columns and pronouncements about the Scopes trial than would ever read the transcript, which was printed by a Chattanooga newspaper and syndicated around the world every day. The immensely entertaining, witty, and fashionable Mencken wanted to write about the Monkey Trial. So from the first, Mencken's clever *bon mots*—written for the enjoyment of his audience and the further enhancement of his popularity, with no thought given to historical accuracy—became nevertheless a foundation of the "historical" record. Mencken made no effort at deception; he was a columnist, not a historian, and never pretended to be anything else. But his characterization of the trial as a battle between inbred Fundamentalist mountaineer buffoons on one side and truth and common sense on the other became the historical template generations of people would accept without question.

Here is another sampling from his June 29, prearrival column:

> [The] great masses of men [outside the] educated minority [are] ignorant, they are dishonest, they are cowardly, they are ignoble. They know little if anything that is worth knowing, and there is not the slightest sign of a natural desire among them to increase their knowledge. . . . The so-called religious organizations which now lead the war against the teaching of evolution are nothing more, at bottom, than conspiracies of the inferior man against his betters. . . . Whatever lies above the level of their comprehension is of the devil. A glass of wine delights civilized men; they themselves, drinking it, would get drunk. *Ergo,* wine must be prohibited. The

hypothesis of evolution is credited by all men of education; they themselves can't understand it. *Ergo,* its teaching must be put down.

This simple fact explains such phenomena as the Tennessee buffoonery. Nothing else can.

After he arrived in Dayton but before the trial began, Mencken filed a story on how the trial provided "almost a miraculous chance to get Dayton upon the front pages, to make it talked about, to put it on the map." But now on the eve of the big event, he believed the city fathers had realized their tragic mistake. The affair "must be managed discreetly, adroitly, with careful regard to psychological niceties. The boomers of Dayton, alas, had no skill at such things, and the experts called in were all quacks. . . . Two months ago the town was obscure and happy. Today it is a universal joke."

Whatever benefit Dayton might gain from the trial would be, Mencken thought, both meager and temporary. Would visitors "bring any money with them? . . . Will they light the fires of the cold and silent blast furnace down the railroad tracks? On these points, I regret to report, optimism has to call in theology to aid it. Prayer can accomplish a lot. It can cure diabetes, find lost pocketbooks and restrain husbands from beating their wives. But is prayer made any more efficacious by giving a circus first? Coming to this thought, Dayton begins to sweat."

Here's more of Mencken's description of Dayton residents: They were "rustic japes" and "yokels" in a "ninth-rate country town" who "believe, on the authority of Genesis, that the earth is flat and that witches still infest it." Mencken declared that there was an educated minority in Dayton and in Tennessee that saw the issue in the right light. He also had compliments for Scopes. But he invariably described the townspeople in general as lowbrow hicks, pitiful and even frightening in their ignorance.

This view was the only one many would ever glimpse of the Scopes trial: the opinion of a great writer and commentator playing to his audience with no concern for the facts. Other reporters put their own spins on the events or staged them completely from scratch.

Reporters from Nashville and other nearby cities saw the scene with a more familiar and sympathetic eye. The wire service reporters stuck more to the facts, filling their dispatches with quotations and trial transcripts. But it was Mencken's entertaining and outrageous characterizations that captivated the public and that people remembered and talked about.

Thirty years later the play *Inherit the Wind* cemented those caricatures by depicting town residents as almost rabid advocates for the Bryan character and foes to the finish of the Darrow character. The movie version five years afterward heightened the depiction with marching crowds singing praises to the great orator and Christian apologist Matthew Jefferson Brady in one scene, then burning the Scopes character (who was in jail) in effigy as they raucously sang, "We'll hang Bert Cates from a sour apple tree!" To most of the audience, this was history; consciously or unconsciously, in the absence of the facts they accepted this depiction as the way it was. Thus fiction gradually supplanted fact in the public record, and citizens of Dayton were marked by history as backward, closed-minded, uneducated, hopelessly dull-witted mountain rubes.

Movie and theater watchers would never suspect that Bryan and Darrow were both guests of honor at welcoming banquets, that Scopes was the friend of all who knew him, and that the crowds at the trial cheered both sides.

CHAPTER 6

"Armed Clowns . . . Have Begun to Shoot"

WITH NO COURT PROCEEDINGS on Saturday, the spectators, reporters, and other strangers—maybe three or four thousand in all—went in search of entertainment. Alcoholic beverages had been illegal throughout the United States since 1920, so Dayton had no place to congregate other than Robinson's, where a crowd swirled constantly in and out, ordering cold drinks and ice cream to beat the heat and reading dispatches, notes, and announcements taped to the storefront windows.

Plenty of illicit homemade liquor was for sale; the hollows of Tennessee were famous for their moonshine. No doubt many visitors had experiences similar to Mencken when he reported, "Ten minutes after I arrived a leading citizen offered me a drink made up half of white mule and half of Coca-Cola." Some visitors cruised the souvenir stands while others swam in the Tennessee River, waded in Richland Creek, or poked around the abandoned railroad tracks and mine entrances of the old Dayton Coal and Iron Company.

Others, visitors and locals alike, drove a few miles west to the hills near Walden Ridge where small resorts clustered around springs that dotted the region. The hotel in Morgan Springs, ten miles from

Dayton, had a dance every Saturday night in the summer. The biggest crowd anybody could remember swarmed over the dance pavilion and hotel grounds, swaying to the music of the house orchestra.

Driving a snappy yellow roadster lent by a friend, John Scopes arrived for the dance in hopes of putting his celebrity behind him for a few hours and enjoying the company of other young people. In the pavilion, which was separate from the hotel, he met a girl he had dated in the past, and they began talking. Then she asked him if he would escort her from the pavilion across the dark lawn to the hotel. "Although we hadn't gone to the dance together," Scopes later observed, "her request seemed a normal and reasonable one."

But Scopes the celebrity was too tempting a target. He continued the story:

> As we were walking in darkness, she suddenly wrapped her arms around my neck and started kissing me. She caught me totally by surprise and as I stood there, momentarily paralyzed, floodlights flashed on. Was it coincidence that a photographer happened to be handy, and that as the lights went on, he took a picture of us? The next day papers all over the country showed me in the arms of the girl. . . . I knew now that almost anything could lead to a setup for either reporters or cameramen. The pressure of publicity never let up.

Though the pace of activity slowed on Sunday when all the stores and businesses in town were closed, it was standing room only at the Southern Methodist church a few blocks down Market Street from the courthouse. William Jennings Bryan had been invited to deliver the sermon that morning, and since he hadn't spoken yet in the trial, it would be the most formal and officious setting thus far for a speech by the Great Commoner.

To the surprise of visiting reporters, John R. Neal, Bryan's opponent in the courtroom, shared the platform as a guest of honor, and Judge Raulston and his two daughters sat near the front. Some in the congregation came to hear Bryan defend his beliefs, but others came simply to see such a famous man in person or to hear the legendary

Bryan voice. It was true what they'd heard: Bryan never seemed to shout, but everyone in the building could understand every word perfectly. Almost eighty years later Eloise Purser Reed, whose brother was one of John Scopes's tennis partners, vividly remembered how excited she was to hear him speak, then worm her way through the crowd of well-wishers afterward to shake his hand; she was so awed by his celebrity that she didn't recall a thing he said.

Bryan ate lunch in a pleasant house four blocks further down Market Street where he, his wife, Mary (confined to a wheelchair by arthritis), and William Jr. were living for the duration of the trial. It was the home of F. R. Rogers, who worked for Doc Robinson in his drugstore and who moved his family out temporarily so the Bryans could have it to themselves. Later in the day Bryan addressed a throng of three thousand on the courthouse lawn, almost twice Dayton's normal population, from the platform along the north side of the building. H. L. Mencken reported that Bryan was "presenting the indubitable Word of God in his caressing, ingratiating way. . . . What Bryan says doesn't seem to these congenial Baptists and Methodists to be argument; it seems to be a mere graceful statement of the obvious."

The Baltimore reporter, who boarded with a local dentist named A. M. Morgan, had quickly soured on Dayton as well. Mencken wrote on July 9, the day after his arrival:

> The town, I confess, greatly surprised me. I expected to find a squalid Southern village, with darkies snoozing on the horseblocks, pigs rooting under the houses and the inhabitants full of hookworm and malaria. What I found was a country town full of charm and even beauty. . . . The houses are surrounded by pretty gardens, with cool green lawns and stately trees. . . . The stores carry good stocks and have a metropolitan air, especially the drug, book, magazine, sporting goods and soda-water emporium of the estimable Robinson. . . . [T]he younger bucks are very nattily turned out. Scopes himself, even in his shirt sleeves, would fit into any college campus in America save that of Harvard alone.

Two days later Mencken had returned to sneering, as his July 11 column revealed:

> It would be hard to imagine a more moral town than Dayton. . . . But what of life here? Is it more agreeable than in Babylon? I regret that I must have to report that it is not. The incessant clashing of theologians grows monotonous in a day and intolerable the day following. One longs for a merry laugh, a burst of happy music, the gurgle of a decent jug. Try a meal at the hotel; it is tasteless and swims in grease. Go to the drug store and call for refreshment: the boy will hand you almost automatically a beaker of Coca-Cola [very much a Southern regional drink in 1925]. Look at the magazine counter: a pile of *Saturday Evening Posts* [decidedly middlebrow compared with the *American Mercury*] two feet high. Examine the books: melodrama and cheap amour. Talk to a town magnifico; he knows nothing that is not in Genesis.

News reports had little to say in comparison about Clarence Darrow. He and his wife stayed in a house at the corner of Walnut and Second Streets owned by Luke Morgan, whose son, Howard, was one of the students set to testify against Scopes. Darrow spent the majority of the weekend at the old mansion where the defense team was boarding, discussing their strategy and planning for Monday's proceedings. Because Darrow arrived in town only the day before the trial, he and his New York co-counsel had had almost no time to consult ahead of time with local attorneys John Neal, Gordon and Ben McKenzie, and the Hicks brothers.

Monday, July 13, was another scorcher. The courtroom was already uncomfortably warm by the time the proceedings came to order at nine o'clock. Once again the official record began with a prayer: "O God our Father, Thou who art the creator of the heaven and the earth and the sea and all that is in them." The bailiff, Chattanooga police officer Kelso Rice, summoned the jury, still not sworn in. Neal immediately presented a motion to quash the indictment against Scopes.

This motion set off a chain of confusing events over the next several minutes. In reply to Neal, the judge said the indictment should be read first and that he could then submit his motion when the judge called for his plea. But then Tom Stewart asked the judge's permission to reexamine one of the jurors. Agreeing to the request, Raulston directed the sheriff to remove the other jury members, who had scarcely settled in their seats, from the courtroom. This caused a rumble of reaction from the packed gallery of spectators; the judge couldn't find his gavel at first, and it took him a moment to restore order.

Then Clarence Darrow objected to reexamining a juror, stating that Stewart had already examined him. The judge replied that since the jury had not yet been sworn, which Darrow had also objected to the Friday before, either side could examine jury members further. Stewart had heard a rumor that the juror had expressed an opinion about the trial to someone and wanted to know if he'd already made up his mind. The juror insisted he hadn't. The rest of the jury returned to the room.

The judge ordered the indictment read but stopped it when someone said a juror was still missing. Darrow asked if the jury shouldn't be sworn in before the indictment was read. The judge replied that he normally did that after the indictment was read and the defendant's plea was entered. Then Tom Stewart spoke up to say the defense motion to quash should be decided before the indictment was read.

Judge Raulston tried to stay in control in the midst of so many starts and stops. He asked his attorney general, "Wouldn't [the motion to quash] come when I call upon them to plead? I can proceed either way." "Our practice has been to dispose of that even before the jury was impaneled," Stewart answered. Without further comment the judge ordered the indictment read, and Stewart did so. "What is your plea, gentlemen?" asked the judge, looking at the men wedged around the defense table.

Neal replied with another request to quash the indictment against his client and asked that such a ruling be made later. Stewart insisted any motion to quash must be heard first. The judge agreed, and Neal submitted a lengthy written motion to dismiss all charges against the defendant. His first reason for requesting dismissal was that the Butler

Act violated the Tennessee state constitution, and he went on to cite ten specific passages that he said invalidated the law, including Article XI, Section 12, which required the government "to cherish literature and science." Also, Article I, Section 3 stated that "all men have a natural and indefeasible right to worship Almighty God according to the dictates of his own conscience; . . . no human authority can, in any case whatever, control or interfere with the right of conscience." Article I, Section 19 affirmed that "every citizen may speak freely, write and print on any subject, being responsible for the abuse of that liberty."

The defense also moved to dismiss the indictment because the wording was "so vague as not to inform the defendant of the nature and cause of the accusation against him." Neal's third point was that the law violated the Fourteenth Amendment to the U.S. Constitution guaranteeing protection against loss of "life, liberty or property, without due process of law."

Neal and Darrow proposed that the judge rule on the motion to quash after evidence had been presented; Stewart pressed for an immediate ruling that, if affirmative, would deny the defense the chance to make its case in favor of evolution. It would also abruptly end Dayton's moment in the headlines around the world.

The judge allowed Neal to explain why he thought the law itself was illegal, going down the constitutional points one by one. When Neal made it to Article I, Section 3 about each citizen's right to worship God in his own way, he said, "We do not for one moment in this case question the right of the state of Tennessee . . . to supervise and control its schools. We think, of course, the curriculum in that school must be fixed by some authority" but that in the Butler Act "there is made mandatory the teaching of a particular doctrine that comes from a particular religious book, and to that extent it places the public schools of our state in such a situation, in regard to particular church establishments, that they contravene the provisions of our constitution."

Tom Stewart interrupted Neal to move that the jury be excused during the argument over the motion to quash. Should the judge rule in Neal's favor and allow the trial to proceed, Stewart feared the prosecution's case might be compromised if jurors began to doubt the constitutionality of the Butler Act.

Darrow in turn objected to the jury retiring. Neal chimed in as well, insisting, "The jury is the judge of the law and the facts." Stewart fired back, "Oh, that is all foolishness!"

After further discussion Judge Raulston excused the jury, with the judge assuring Darrow that he could repeat points from the motion in his opening statement before the jury later on. The jurors filed out, stepping over the ropes that cordoned off their seats from the throng, and went outside. Some jurors joined the large audience on the courthouse lawn listening to the testimony on loudspeakers.

With the jury gone Neal resumed his argument. When he finished, Arthur Garfield Hays picked up the torch, touching on various technical details of the law's shortcomings. After Hays spoke came another round of discussion about when the ruling on the motion to quash should be made and when the accused should enter his plea.

Debate on the motion continued, with Stewart and his semiretired predecessor as attorney general, Ben McKenzie, defending the appropriateness and legality of the statute. "Under the law you cannot teach in the common [public] schools the Bible," McKenzie argued. "Why should it be improper to provide that you cannot teach this other theory?"

He also tossed a small barb at the outsiders on the defense: "The questions have all been settled in Tennessee, and favorable to our contention. If these gentlemen have any laws in the great metropolitan city of New York that conflict with it, or in the great white city of the northwest that will throw any light on it, we will be glad to hear about it."

Dudley Field Malone, the only lawyer at either table still wearing his suit coat in the withering heat, took exception to the reference to their out-of-town status: "I do not consider further allusion to geographical parts of the country as particularly necessary. . . . We are here, rightfully, as American citizens."

When the judge tried to smooth Malone's feathers, assuring him he was a guest who would be accorded every reasonable privilege, Malone replied that "we want it understood that while we are in this courtroom we are here as lawyers, not as guests."

Darrow spoke next, complimenting the state's "broad and plain" constitution but warning that if the antievolution law were held to be valid, then there was "no law, no matter how foolish, wicked, ambiguous, or ancient, but can come back to Tennessee. All the [constitutional] guarantees go for nothing." He harangued for more than two hours, while Bryan sat silent and virtually motionless. At last the judge interrupted him to say it was time to adjourn for the day.

Continuing on sheer momentum for another moment, Darrow warned, "If today you can take a thing like evolution and make it a crime to teach it in the public schools, . . . the next session you may ban books and newspapers. . . . After a while, your honor, it is the setting of man against man and creed against creed until with flying banners and beating drums we are marching backward to the glorious ages of the sixteenth century" when "men who dared to bring any intelligence and enlightenment and culture to the human mind" were burned at the stake.

Unexpectedly, the judge then asked both sides for written briefs of their argument over quashing the indictment. After court adjourned, the defense spent the rest of the afternoon and early evening working on their presentation. Darrow left his wife at their rented house for dinner and a strategy session at the old mansion with his colleagues. City water service had been interrupted all over town earlier in the day, then the electricity failed, leaving Dayton's eighteen hundred residents and perhaps twice as many visitors—including the lawyers and expert witnesses in the mansion—to make do with candles.

Though a few in the gallery had hissed Darrow at the end of his lengthy speech that afternoon, others said it was a masterpiece, including Mencken, who also saw a prejudice against Scopes that transcended all reason or argument. He led off his July 14 dispatch with a pronouncement on the subject: "The net effect of Clarence Darrow's great speech yesterday seems to be precisely the same as if he had bawled it up a rainspout in the interior of Afghanistan. . . . You have but a dim notion of it who have only read it. It was not designed for reading, but for hearing. The clanging of it was as important as the logic. It rose like a wind and ended like a flourish of bugles. The very judge on the bench, toward the end of it, began to look uneasy. But the morons in the audience, when it was over, simply hissed it."

Mencken felt that Bryan had already won the trial without saying a word: "The case will not be decided by logic, nor even by eloquence. It will be decided by counting noses—and for every nose in these hills that has ever thrust itself into any book save the Bible there are a hundred adorned with the brass ring of Bryan. These are his people." Mencken abandoned any argument of the facts of the case in favor of slandering country people who made easy targets. Not discerning that a Rhea County crowd had its fair share of well-educated and well-read citizens with diverse views, Mencken wrote comments as insular and closed-minded as he accused others of being.

Scopes would be convicted, Mencken believed, because right-thinking men had done nothing when antievolution forces first showed themselves. Those forces were growing and would soon be unstoppable: "You probably laughed at the prohibitionists, say, back in 1914. Well, don't make the same error twice." Educated, rational men had known what was going on and except for a handful of them, they had done nothing. The "civilized minority" had neglected to smother this dire threat to intellectual freedom in its crib.

"The Baptist preachers ranted unchallenged," Mencken deduced. "Their buffooneries were mistaken for humor. Now the clowns turn out to be armed, and have begun to shoot."

CHAPTER 7
Face-off

OTHER PRESS OBSERVERS shared Mencken's admiration for Darrow's speech without his worry that it had been wasted. Telegraph operators sent 200,000 words from Dayton that day, a record that was never broken. The *New York Times* exulted, "Clarence Darrow bearded the lion of Fundamentalism today, faced William Jennings Bryan and a court room filled with believers of the literal word of the Bible and with a hunch of shoulders and a thumb in his suspenders defied every belief they hold sacred. . . . While he was talking there was absolute silence in the room except for the clicking of telegraph keys. His words fell with crushing force, his satire dropped with sledge-hammer effect upon those who heard him." Joseph Wood Crutch of the *Nation* showed his bigotry in writing about the reaction to Darrow's closing comparison of the charges against John Scopes and the superstition of the sixteenth century: "even Dayton stopped to think."

As the court convened for a third day on Tuesday, July 14, the sharp division between the defense and prosecution over the subject matter of the trial appeared as soon as the bailiff rapped for order. Judge Raulston called for a minister to open with prayer, but before

Reverend Stribling could say a word, Darrow objected both to the prayer and to the jury being present to hear his objection. The judge delayed bringing in the jury and let Darrow speak.

Darrow acknowledged that Raulston traditionally began his court sessions with a prayer, but seeing that in this case "it is claimed by the state that there is a conflict between science and religion, above all other cases there should be no part taken outside of the evidence in this case and no attempt by means of prayer or in any other way to influence the deliberation and consideration of the jury."

Attorney General Stewart disagreed: "The state makes no contention, as stated by counsel for the defense, that this is a conflict between science and religion insofar as the merits are concerned; it is a case involving the fact as to whether or not a schoolteacher has taught a doctrine prohibited by statute." Turning the tables on the defense team, which contended that the Butler Act unfairly promoted a specific religious belief, Stewart added, "We for the state think it is quite proper to open the court with prayer if the court sees fit to do it, and such an idea extended by the agnostic counsel for the defense is foreign to the thoughts and ideas of the people who do not know anything about infidelity [to the Bible] and care less."

Dudley Field Malone responded that the prayers opening the previous two days of the trial were "argumentative" and helped "to increase the atmosphere of hostility to our point of view."

Stewart stood firm: "There is still no question involved in this lawsuit as to whether or not Scopes taught a doctrine prohibited by the statute. . . . So far as creating an atmosphere of hostility is concerned, I would advise Mr. Malone that this is a God fearing country."

That remark raised the Irish lawyer's hackles, but Malone was cut off by the judge. Darrow continued to explain his position that because the case involved the divine account of creation in the Bible, "There is no question about the religious character of these proceedings."

Insisting that prayer before the session was "a matter wholly within the discretion of the court" and that he intended no "bias or prejudice," the judge overruled Darrow's objection and ordered the minister to give his prayer. It was, however, a much more general prayer than the previous two had been, asking for "minds that are willing to be directed in the way Thou wouldst have us do," though Reverend Stribling also prayed that there would be in every heart and mind "a reverence to the Great Creator of the world."

The prayer debate took up almost the whole morning. It was then that Judge Raulston told the attorneys that because of the electrical failure the night before (the water service was still out; the new courthouse drinking fountains and toilets were not working) he had not been able to finish his deliberations on the defense motion to quash the indictment.

The judge would take more time to consider his ruling, he said, but before he could call for the midday recess, Darrow asked that the record show his objection to prayer every morning. The judge agreed: "Let the record show that it will be treated as made and overruled every morning."

Court adjourned for lunch, and as Scopes started down the courthouse stairs, he saw William K. Hutchinson, a young reporter for the International News Service with whom he had become friendly. Hutchinson invited Scopes to join him for lunch but, quickening his pace, said he first had to catch up with Judge Raulston and ask him something. The two young men threaded their way through the dispersing crowd and caught up with the judge on the way back to his room at the Hotel Aqua. Scopes recorded the scene in his memoirs more than forty years later.

> We caught up with the judge and, as we marched along, Hutchinson praised him for his efficient conduct of the trial. This made the judge feel good. Hutchinson noticed a bundle of papers under the judge's arm.
>
> "Is that your decision on the motion to quash?"
>
> "No, that's being copied by a stenographer now," replied the judge.
>
> I could sense that Hutchinson knew he was close to a good story. He asked, "Will you read that decision this

afternoon?"

"That is my intention," said Judge Raulston.

"Then, after you adjourn until tomorrow, you'll take up the admissibility of expert testimony next?"

"Yes," was the reply.

If the judge had approved the motion to quash, the trial would end immediately with no adjournment "until tomorrow." That meant Raulston was denying the motion. Before Hutchinson and Scopes had lunch, the reporter excitedly phoned in his scoop.

By one o'clock the defendant and his friend were back in the sweltering, malodorous courtroom. The three little electric fans in the room now all had electrical cords of about the same length and were clustered in one place around the judge's bench. The day was the hottest yet and the crowd the biggest. The sun baked down, making hundreds of small, stark shadows directly under the trees and bystanders on the courthouse lawn.

Instead of the figure of Judge Raulston in his light summer suit, a policeman stepped to the bench and called for order. "The court will reconvene at 2:30 o'clock PM," he announced. Since no one wanted to lose his seat in the courtroom, the crowd settled in to wait, smoking—permitted in the room as long as the court wasn't in session—and drinking iced soft drinks.

Judge Raulston returned to the bench fifteen minutes early but stayed only long enough to remind his listeners of his "strict instructions" not to release any information about his ruling on the motion to quash until he himself announced it in court.

The judge was gone an hour and a half, while, as the Memphis *Commercial Appeal* reported, "The hot, bustling crowd puffed, fanned, smoked and drank red soda pop." At 3:45 Judge Raulston returned. His first order of business, over the vehement objection of Attorney General Stewart, was to consider a petition by Unitarian and Congregationalist pastors and a rabbi to "select the officiating clergyman" for the daily opening prayer "from other than fundamentalist churches in alteration with fundamentalist clergymen."

Amidst laughter and loud applause, the judge referred the petition to the local pastors' association. Then, adapting a more serious tone, Raulston announced that he had already read newspaper accounts of his decision on the indictment to quash, despite the fact he had not announced his ruling. Angrily he informed the packed courtroom that he would announce his ruling the next day but in the meantime wanted to meet privately with the reporters and attorneys.

After the room was cleared of spectators, Malone asked once more if the judge would rule on the admissibility of expert witnesses, as the defense had several standing by and more on the way. "No sir, not until the proof is offered," the judge replied with a note of finality. Raulston then adjourned the court and addressed the reporters alone.

He held up a telegram, then read it to the group of men and women crowded around him. "*St. Louis Star* out final, carrying story law been held constitutional by judge." Raulston appointed a committee of five reporters to find out where the leak was and report to him. Then the judge dismissed the press corps and returned to his room at the Hotel Aqua. The reporters went their separate ways except for the five investigators, who spent the evening dining, drinking bootleg liquor, and playing cards. They already knew who the culprit was, and had no doubt the judge would go easy on him when the time came.

In Dayton that night some thought the Scopes trial could still be a public relations blockbuster. Yet over the weekend, after only one day of testimony, the United Press reported "a wave of disappointment running through Dayton" at the small size of the crowds. Some had predicted thirty thousand visitors—city leaders beseeched the Southern Railway to schedule special trains from Chattanooga for the duration of the trial—but most final estimates were closer to three thousand. One listener estimated the audience that heard Bryan on Sunday afternoon at five thousand; that was perhaps the biggest serious estimate by an eyewitness. Five thousand or three thousand still made a big crowd in a town of eighteen hundred, but somehow it all seemed smaller in scale than the townspeople had figured on.

Newspapers and magazines reported that the initial reaction overseas to the trial was largely negative. The London *Daily Mail* sniffed,

"To English eyes there is something comic about this storm in a teapot, but it has a serious aspect, too. The attempt to stifle liberty of thought and speech is doubtless doomed to ultimate failure." *Nature* quoted the bishop of Birmingham as saying, "As one who values intellectual freedom, I am shocked that Anglo-Saxon communities should seek by legislation and prosecution to prevent the spread of knowledge."

Sir Arthur Keith, identified as one of England's foremost scientists, declared, "Only penal servitude for life will prevent men from searching the rocks and discovering the record kept there, detailing history of plant, beast and man, and all these records shout aloud that evolution is true." A Viennese scientist explained to the Associated Press how "German theology and German science have both continued to labor undeterred for the greater glory of the Christian faith."

Back in Dayton, visitors were often elbowing away residents from the action. Writing for United Press, John Moutoux observed, "The home folks found themselves barred from the courtroom by out-of-town newspaper men. There was a dearth of visitors except for their own kin." But now that the trial was heating up, spirits were on the rise, particularly at the prospect of a face-off between Darrow and Bryan. Moutoux wrote that "throngs on the criss-crossing main streets talked of nothing else."

H. L. Mencken agreed: "The basic issues of the case, indeed, seem to be very little discussed at Dayton. What interests everyone is its mere strategy. By what device, precisely, will Bryan trim old Clarence Darrow? Will he do it gently and with every delicacy of forensics, or will he wade in on high gear and make a swift butchery of it? For no one here seems to doubt that Bryan will win."

Public discussion was at a high pitch by the end of the day Tuesday. Darrow had spoken eloquently and at length in the courtroom while Bryan had yet to speak at all. Reports circulated about the work Bryan had done at his "palatial Miami estate" preparing his courtroom presentations. Anticipation to hear them grew with each passing hour.

Wednesday's session began with Judge Raulston asking his pastors' committee for their selection to say the opening prayer. To the surprise of many, the committee picked Charles Francis Potter, a

Unitarian pastor who had traveled with Malone and Hays from New York to be one of their expert witnesses. Potter had earned some local notoriety the Sunday before when asked by a local Northern Methodist minister to preach in his church as Bryan was preaching in a Southern Methodist one. But the Northern Methodist congregation balked, withdrew the invitation, and sent its preacher packing. Potter's opening prayer was two short sentences in supplication to "Whom all pray and for Whom are many names" for "the progress of mankind toward Thy truth."

Revisiting the previous day's argument, John R. Neal again objected to prayer in court, explaining that any prayer "must necessarily be of one particular faith" and might influence the proceedings. Sue Hicks responded for the state, declaring once again that "we maintain that there is no religious controversy in this case." The defense, Hicks continued, had first insisted that evolution did not contradict the Bible and Christianity. "Why are they objecting to prayers if it doesn't contradict the Bible?"

Before the opposing sides got on too much of a roll yet again about the matter of opening prayer, Raulston interjected himself, insisting there was no intention or likelihood of influencing the trial: "I don't think it hurts anybody and I think it may help somebody. So I overrule the objection."

The next principal matter was the report of the press committee, which was read by Richard Beamish of the *Philadelphia Inquirer,* a short, heavyset man with pince-nez who served as committee chairman. (According to Scopes, another member of the committee, Philip Kingsley of the *Chicago Tribune,* caused the whole uproar. Furious at being scooped by Hutchinson, he had alerted the judge to the leak as an act of revenge.)

Beamish told the court that the news bulletin on the judge's decision was based on information the sender considered truthful and that "the sender did not obtain this information from your honor's stenographer, nor in any improper or unethical manner."

Raulston was not satisfied. "I think this court is entitled to know how this information was had."

Beamish testified that the information "came from the court" and explained the incident in detail. At the judge's order, Beamish identified Hutchinson as the source. Perturbed, the judge admonished the newsmen against asking anything other than a question for "direct information." Eventually he let the matter drop.

After posing once more for pictures, the judge read his decision on the defense motion to quash the indictment because, among other things, the law violated the Tennessee constitution. The typewritten opinion filled nineteen legal pages. Among the long stretches of boilerplate were several key statements, including:

"The courts are not concerned in questions of public policy or the motive that prompts the passage or enactment of any particular legislation. . . . [These questions] address themselves to the legislative department of the state, and not the judicial department."

"I cannot conceive how the teachers' rights [under the Tennessee constitution] would be violated by the act in issue. There is no law in the state of Tennessee that undertakes to compel this defendant, or any other citizen, to accept employment in the public schools . . . and if his conscience constrains him to teach the evolution theory, he can find opportunities elsewhere in other schools in the state to follow the dictates of his conscience."

The judge took each of the fourteen points of the defense motion in turn, citing the statutes and in some instances quoting from cases, then declaring them overruled. Finally he read, "The court, having passed on each ground chronologically, and given the reasons therefore, is now pleased to overrule the whole motion and require the defendant to plead further."

Wearied from reading his motion in the ovenlike atmosphere and wanting to give the defense time to prepare some paperwork, the judge declared a recess until one o'clock.

"Now it was official," John Scopes later recalled, "the trial would continue." Looking back from a historical perspective, Scopes wrote that Raulston was a well-meaning country judge who was in over his head, considering the constitutionality of a law he didn't know based on testimony he couldn't understand. "Furthermore," Scopes concluded, "and this was crucial, he occupied an elective office and if he had made a decision that the voters didn't like, he might have been kicked out of a job rather swiftly. All factors considered, he conducted himself well."

Besides, Scopes and everybody else assumed the case would soon be heard in the U.S. Supreme Court. This was only the first round; meaningful results wouldn't come until later.

Looking for relief from the heat, Scopes took off for a swim between sessions. William Jennings Bryan Jr. and local prosecutor Wallace Haggard (who had been part of the case since the early meetings at Robinson's) went with him, and the three had a refreshing dip in a mountain pond. The trio lost track of the time, and by the time they reentered the courtroom, the court was already in session.

"Where the hell have you been?" Arthur Garfield Hays demanded, explaining Scopes could be arrested for contempt for being late. Inching his way through the packed room to the defense table, the young defendant was too embarrassed to argue. The judge also noticed his tardiness, but before he could speak, Clarence Darrow rose and distracted him.

Scopes wasn't the only one who was late. The prosecutors had some last-minute trouble rounding up all the witnesses they had subpoenaed. After a few confusing minutes, everyone was finally accounted for.

Hundreds of spectators stood in the doorway, squirmed around the perimeter of the room, and sat in the large open windowsills. The clicking of telegraph keys and the clattering of typewriters covered the soft whir of hand-cranked newsreel cameras. Some reporters, including Mencken, stood on tables. The hum and rustle of a thousand people made a constant low-level commotion. The three little electric fans whirred bravely against the stifling atmosphere, rustling the fresh flowers on the judge's bench, the one blaze of freshness and color in the scene.

Judge Raulston looked around the room as a policeman rapped for order, paused for a moment, and said, "Let the clerk call the jury."

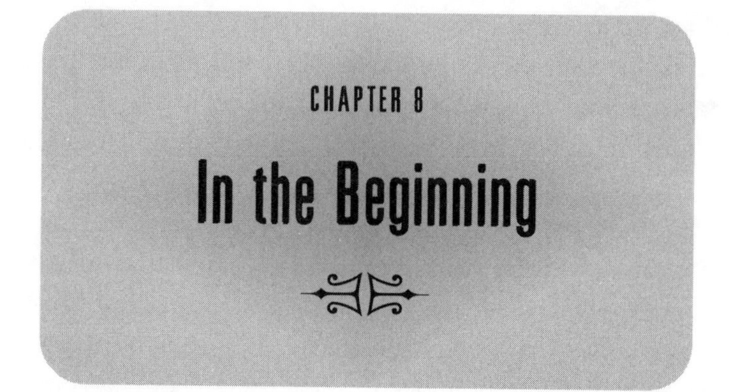

CHAPTER 8
In the Beginning

JOHN SCOPES WAS ON TRIAL in Dayton, Tennessee, but so were the doctrines of creation and evolution. In a larger sense the Bible itself was on trial. Is it reliable? Are its accounts mythical?

How had Western civilization come to this point? And why did journalists see Darwinism as the cutting edge and the Bible as something to be embraced only by rural, behind-the-times folks?

Let's start with this: "Man is the measure of all things." So declared the Greek philosopher Protagoras in the fifth century BC, expressing with classical simplicity the idea that man, not God or any other supernatural force, was the ruler over all creation. Man, not God or gods, defined values of good and evil, right and wrong, and established the standards for living in the world. One man's truth was as valid as another's, and what was true for someone today might not be true tomorrow. The desires of his listeners' Athenian gods were unknown and unknowable, so worrying about them was useless.

Though his historic quotation famously summarized the point of view that all standards are relative, Protagoras nevertheless tried to persuade his students that certain viewpoints and perceptions were better than others because they led to more desirable results. Even if man was the ultimate source of right and universal truth did not exist, one way of looking at the world might be more fulfilling and suitable than another.

Twenty-four centuries later in a Tennessee courtroom, mankind was still puzzling over the tension between the urge to claim a place as king of the universe and the sense that there must be more to creation than what man can explain, comprehend, and control.

The ideas and writings of Charles Darwin, so much in the news and so hotly debated in the summer of 1925, derived from a scientific establishment that had discarded religious mystery as backward and ignorant in favor of the exciting discoveries and philosophical turns of the Age of Enlightenment, that period during the late seventeenth and eighteenth centuries when scientific advancements led the world to believe the universe could be defined in mechanical (also called "material") terms.

The age was shaped by great thinkers like Sir Isaac Newton, who developed laws of motion describing force, inertia, and the discovery that every action has an equal and opposite reaction. His experiments and calculations with gravity revealed the relationships among force, mass, and distance. He proved that white sunlight was made up of a spectrum of colors. He also refined and consolidated work by earlier scientists, including Copernicus and Galileo.

To such enlightened minds the physical realm was no longer the mysterious, inscrutable place it had always been; rather, it could be explained in material terms down to the last detail. The world worked on mechanical principles; the very light of the sun was a collection of colored particles. In 1747 the French scientist Julien La Mettrie published *Man a Machine,* describing the human body as an "automaton," guided by a mind that reasoned by virtue of "a complex organization of matter." His was the first comprehensive description of man as a purely materialistic collection of mechanical components.

John Locke's theory that all ideas were the result of experience was the psychological parallel to Newton's radical new picture of the physical world. Locke also theorized that all human sensation came from tiny invisible particles affecting the nervous system. Thought, therefore, was a product of physical stimulation, a mechanical response to a mechanical environment.

Even though Newton wrote as a Christian, some thought his explanations about matter made a supernatural explanation unnecessary. Where God had once been the center of the universe, Enlightenment science declared him surplus. Earlier in the Christian era architects and artisans of the great European cathedrals worked anonymously because they believed their identity was unimportant: they labored not for recognition but for the glory of God. By the time of the Renaissance, great painters, sculptors, and architects were not only public figures but celebrities, building reputations and attracting ever more spectacular commissions on the basis of their fame.

By the eighteenth century some men could boldly claim that, while religion might still have a place in the affairs of society, science had unlocked the secrets of life, examined the recesses of the universe, and discovered it was all built on laws and particles and mechanical absolutes. There was no need for a Creator. Others disagreed: The leading thinker of the early eighteenth century, Jonathan Edwards—some call him the greatest American thinker ever—did not fall into the trap of believing that science could replace the supernatural hand of God in world events.

In America the Great Awakening of the 1730s and 1740s and the Second Great Awakening early in the nineteenth century led many to return to the Bible as their guide in every aspect of life. The Methodist revival in eighteenth-century England, and William Wilberforce's work among the London elite from the 1780s to the 1830s, had an important impact on both sides of the Atlantic. But as the nineteenth century began, many intellectuals were assigning God a role in creation while suggesting that his services beyond that were no longer needed.

He compared this hypothetical watch to an eye, so beautifully and specifically made that it never could have happened by accident. The eye, Paley concluded, had to have had a designer. Similarly, all life on earth gave evidence of a designer, as the watch gave evidence of some invisible and unknown watchmaker, because it was too perfect to have come from nothing.

But was it possible in some way for the watch to have built itself? By the time Charles Darwin, born in 1809, received his B.A. from

Cambridge in 1831, British intellectuals were asking that question and yearning for someone to come up with a believable theory.

Darwin's father, Robert Waring Darwin, was a wealthy and successful doctor who wanted Charles to take up medicine as well. But Darwin failed miserably at his medical studies, partly because he couldn't stand to watch operations (anesthesia was still about fifteen years in the future). He turned to the ministry, preparing for ordination as a Church of England clergyman, "the last resort for failures in rich families," as one reference describes it. In later years people would argue that Darwin had been lured away from a career as a minister by the theory of evolution. The fact was that Darwin studied for the ministry because it was one of only a handful of options for the sons of wealthy English families of the era. He evidently spent most of his time during those years riding and shooting.

Between December 1831 and October 1836, Darwin sailed on a scientific voyage around the world aboard the *H.M.S. Beagle.* On this trip he first formed his theory of evolution. According to Darwin's biographer, Sir Gavin de Beer, Darwin made three observations that transformed his thinking about the origins and development of life.

First, he found fossil skeletons of extinct animals that were essentially the same as living animals; extinct species of sloths, for example, were similar to sloths living in South America. Second, he observed that various species of an animal on the same continent had similarities that the species on a different continent did not have. Third, he found that the animals on islands most closely resembled those on the nearest continents. These observations, in de Beer's words, "led Darwin to wonder why—if species were created separately—such similar species happened to be created in successive time periods or in adjacent geographical areas."

Charles's marriage in 1839 to his cousin Emma Wedgwood—niece of Josiah Wedgwood, inventor and namesake of the distinctive stoneware pottery—brought him a comfortable income and the leisure to write and experiment for the next twenty years on his theories of evolution and natural selection. He came to believe that the fossil record, the work of plant and animal breeders, and his own study all pointed toward a system of natural selection within which living specimens with a particular characteristic would thrive and multiply over time, while those without the characteristic would gradually disappear. Once these distinctive characteristics were firmly ingrained, Darwin deduced, new species of plants and animals would be established. As he explained early in his research, "There is a force like a hundred thousand wedges trying to force every kind of adapted structure into the gaps in the economy of nature, or rather forming gaps by thrusting out weaker ones."

In 1858 Darwin received a letter from a naturalist working in the Malay Archipelago describing the very evolutionary theory Darwin had developed. Spurred by the thought someone else would claim credit for the theory he had been working out for years, Darwin began writing what he called an "abstract" of the idea. In the fall of 1859, he published the result, *On the Origin of Species by Means of Natural Selection, or the Preservation of Favoured Races in the Struggle for Life.* It was a tremendous success; the printing sold out immediately, and by 1872 the work had gone through numerous printings and six editions and was famous throughout the world.

In the last chapter, Darwin wrote that he had no designs against Christianity or the church in proposing his theory:

> I see no good reason why the views given in this volume should shock the religious feelings of anyone. It is satisfactory, as showing how transient such impressions are, to remember that the greatest discovery ever made by man, namely, the law of the attraction of gravity, was also attacked . . . as "subversive of natural, and inferentially of revealed, religion." A celebrated author and divine has written to me that he has "gradually learnt to see that it is just as noble a conception of the Deity to believe that He created a few original forms capable of self-development into other and needful forms, as to believe that He required a fresh act of creation to supply the voids caused by the action of His laws."

Other than these brief comments, Darwin had little to say to critics who opposed him on religious grounds, though he was quick to offer thorough replies to scientists who questioned his methods or conclusions. As many evolutionary scientists would do in later years, Darwin seemed to think of religious opposition as intellectually lightweight and not much worth bothering about.

One offshoot of his work that perhaps Darwin had not anticipated was that social and behavioral scientists adapted his theory of natural selection into a sociological concept justifying unrestrained, even ruthless, competition in the struggle for existence. When sociologist Herbert Spencer described this social Darwinism as "survival of the fittest," which implied an aggressiveness and purposefulness Darwin's original theory never had, many Christians saw the theory as a serious threat.

In the United States one of Darwin's most enthusiastic supporters was Asa Gray, a former medical doctor who was a professor of natural history at Harvard and director of the Harvard Botanic Garden. Gray and Darwin began corresponding several years before *The Origin of Species* was published, and the two of them discovered they had many ideas in common. After *Origin* was published, Gray became one of Darwin's strongest defenders in America, though Gray insisted that natural selection did not threaten the concept of a divine Creator. He believed that life systems continued on the strength of "forces communicated at the first" until "now and then, and only now and then, the Deity puts his hand directly to the work." It was a compromise that made Darwinism more palatable to people who had to have a supernatural presence in there somewhere.

Darwin's chief challenger in America was Asa Gray's Harvard colleague Louis Agassiz, born in Switzerland, who began teaching at Harvard in 1848, six years after Gray. Agassiz was a zoologist, fossil authority, and glacier expert who insisted that life on Earth was designed and formed according to a divine plan. He was a steadfast antievolutionist even though his own studies of glaciers and their slow but dramatic changes could be used to support parts of Darwinian theory. Agassiz was a gifted teacher and lecturer, a commanding presence on the platform, and a writer who knew how to explain scientific principles in familiar terms to a popular audience. By the time he died in 1873, he had become the best-known opponent of Darwinism in the country.

Despite this opposition Agassiz did not necessarily support the traditional Christian account of creation: he did not believe in the literal creation story in Genesis. He claimed instead that there were more origins to human life than Adam and Eve, that a series of worldwide catastrophes had periodically depopulated the earth, and that living species had no genetic connections with their fossilized supposed ancestors. Near the end of his life, even Agassiz admitted that the Darwinian viewpoint had achieved "universal acceptance."

Other American men of science agreed that by the mid-1870s, the Darwinian theory of evolution had taken the high ground. As paleontologist Edward Drinker Cope wrote, "The modern theory of evolution has been spread everywhere with unexampled rapidity, thanks to our means of printing and transportation. It has met with remarkably rapid acceptance by those best qualified to judge its merits." Clearly Darwin had filled in not only several scientific holes but also a theological gap among those who had lost faith in the Bible and were looking for some other explanation of origins.

While Darwinism ascended, no one stepped into Louis Agassiz's shoes in the scientific community to challenge it. A few critics gained some degree of professional stature, John McCrady at the College of Charleston and John William Dawson at Princeton for example, but none had the commanding presence and clarity of thought to carry the creationist case to a wider audience in the face of overwhelming Darwinian momentum. Since theologians and clergymen had no standing in the world of natural science, their criticisms had no significant effect on the spread of Darwinian belief and no real impact on what the scientists at Harvard and Princeton and everywhere else taught their students.

By the end of World War I, evolution theory was the basis for college science courses throughout the United States. A 1919 survey of other Midwestern college presidents by Charles A. Blanchard, president of Wheaton College in Illinois, revealed that nearly three-fourths of the schools' science faculties taught evolution; fewer than 8 percent taught only creation science; the rest taught something in between or did not answer the question.

Colleges in the conservative, Baptist-populated South also promoted evolution. William Louis Poteat at Wake Forest, his pupil John Louis Kesler at Baylor, and other professors at church-affiliated colleges taught evolution as a proven fact without any complaints from the students, parents, faculty, or sponsoring denominations. As several fellow college presidents told Dr. Blanchard in his survey, they had little choice but to teach evolution because all the textbooks included it.

Science faculty members and science books had a chicken-and-egg relationship: the evolution-oriented texts Dr. Blanchard's respondents noted were largely written by their own students, colleagues, or peers. Those books in turn produced another wave of young scientists who believed evolution as a proven fact. One such book was *A Civic Biology: Presented in Problems* by Dr. George William Hunter, professor of biology at Carleton College in Minnesota. Before his appointment at Carleton, Hunter headed the department of biology at De Witt Clinton High School in New York City.

In his "Foreword to Teachers" Hunter observed, "In a course in biology the difficulty comes not so much in knowing what to teach as in knowing what *not* to teach. The author believes that he has made a selection of the topics most vital in a well-rounded course in elementary biology directed toward civic betterment."

The book wasn't only about animals and biological systems. It covered the importance of the environment and heredity in human comfort and happiness. Across from the title page were two pictures, one of a busy street in a big city and the other of a large house in the country beside a tree-lined road. The caption under them read, "Compare the unfavorable artificial environment of a crowded city with the more favorable environment of the country."

Hunter integrated moral lessons and contemporary value judgments throughout his book. One noteworthy place was in his section on eugenics, which he defined as "the science of being well born." He explained:

> When people marry there are certain things that the individual as well as the race should demand. The most impor-

> tant of these is freedom from germ diseases which might be handed down to the offspring. Tuberculosis, that dread white plague which is still responsible for almost one seventh of all deaths, epilepsy, and feeble-mindedness are handicaps which it is not only unfair but criminal to hand down to posterity. . . .
>
> Studies have been made on a number of different families in this country. . . . [One particular woman] had a feeble-minded son from whom there have been to the present time 480 descendants. Of these 33 were sexually immoral, 24 confirmed drunkards, 3 epileptics, and 143 feeble-minded. . . . The evidence and the moral speak for themselves! . . .
>
> The cost to society of such families is very severe. . . . They not only do harm to others by corrupting, stealing, or spreading disease, but they are actually protected and cared for by the state out of public money. . . .
>
> If such people were lower animals, we would probably kill them off to prevent them from spreading. Humanity will not allow this, but we do have the remedy of separating the sexes in asylums or other places and in various ways preventing intermarriage and the possibilities of perpetuating such a low and degenerate race. Remedies of this sort have been tried successfully in Europe and are now meeting with success in this country.

Hunter's view of eugenics, widely accepted early in the twentieth century, was a common deduction drawn from and associated with Darwinian theory. Earlier in his book Hunter had explained Darwinian evolution over five pages, then moved later to a section on "heredity and variation" that included eugenics. This popular connection between natural selection and social engineering would soon fan the flames of opposition to teaching Darwinism, particularly in light of the "remedies" that had "been tried successfully in Europe" on the eve of World War I, including sterilizing mental patients, criminals, and other genetic "contaminants."

But school districts across the country saw no problem with Hunter's approach to biology, society, or evolution and approved the book for their classrooms. Tennessee schools began using the book in 1909, adapting a revised edition in 1914. It was a text that contemporary readers and school administrators considered very much in the mainstream.

And that, according to others, was precisely the problem.

CHAPTER 9
The Stakes

HISTORY USUALLY PORTRAYS Charles Darwin as a scientist whose field research and detailed analysis led to a revolution in religious thinking. Yet he admitted from the beginning that one of his main purposes was to separate God from creation. Darwin observed that if God truly were the all-powerful Creator, there shouldn't be such evil in the world. God the perfect Creator could have created a perfect world, yet the world obviously was far from perfect. It seemed to Darwin that either God was unaccountably allowing evil into the world or incapable of keeping it out.

Relieved of the responsibility for creation, God could be perfect even though the world of mankind was hopelessly flawed. In a universe ruled by purposeless random selection, anything made sense. As Darwin explained in his autobiography:

> Suffering is quite compatible with the belief in Natural Selection, which is not perfect in its action, but tends only to render each species as successful as possible in the battle for life with other species, in wonderfully complex and changing circumstances.

> That there is much suffering in the world no one disputes. Some have attempted to explain it in reference to human beings, imagining that it serves their moral improvement. But the number of people in the world is nothing compared with the numbers of all other sentient beings, and these often suffer greatly without any moral improvement. A being so powerful and so full of knowledge as a God who could create the universe is to our finite minds omnipotent and omniscient. It revolts our understanding to suppose that his benevolence is not unbounded, for what advantage can there be in the sufferings of millions of lower animals throughout almost endless time? This very old argument from the existence of suffering against the existence of an intelligent First Cause seems to me a strong one; and the abundant presence of suffering agrees well with the view that all organic beings have been developed through variation and natural selection.

This is not science but theology, evidence of the revolution that Darwinism sparked in the relationship between science and religion. From the High Renaissance to *The Origin of Species,* faith and science were not opposing forces but cultural and intellectual allies. Most scientists were Christians whose observations and deductions tended to confirm the divine beauty and perfection of creation wherever they looked.

Darwin cast science and faith as opposites. Copernicus, Newton, and Galileo saw science as proof of a divine order regardless of their scientific conclusions. By contrast Darwin saw a world irreconcilable with his notion of a perfect God. Instead of concluding that he could not fathom the mind and will of God, Darwin believed that an all-powerful God would never rule over a world filled with evil.

Science writer Cornelius Hunter (who has a different worldview from the George William Hunter who wrote *A Civic Biology*) calls this Darwinism "a description of reality based on a metaphysical presupposition, and as such makes truth claims as no scientific theory can." From Darwin's time forward, evolutionists railed against any "religious" challenge to random mutation and natural selection as "unscientific" and "unprovable." Yet the theory emerged not out of science but from

Darwin's metaphysical assumption that a loving and all-powerful God would never create such an imperfect world.

Darwin's conclusions marked the transformation of religion from an ally of science and the center of absolute truth to a subjective, symbolic collection of myths and maxims. Science became a world of physical materialism where metaphysical notions had no place. Darwin's ideas about religion led him to his theory, yet all his later defenders insisted that metaphysics had no part in the materialistic world of science.

Scientific arguments have raged for centuries about the nature of light, the mechanism of heredity, the relationship between speed and time, and a long list of other matters. But what made Darwinism so important and impactful was theological and not scientific: it pulled the foundation of moral absolutes out from under every law, action, and relationship. If God is sovereign, his law as given in the Bible is the absolute standard; if God is an uninterested or helpless bystander and pointless random chemical reactions underlie all of life, God's law is superfluous.

The abandonment of absolute standards of morality and behavior eventually transformed the American cultural and legal landscape. Pornography became free speech, with public decency standards ("*Whose* standards?") marginalized. The destruction of moral absolutes paved the way for welfare programs that held no one accountable for his actions or choices and set out to apply materialist solutions—money—to metaphysical problems of the heart and the spirit.

Materialist responses will never solve a metaphysical problem. Yet to many people the thought that Darwinism is a hollow myth and that they are ultimately accountable only to God must be horrifying and scarcely imaginable. They can't bear to recognize standards other than their own. A contemporary of Darwin predicted as much. Reverend Adam Sedgwick, president of the Geological Society of London and a popular lecturer at Cambridge, was both a clergyman and a scientist. Like many educated people at that time (and before), he believed materialism and the spiritual world were on equal footing and that the unmistakable hand of God as Creator was on both: "In the material world we see in all things the proofs of intelligence and power; so also, that in the immaterial world we find proofs, not less strong, that man is under the moral government of an all-powerful, benevolent, and holy God."

As Cornelius Hunter asserts in *Darwin's God,* Victorians saw God as a wise and benevolent figure whose wrath and refining fire were seldom mentioned. Sedgwick concentrated on the forgiving and gracious God who prescribed universal laws for living. He wrote Darwin that absolving God of any responsibility for creation, in Hunter's words, "was disregarding the moral imperative":

> There is a moral or metaphysical part of nature, as well as physical. A man who denies this is deep in the mire of folly. 'Tis the crown and glory of organic science that it does through final cause link material and moral; and yet does not allow us to mingle them in our first conception of laws; and our classification of such laws, whether we consider one side of nature or the other. You have ignored this link; and, if I do not mistake your meaning, you have done your best in one or two pregnant cases to break it.

Hunter concludes that the difference between Sedgwick and Darwin "lay not in their conception of God but in the metaphysical problem that colored their study of nature. Sedgwick was concerned with morality, and Darwin was concerned with evil." A century and a half later evolutionist Stephen Jay Gould expressed a logical extension of Darwin's viewpoint that the world just doesn't make enough sense for an intelligent God to have created it: "Odd arrangements and funny solutions are the proof of evolution—paths that a sensible God would never tread but that a natural process, constrained by history, follows perforce."

The claim here that God is too "sensible" to have created the world we know is purely subjective and religious. And so despite longstanding assertions to the contrary, Darwinism did not divorce science from metaphysics after they had coexisted together for centuries. Rather Darwin, to use Hunter's term, "merely switched the metaphysics." He started with a theological premise, and his defenders have followed suit ever since, gaining such confidence in the process that they lambasted as stupid anyone who did not go along.

By the time Darrow and the rest of the defense team needed to assemble a crew of top scientists in Dayton to make their case for evolution, the task was easy. The academic credentials were impressive: Charles Hubbard Judd, director, School of Education, University of Chicago, former professor of psychology at Yale, Ph.D. from Leipzig University, twice president of the Society of College Teachers of Education; Fay-Cooper Cole, anthropologist, University of Chicago, graduate studies at the University of Berlin, Ph.D. from Columbia; Wilbur A. Nelson, president of the American Association of State Geologists and chairman of the department of geology at the University of Virginia; Kirtley F. Mather, chairman of the Department of Geology, Harvard University; and many more.

In their written testimony to the court, defense attorneys not only presented Darwinian evolution as an absolute fact, but they also suggested that anyone who disagreed with its conclusions was either too dim-witted to accept the truth or too uninformed to know it. Many of the scientists also minimized the theological consequences of their views. Dr. Maynard Metcalf, the one expert allowed to speak briefly on the stand, submitted a written statement declaring that nothing having to do with evolution

> has any bearing upon the question of God as the creator of the universe. It is only a matter of the method He has chosen in creation—whether immediate fiat or gradual growth accompanied by divergence. The evidence is overwhelming that the latter was and is His method. . . . There is no conflict, no least degree of conflict, between the Bible and the fact of evolution, but the literalist interpretation of the words of the Bible is not only puerile; it is insulting, both to God and to human intelligence.

Metcalf continued: "The fundamentalist would do much worse than insult God. He is in reality, although he doesn't realize this, trying to shut man's mind to God's ever-growing revelation of Himself to the human soul. He teaches, in effect, that God's revelation of Himself was completed long ago, that He long ago ceased to unfold His mind to men in new revelation. This is evil influence, criminal damnable. Truth is sacred and to hinder men's approach to truth is as evil a thing, as un-Christian a thing, as one can do."

Even at this early stage in the history of the Scopes trial, Dr. Metcalf used his platform as a scientific expert—an expert in the materialist world—to make some very metaphysical statements for the record. The rest of the scientific experts in Dayton and many of their American colleagues stated at various times that though God was the Creator, Darwin's random mutation and natural selection were his tools. At least one of the expert witnesses, Dr. Mather of Harvard, was a Baptist Sunday school teacher who saw no conflict between evolution and the Bible.

Reporters buttonholed college professors, divinity school presidents, and high-profile personalities for statements inevitably branding creationism as the refuge of fools. Dr. Winterton C. Curtis, a Dayton witness and professor of zoology at the University of Missouri, submitted a letter to the court from the late former U.S. president Woodrow Wilson, written on August 29, 1922, stating, "May it not suffice for me to say, in reply to your letter of August 25th, that, of course, like every other man of intelligence and education, I do believe in organic evolution. It surprises me that at this late date such questions should be raised."

Evolutionists and the media emphasized the Darwinians' academic credentials, their respect nonetheless for the Bible, and the seemingly overwhelming evidence in the fossil record and other scientific quarters that supported evolution. Yet as they made their case, they established some of the misunderstandings that continue to cloud the issue. For example, in his written brief to the court defending evolution, Professor Metcalf wrote, "Not only has evolution occurred; it is occurring today and occurring even under man's control. If one wishes a new vegetable or a new flower, it is, within limits, true that he can order it from the plant breeder and in a few years he will produce it."

What Metcalf either minimized or purposefully ignored was the glaring differences between what he described and Darwin's theory. Darwin's random, purposeless mutation and natural selection assume exactly the opposite of plant breeding "under man's control." In the latter case an intelligent force, the breeder, is working toward a specific end, a disease-resistant tree or a new color of rose. Also a "new" vegetable or flower "within limits" describes small changes or modifications to characteristics that are already there. Breeding might make a ten-petal rose from an eight-petal rose, but it can't produce a petal from nothing and will never transform an apple into a tomato.

Glaring differences aside, these statements of "scientific fact" from expert witnesses bearing world-class academic credentials established Darrow's position for the evolution side. Meanwhile, they put creationism on trial and found it guilty of inconsistency, hypocrisy, and general muddle-headedness. They were so successful that within a generation Darwin's theory would become so popular that it needed no justification at all.

Let's go back to *Darwin's God,* in which Cornelius Hunter articulates two ideas that blossomed over the past century. First was the law of divine sanction, a version of the theory that God is a watchmaker who made the universe, then left it alone to run on its own. The God of divine sanction, Hunter explains, "is seen as being all the greater for designing a world that works on its own rather than requiring divine intervention."

The second idea that helped the ascendancy of Darwinism was the law of intellectual necessity, the viewpoint that led ultimately to scientist Richard Lewontin's recent warning that scientists can't risk letting a divine foot in the door. Intellectual necessity holds that science has to restrict God to natural laws and disallow the supernatural because "only this ensures that meaningful scientific inquiry is possible. If natural laws are liable to violation, then we cannot discern the law from the exception."

One of the chief legacies of the Renaissance and the Enlightenment was that man recognized reason as a means to change his relationship with God. Before, God was the mysterious, incomprehensible, all-powerful ruler of the universe. In the wake of the Enlightenment, man confidently claimed sufficient reason to understand God and interpret his motives. The Age of Reason produced a God of reason that presumably made rational sense according to the standards of the newly self-aware human mind.

And what rational person could accept evil in a world created by a perfect, all-loving God? Early thinkers could explain moral evil—warfare, murder, and other man-made disasters—as the by-product of human sinfulness. But what about natural evil? What about earthquakes, birth defects, and parasites that kill their host? Beginning with René Descartes in the seventeenth century, philosophers looked for a materialist, mechanical solution to the origins and development of life and for a way to explain what part evil played in the whole equation. The German philosopher Gottfried Leibniz described a universe that was self-correcting because punishment and morality were built into the mechanics of creation: "Sins carry their punishment with them by the order of nature and by virtue of the mechanical structure of things itself; and . . . in the same way noble actions will attract their rewards by ways which are mechanical as far as bodies are concerned."

Scientists, philosophers, and theologians struggled and argued endlessly about the relationship between a perfect God and an imperfect world that he might or might not have created. The eighteenth-century philosopher David Hume asserted that miracles were impossible because they violated natural law and the theory of uniformitarianism and that all the physical conditions in the world today have been the same throughout history. Two hundred years later theologian Rudolf Bultmann's claims showed that Hume's arguments were accepted as fact: "The historical method includes the presupposition that history is a unity in the sense of a closed continuum of effects in which individual events are connected by the succession of cause and effect. . . . This closedness means that the continuum of historical happenings cannot be rent by the interference of supernatural transcendent powers and that therefore there is no 'miracle' in this sense of the word."

According to Bultmann, whether there is any proof to support reported miracles is immaterial because of a "presupposition" that history is a closed time line where the rules are always the same. Nothing happens outside the rules; therefore miracles don't exist. Bultmann here is making his own rules; if rules could change, empirical, material, scientific conclusions alone would be insufficient to prove a theory, and scientists would lose their power to declare what was true and what was not. This is where science calls a halt to the debate. Unfettered discussion, inquiry, and conclusion are all nipped in the bud by stacking the metaphysical (and not the scientific) deck against any challenge to the absolute primacy of materialism and uniformism.

One of Charles Darwin's favorite books was *Paradise Lost,* the great epic by John Milton first published in 1667. Though it included non-Christian elements, such as a classically inspired invocation to the Greek goddesses of poetry and the literary device of sending the angel Michael to Eden after the fall to explain God's plan of salvation to Adam, it strongly affirmed the biblical teaching that God created all the universe. What Darwin may have appreciated about the story was that from Milton's perspective God didn't cause evil in the world. According to *Paradise Lost,* evil originated with Satan, who caused the fall and ruined mankind in retribution for God throwing him out of heaven and into a lake of fire in hell.

Poetic license puts this account somewhat at odds with the Bible's own version of the story, as Milton must have known, but having Satan work his evil on Adam and Eve comfortably distanced God from original sin. Through Jesus, God could then redeem Adam from sin and lead him to the promise of a personal paradise in heaven even greater than unspoiled Eden would have been. Darwin believed God would never have created suffering; *Paradise Lost* offered the comforting suggestion that evil in the world was Satan's fault, a terrible blow delivered to God's perfect creation in defiance and retribution. God's answer was to send his Son, Jesus, to atone for all sin.

The Bible is filled with examples of both moral and natural evil that exist so that God may reveal his perfect will by triumphing over them: Joseph's brothers sell him into slavery, where he eventually saves their lives and the lives of all Israel (Genesis 37); Jesus restores sight to a man born blind (John 9) and raises Lazarus from the dead (John 11–12), using blindness and death to show his power and compassion. In a world brought down by the Fall, God shows himself and his power most clearly by providentially or miraculously overcoming evil.

Two essential characteristics of God were incompatible with a Victorian society that pictured God as a kind, grandfatherly figure and Jesus as a gentle shepherd. First is the idea that mankind is born in sin and therefore no matter how terrible someone's life is, it's better than he deserves. No mortal is good enough to "earn" God's approval. Jesus died as an atonement for all sin; the way God applies that gift of atonement is not for his creation to judge.

The second characteristic, which has been challenged from the Renaissance onward, is the idea that mortal minds cannot comprehend the mind of God. From a human perspective war and famine cannot be justified; murder is irreconcilable with a world created by a loving God. But man cannot know the purposes of the Creator and cannot assume he would reason out matters as we would. God's omniscient reason begins at the limit of our own; what seems unspeakably horrible to us is part of a universal picture we can never see. Hume, Darwin, and all the rest struggled mightily to explain why God would do something, but we need to recognize that as his creations we are always smaller than and subservient to him. Some whys will always be beyond our ability to answer. The material scientist, it seems, would rather have the wrong answer based on "presuppositions" than no answer at all.

Alfred, Lord Tennyson, wrote the poem *In Memoriam* in 1850 when he was already poet laureate and the most honored poet of his generation. An excerpt reflects the cultural mind-set of Darwin's time, musing on God's evident indifference:

> Are God and Nature then at strife,
> That Nature lends such evil dreams?
> So careful of the type she seems,
> So careless of the single life;
>
> That I, considering everywhere
> Her secret meaning in her deeds,
> And finding that of fifty seeds
> She often brings but one to bear . . .
>
> "So careful of the type?" but no.
> From scarpéd cliff and quarried stone
> She cries, "A thousand types are gone:
> I care for nothing, all shall go" . . .
>
> Man, her last work, who seemed so fair,
> Such splendid purpose in his eyes,
> Who rolled the psalm to wintry skies,
> Who built him fanes [temples] of fruitless prayer,

> Who trusted God was love indeed
> And love Creation's final law—
> Tho' Nature, red in tooth and claw
> With ravine [violent force], shrieked against his creed—

Poetry, arguably the most subjective of all intellectual pursuits, here expresses what Darwin transformed into science: the world is too wasteful, fruitless, and violent for God to have created it. As Hunter terms it, "Evolution is intellectually necessary because divine creation cannot be investigated and analyzed. For Isaac Newton and many other scientists the idea that God created the world has been a stimulus to scientific inquiry, but for today's evolutionists it is anathema."

In *Darwin's God* Hunter concludes:

> We often hear that evolution is an objective, scientific theory. . . . But this is a great myth of our time. Evolution is not a story of a bold scientific stroke that has been beautifully borne out by the advancement of science, against metaphysical resistance. It is nearly the exact opposite. It is not that evolution is utterly unscientific or that it completely lacks evidence. Evolution can be properly formulated as a scientific theory with plenty of supporting evidence, but as such it is unremarkable. Evolution's supporting evidence is outrun by the counterevidence. . . . Evolution's compelling arguments, and the reason for its stunning success, come not from its scientific support but from indirect arguments against creation.
>
> Evolution provides a theological solution to a theological problem, and the science is sandwiched somewhere in between. But the theological premises are denied, so the theological result is seen as coming from science, and science inappropriately attains the status of truthgiver. Philosophy and science have always been influenced by theology. This is especially true for evolution. The difference is that evolution denies the influence.

Now that we've briefly discussed why the issues raised in the Scopes trial were so crucial, let's return to the action.

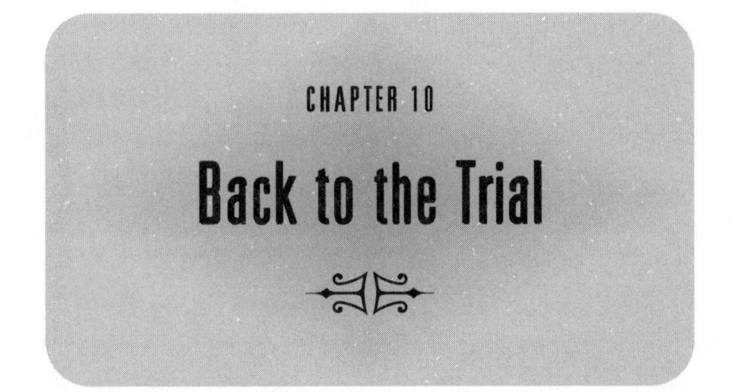

CHAPTER 10
Back to the Trial

BY THE BEGINNING of the afternoon session on Wednesday, July 15, the so-called trial of the century, in a spot derided by the intellectual elite of the century, had produced a lot more smoke than fire. For all the ink the Scopes story commanded around the world, citizens of Dayton and Tennesseans at large were surprised and disappointed to see how much of it was negative. The president of Columbia University, for one, declared his prestigious institution would no longer accept students from Tennessee high schools if they couldn't be taught Darwinian theory.

U.S. president Calvin Coolidge, a Congregationalist, also decried the state ban on teaching evolution though, like so many other Americans, his focus was on William Jennings Bryan and not on the legal particulars. The president objected to "the possibility of interjection of 'mob psychology' into the evolution controversy," according to wire service reports, and also worried about the polarizing prospect of a constitutional amendment against teaching evolution "that inevitably would bring about even greater differences than the prohibition amendment."

Crowded though the town was, reporters continued to interview disappointed merchants and opportunists. "The Scopes trial has been a failure from the concessionaire's point of view," according to an Associated Press dispatch describing the temporary refreshment and souvenir stands that covered the area around the courthouse. "Built cheaply, there was not any great investment required for the construction of the stands, but despite the small expenditures, many of the men declared they have failed to earn enough to authorize the investment. . . . The town prepared to entertain thousands and the crowds came by hundreds."

As the afternoon session of the eighteenth circuit court was called to order, someone took every available space. Reporters asked the judge for more chairs; the defense attorneys called out for their chairs to be returned, with Ben McKenzie jovially suggesting that Judge Raulston ask spectators "that they not carry off the chairs of the attorneys. We are a necessary evil in the courtroom, supposed to be a part of it."

Later Judge Raulston ruled that no more people would be allowed in the courtroom than there were chairs; beginning the next day everybody without a seat would have to listen to the trial on the speakers outside. That Wednesday afternoon was not only the most crowded session but by all accounts the hottest. A high pressure weather system gripped Tennessee from the Mississippi River to the Cumberland Mountains. The heat was worse in Texas, where triple-digit temperatures simmered Dallas and Wichita Falls, but the thermometer also hit 100 degrees in Idaho, and Phoenix topped out at 114.

In the swarm of people, packed almost too close to move, it took a moment for Attorney General Tom Stewart and defense counsel Clarence Darrow and Dudley Field Malone to make sure everyone they had subpoenaed was present. Then at last, and no doubt to Clarence Darrow's immense relief, the judge called for the jury to be seated. Darrow had been frustrated by Judge Raulston's insistence that the debate about the constitutionality of the law, the appropriateness of courtroom prayer, and other matters up to this point be argued without the jury. Now jurors would at least hear something of the case, though the judge still held that they would not be sworn in until the issues were "made up" by opening statements from both sides.

Turning to the defense table, Raulston asked, "What is your plea, gentlemen?" "Not guilty, may it please your honor," John R. Neal replied. The judge then asked each side for a brief opening statement outlining "what your theory is in the case."

Tom Stewart saw the accusation as a simple violation of a simple statute. His entire opening statement took two sentences: "It is the insistence of the state in this case that the defendant, John Thomas Scopes, has violated the antievolution law, what is known as the antievolution law, by teaching in the public schools of Rhea County the theory tending to show that man and mankind is descended from a lower order of animals. Therefore, he has taught a theory which denies the story of divine creation of man as taught in the Bible."

As far as Stewart was concerned, whether biblical creationism was true was entirely beside the point. If John Scopes taught it in the public schools, he was guilty because the law said he couldn't.

Evidently surprised by the brevity of Stewart's opening statement, Dudley Field Malone warned the judge that his opening would be far longer. "I just want a brief statement of your theory," Judge Raulston replied.

"I understand that, your honor," Malone answered back and began an opening statement that took half an hour. The essence of his position was that it was possible to believe in both the Bible and evolution. While admitting that the defense considered the two irreconcilable, Malone explained that "men learned in science and theology" would testify "that there are millions of people who believe in evolution and in the stories of creation as set forth in the Bible and who find no conflict between the two." Just because Scopes taught Darwinian theory did not mean he necessarily taught against the story of divine creation.

"We believe there is no conflict between evolution and Christianity," Malone continued, insisting that the prosecution had a burden to prove exactly what "evolution" was. "There may be a conflict between evolution and the peculiar ideas of Christianity which are held by Mr. Bryan as the evangelical leader of the prosecution, but we deny that the evangelical leader of the prosecution is an authorized spokesman for the Christians of the United States."

Going further, Malone read from the commentary of a "great political leader" on Thomas Jefferson's "Statute of Religious Freedom" that concluded:

> The regulation of opinions of men on religious questions by law is contrary to the laws of God and to the plans of God. [Jefferson] pointed out that God had it in His power to control man's mind and body, but that He did not see fit to coerce the mind or the body into obedience to even the Divine Will; and that if God Himself was not willing to use coercion to force man to accept certain religious views, man, uninspired and liable to error, ought not to use the means that Jehovah would not employ. Jefferson realized that our religion was a religion of love and not a religion of force.

Malone then added his zinger: "These words were written by William Jennings Bryan, and the defendant appeals from the fundamentalist Bryan of today to the modernist Bryan of yesterday."

Without waiting for a rejoinder from Bryan or a reaction from the audience, Malone charged ahead, claiming that evolutionary theory was essential to teaching every branch of science, including agriculture and livestock breeding. All scientific truth, he said, could not be in the Bible since so many scientific discoveries had been made since biblical times: "Moses never heard about steam," he continued, "electricity, the telegraph, the telephone, the radio, the aeroplane, farming machinery, and Moses knew nothing about scientific thought and principles from which these vast accomplishments of the inventive genius of mankind have been produced."

Malone plowed on: "The defense denies that it is part of any movement or conspiracy on the part of scientists to destroy the authority of Christianity or the Bible. The defense denies that any such conspiracy exists except in the mind and purposes of the prosecution. . . . The narrow purpose of the defense is to establish the innocence of the defendant Scopes. The broad purpose of the defense will be to prove that the Bible is a work of religious aspiration and rules of conduct which must be kept in the field of theology."

Stewart interrupted Malone to object to the defense mentioning Bryan's name. Malone was skillfully working to use Bryan's fame and notoriety against him. But it was not easy to turn popular opinion against the Great Commoner. Having sat in silence for four days, fanning himself with a palm leaf fan carrying an advertisement for Robinson's Drug Store, Bryan spoke at last in response to Judge Raulston's ruling that references to Bryan be deleted from the record.

He said, "The court can do as it pleases in carrying out its rules, but I ask no protection from the court. And when the proper time comes, I shall be able to show the gentlemen that I stand today just where I did, but that this has nothing to do with the case at the bar."

This short, innocuous statement brought a thunderous roar of applause from the spectators. It further whetted the appetites of the thousands upon thousands who were waiting for the glorious battle they knew was coming between Darrow and Bryan. Raulston threatened to remove applauders from the room, saying he could not allow an expression of opinion in front of the jury. The fact that Bryan had spoken at all made headlines coast to coast the next day.

Malone returned to his opening statement, now reading from page 4 of his typewritten text. Again Stewart objected to arguing the question of religion, and Ben McKenzie added that the New Yorker was trying to influence the jury improperly, insisting no discussion of science versus religion was proper until Judge Raulston ruled on whether the scientific experts would be allowed to testify for the defense. McKenzie argued that while the prosecution had simply stated its position as ordered by the judge, the defense was now arguing its position in detail.

Malone responded, "The jury, we believe, is an intelligent body of citizens that know the difference between testimony taken from the witnesses and oratorical flights of the judge and myself." In trying to affirm he knew as much and, furthermore, knew what he was talking about, McKenzie tripped over his words: "There could not have been anything in the minds of the lawyers—we are not mediocre lawyers—"

Malone cut him off. "That is not what I meant."

McKenzie went on affably: "The only mistake the good Lord made is that he did not withhold the completion of the job until he could have got a conference with you." Malone immediately caught the spirit of the moment. "I rather think you are right." The courtroom rumbled with laughter that broke the tension.

The defense finished its opening statement, the jury was sworn in at last, and the prosecution called its first witness, school superintendent Walter White, who had replaced George Rappleyea as the official complainant against Scopes. Under questioning by Stewart, White testified that John Scopes taught in the public school and had admitted he taught from Hunter's biology textbook. By now the entire world knew about the May 5 conversation in Robinson's Drug Store to which White referred. The whole purpose of it was to establish that young Scopes had taught evolution, though under oath as a witness White never said Scopes had done so.

The way the superintendent described it, Scopes said he had "taught this book, and had reviewed the entire subject, as it is customary for the teacher to do [during a year-end review], and among other things he said he could not teach that book without teaching evolution."

Years later Scopes himself would write that he "didn't remember teaching" evolution and "didn't know technically" whether he had violated the Butler Act. Looking back from a historical perspective, Scopes would claim he had agreed to his arrest because he thought the policies and viewpoints represented by the law were a menace that would only grow more dangerous. "I realized," he explained, "that the best time to scotch the snake is when it starts to wiggle."

Superintendent White's testimony, in essence, was that if Scopes taught biology he had to have used the state textbook, and if he covered everything in the state textbook, he had to cover Darwinian evolution because it was included in the material.

Stewart then proposed to submit a copy of the Bible as an exhibit showing what the law meant when it referred to that item. Hays objected on the grounds that many versions of the Bible existed and a specific translation could not represent them all. Judge Raulston overruled the objection. Darrow wanted to know what edition the exhibit

Bible was, asking if it were the Scofield edition. Stewart answered by reading aloud from the title page, "Holman's Pronouncing Edition of the Holy Bible. . . . Text conformable to that of 1611, known as the Authorized or King James Bible," published by A. J. Holman & Co. of Philadelphia. It was available, Stewart told Darrow, at Robinson's if he wanted an identical copy. Barring further objection, the Holman King James Bible would be the official Bible of the Butler Act.

Under cross-examination by Darrow, superintendent White revealed how transparent the case against Scopes was, though none of the reporters or commentators seemed to pick up on these telling details of testimony.

First, Darrow asked whether the state textbook commission had officially approved the Hunter textbook. "That was the official book adopted by the Tennessee textbook commission in 1919," White replied, "but the contract expired August 31, 1924." Darrow then asked, "Had any other book been adapted in the meantime?" "No, sir," was the response.

Darrow then asked where this and other textbooks were for sale. "Certain depositories in Tennessee," White answered. "The Robinson store was one of those depositories, was it?" Darrow queried. "Yes, sir." Robinson further testified that he had never heard any complaints against Scopes as a teacher, and that *A Civic Biology* had been used in Tennessee since 1909, ten years before it was officially endorsed by the state commission.

So according to the first prosecution witness, the accused taught from the state-sanctioned textbook, which was purchased by students from Doc Robinson, chairman of the school board. Nothing White said directly implicated Scopes, who seemed guilty of nothing more than teaching out of a book that had been used since he himself was in grade school, the purchase of which put money in the pocket of the school board chairman.

Stewart's next witness was Howard Morgan, son of Darrow's host in Dayton, looking serious and somber, his white shirt freshly pressed, his cap in his hand. He was fourteen, a student at Central High. Morgan testified that Professor Scopes taught him from a textbook titled *General Science* by Lewis Elhuff, which said that "a little germ of one cell organism formed, and this organism kept evolving until it got to be a pretty good-sized animal, and then came on to be a land animal, and it kept on evolving, and from this was man."

The boy admitted, though, that he couldn't find anything about evolution in the book and didn't remember what mammals were. On cross-examination Darrow gently questioned Morgan further about what he remembered of the course Scopes had taught him. At that moment Morgan couldn't remember much of anything except the organism evolving into man. The student's testimony strongly supported later claims that he and his classmates who were called to testify were coached. What fourteen-year-old boy would otherwise remember such a specific scientific detail, and none other, two and a half months into summer vacation?

At the end of this questioning, Darrow asked of Scopes's teaching, "It has not hurt you any, has it?" "No, sir," the boy replied as laughter rippled through the room. Howard Morgan was excused.

The prosecution called another student, seventeen-year-old Harry Shelton. Professor Scopes, he said, had reviewed his biology class around the middle of April and taught them that "all forms of life begin with the cell."

Cross-examining the student, Darrow asked, "That is all you remember that he told you about biology, isn't it?" "Yes, sir," he answered. Darrow continued, "You didn't leave church when he told you all forms of life began with a single cell?" Again the answer, "No, sir." Laughter and chuckles bubbled up in the courtroom; the judge called for silence. Shelton was excused.

Next up for the prosecution was Doc Robinson, who corroborated Walter White's testimony that John Scopes said "any teacher in the state who was teaching Hunter's *Biology* was violating the law." When it was Darrow's turn, the defense counsel asked Robinson whether he sold the Hunter text. The druggist admitted he did. "And you were a member of the school board?" "Yes, sir."

Tom Stewart interjected, "The law says teach, not sell!" The spectators broke out in laughter, but Darrow went on, reading passages in the text having to do with Darwin and the classification of species.

Then Darrow asked Robinson, "How many of those [textbooks] did you have for sale?" "I have been selling that book for six or seven years," Robinson answered. "Have you noticed any mental or moral deterioration growing out of that thing?"

Attorney General Stewart objected to the question, and the judge sustained his objection.

Darrow went on, "How do you get them, Mr. Robinson?" "From the depository at Chattanooga for this county." They were, Robinson admitted, the state-sanctioned books for the high school, and his store was the only place in Dayton that stocked them.

In response to Darrow reading extended passages from *A Civic Biology,* Stewart then read the first two chapters of Genesis into the record. Knowing the prosecution had more students waiting to testify and suspecting their testimony would add little to the evidence, Darrow suggested their names be added to the record but that they not be asked to give evidence.

Attorney General Stewart agreed. Turning to Judge Raulston, he said, "The state rests."

CHAPTER 11

Sparring over Experts

CLARENCE DARROW called the first witness for the defense, a zoology professor and research scientist named Maynard M. Metcalf, who had studied at Oberlin and Johns Hopkins, taught both in the United States and abroad, directed a research laboratory, and consulted with the U.S. government on biological and agricultural matters.

Darrow had scarcely gotten under way when Attorney General Stewart interrupted him to say that in Tennessee the procedure was that if the defendant was going to take the stand he had to be the first defense witness.

"Well, you have already caught me on it," Darrow answered. The first witness was already sworn in and testifying on the stand. "That is a technicality," the judge replied. "We have not gone into the merits. I will allow you to withdraw the witness." "Your honor," Darrow observed, "every single word that was said against this defendant, everything was true." "So he does not care to go on the stand?" "No. What's the use?"

Darrow returned to his questions for Dr. Metcalf. And so John Scopes, as he said later, would be "a ringside observer at my own trial." Actually Darrow and his colleagues knew Scopes couldn't afford to take the stand. He had to be found guilty to file an appeal to a higher court, which the defense planned from the beginning. His truthful testimony could well have convinced the jury he was innocent.

After leading the zoologist through a description of his work and a short history of his career, Darrow asked, "Are you an evolutionist?" And then, "Do you know any scientific man in the world that is not an evolutionist?"

Tom Stewart sprang to his feet with an objection. Judge Raulston sustained it. Arthur Garfield Hays argued that one of the points of contention was whether the Butler Act "was within the police power of the state," which in turn depended on whether evolution was a "mere guess" or "generally accepted by all scientists" as Raulston framed the matter. As Hays explained, "Our whole case depends upon proving that evolution is a reasonable scientific theory."

Finally the judge allowed Darrow to ask Professor Metcalf whether scientists believed in evolution, but only while crowded privately around the witness table, out of earshot of the jury. The professor answered, "I am absolutely convinced from personal knowledge that any one of these [scientists] feel and believe, as a matter of course, that evolution is a fact, but I doubt very much if any two of them agree as to the exact method by which evolution has been brought about."

When Darrow continued his questions before the whole courtroom, Stewart objected again, insisting that the jury should not hear any argument over whether there was a conflict between evolution and divine creation. Darrow countered that this debate would yield essential evidence for the jury. He was likely frustrated but no longer surprised when the judge asked the jury to leave the room, admonishing them not to listen to the testimony on the radio or loudspeakers. One juror assured the judge that no juryman had heard a single word "pass over the horns out there."

With the jury gone, Dr. Metcalf began a detailed discourse on evolution, starting with the difference between the fact of evolution, which he said was singular, and the theories of evolution, which were many. He traced the development of "organic evolution" through a series of steps he believed had taken as long as six hundred million years, concluding with the opinion that "it would be entirely impossible for any normal human being who was conversant with the phenomena to have even for a moment the least doubt even for the fact of evolution, but he might have tremendous doubt as to the truth of any [one] hypothesis."

Court then adjourned for the day, with a policeman warning the multitude that the next day they were "not going to have any standing room at all"; anybody who couldn't find a seat inside would have to listen on the lawn.

In his column in the next day's Baltimore *Evening Sun,* H. L. Mencken declared Professor Metcalf's explanation of evolution to be the high point of Wednesday's testimony. It was, he wrote, "one of the clearest, most succinct and withal most eloquent presentations of the case for the evolutionists that I have ever heard."

But what seemed to fascinate Mencken even more, what every spectator kept watching, and what the public continued to talk about day after day was William Jennings Bryan. The waiting world saw him as a volcano silently building up pressure for the moment when he would unleash all his passion and eloquence and intellect against this challenge to one of the bedrock beliefs of Christianity. From the beginning neither the narrow legal issues nor the factual specifics, and neither the constitutionality of the Butler Act nor the truth about whether John Scopes taught Darwinian evolution in the public schools received much attention. All eyes were fixed on Darrow and Bryan. Almost all the talk was about what would happen when these two larger-than-life figures collided head-on, reason against the gospel.

Though Bryan had played no part whatever in the trial so far, Mencken could not resist pounding away at him, attacking him with *ad hominem* arguments that had nothing to do with his position on evolution. Bryan hadn't said or done anything in court that Mencken could criticize, so he criticized his very presence. The Sage of Baltimore took obvious pride in considering himself the spokesman for intellectuals and the educated as he hammered away at the Great Commoner sitting silently at the prosecutors' table.

"[Professor Metcalf's testimony] was, to him, a string of blasphemies out of the devil's mass—a dreadful series of assaults upon the only true religion. The old gladiator faced his real enemy at last." Bryan, Mencken declared, feared education and knowledge, and so turned to fundamentalist

> yokels . . . for consolation in his old age, with the scars of defeat and disaster all over him. . . . This old buzzard, having failed to raise the mob against its rulers now prepares to raise it against its teachers. He can never be the peasants' President, but there is still a chance to be the peasants' Pope. He leads a new crusade, his bald head glistening, his face streaming with sweat, his chest heaving beneath his rumpled alpaca coat. One somehow pities him, despite his so palpable imbecilities. It is a tragedy, indeed, to begin life as a hero and to end it as a buffoon.

Mencken had had Bryan in his sights for more than twenty years. The images of Bryan as a washed-up has-been were images Mencken had first used in 1904 when reporting on the Democratic national convention for the *Baltimore Morning and Sunday Herald*. It was the twenty-four-year-old reporter's first presidential convention as an observer and Bryan's third as a prospective candidate; Bryan had won the nomination in 1896 and 1900 and would win again in 1908, but 1904 brought him defeat at the hands of New York commercial interests.

Twenty thousand Democrats had waited through a long, hot July night in St. Louis to hear Bryan speak. As Mencken reported the scene: "For fifty hours he had been tireless and sleepless, struggling in committee room and on the floor, by word and deed, for the things that seemed to him sacred. Now, with his voice a mere whisper, his collar a rag, his hair disheveled, his eyes sunken and his face pallid and deep-lined, the old leader arose before his old retainers and his victorious foes, an imperial and mighty figure, and said good-bye." It was "the funeral of a mighty chieftain."

But even then Mencken acknowledged Bryan's popularity. While by 1925 he considered Bryan's followers yokels and simpletons, in 1904 he had seen them in a less critical light: "As Bryan paused and stepped back, with head erect and eyes flashing fire, there arose a whoop that made the formal cheering for Parker [the eventual Democratic nominee] and the machine-made 'enthusiasm' for Hearst [the powerful publisher, another candidate] seem puny. Again and again his hearers yelled."

Bryan's advocates were still waiting for him to spring into action as the fifth day of the Scopes trial began on Thursday, July 16, amid continued confusion over how Dr. Metcalf and others would testify. Metcalf had testified the day before with the jury absent because Judge Raulston had not yet ruled on whether expert scientific testimony was admissible. Attorney General Stewart and the prosecution continued to insist the testimony be excluded and that the experts say just enough to allow the judge to make a ruling now, then be called back later if necessary to testify for the record; Darrow and the defense wanted experts to testify for the record even if the judge ruled their testimony inadmissible so it would be part of the legal documentation when the case was appealed.

Even the judge was confused. Stewart was explaining the situation as he saw it when Judge Raulston interrupted with, "Let me see what the question was."

Stewart replied, "I say if [expert testimony] isn't competent, now is when we ought to get at once to the issues and let the court pass on the proposition of whether or not it is admissible." The judge responded, "Your plan is, if I was to exclude the evidence, you would want this witness [Metcalf] back and have him reexamined." "Yes, sir, that is our procedure, your honor, always as I understand it." Raulston said, "There was a mix-up here by some kind of agreement or suggestion yesterday."

"That was with the suggestion and understanding as I had it that Mr. Darrow would put before the court sufficient of this evidence to let the court and attorneys on the other side intelligibly understand just what he insisted upon," explained the attorney general, to which Raulston answered, "I thought if I excluded the evidence, you [addressing Darrow] would put this evidence in; then if I excluded the evidence it would all be in the record, and that would be final so far as this proof is concerned." "No, I didn't so understand it," Stewart insisted.

One point of confusion rolled directly into another when Darrow explained to the court that the aim of the defense by using expert testimony was to prove that "men of science and learning, both scientists and real scholars of the Bible . . . expect first to show what evolution is and secondly that any interpretation of the Bible that intelligent men could possibly make is not in conflict with any story of creation, while the Bible, in many ways, is in conflict with every known science, and there isn't a human being on earth believes it literally."

Arthur Garfield Hays added that he intended to support their argument with expert testimony. Stewart replied that "in this matter, the rules of procedure are the same as you made the other day, and the state has the opening and closing" because the state had agreed to take up the question of expert testimony out of the normal procedural order.

Hays quickly answered, "We did not for a moment suppose that you had any idea in your minds that by changing the procedure you would have the opening and closing." That arrangement would guarantee the prosecution, and Bryan in particular, the last volley in the debate, which the defense knew they had to avoid.

After another few minutes the judge allowed Stewart to move to exclude the expert testimony, saying the evidence was immaterial to the issue of Scopes's guilt. But even the act of making a motion was challenged by Hays and Dudley Field Malone. Malone revealed that the two sides had met over the weekend at the old mansion to discuss changing the procedural order back to the original. The argument circled back and forth between the issue of admissibility and the issue of which side would speak last. Raulston insisted it didn't matter what order the two teams spoke in: "Whether you speak in the beginning or in the middle or at the back end does not make any difference to me. I will hear you just as patiently and give what you say the same consideration."

Finally the court moved on to arguments on Stewart's motion against expert testimony. The prosecution's side was argued by William Jennings Bryan Jr., whose famous name seemed scarcely to match his quiet disposition and unassuming good looks. Bryan Jr. was a thirty-eight-year-old Los Angeles lawyer, formerly a U.S. attorney in

Arizona, who avoided publicity and carried on his private practice without fanfare.

Young Bryan's argument was well crafted even if his speaking style was unexciting; John R. Neal asked him to speak louder so everyone at the defense table could hear. Bryan began by repeating the prosecution's position that whether "the theory of evolution as understood by the witness" contradicted "the Biblical account of creation as understood by the witness" was "wholly immaterial, incompetent and inadmissible" because if a witness, no matter how great an expert, "gives a false opinion, there is no way that you can contradict him." Expert testimony was largely "a field of speculation besought with pitfalls and uncertainties."

The judge interrupted next, also asking Bryan to speak louder. Bryan continued, reading at length from cases that established legal precedents, stating there was "no issue of fact raised by evidence; the facts are agreed upon both sides. . . . There is no issue of fact upon which expert testimony is either proper or necessary."

After a short recess following Bryan's presentation, the trial resumed with Judge Raulston warning observers in the packed room not to applaud or make any commotion on account of the tremendous weight upon the floor and the chance that further stress would cause it to give way. Hays rose for the defense to express disbelief at the prosecutors' stance: "First, our opponents object to the jury hearing the law; now, they are objecting to the jury hearing the facts. . . . Jurors cannot pass upon debatable scientific questions without hearing the facts from men who know." Hays insisted that the scientific experts waiting to speak for the defense "are not here, your honor, to give opinions; they are here to state facts."

One of those facts, according to Hays, was that there were two distinct views of Darwinism as explained in a book (by a "Dr. Newman" and otherwise unidentified in the record) from which he read: "The general principle of evolution [which laymen called "Darwinism"] has nothing to do with natural selection [which scientists called "Darwinism"]. . . . But this situation is not at all understood by the antievolutionists, who believe that Darwinism the principle of evolution is inextricably bound up with Darwinism the theory of natural selection." (Darwin's theory of natural selection held that random mutation made individual plants or animals better fit for survival. These mutations continued to the next generation while individuals without the mutation died sooner, leaving fewer offspring. Eventually animals with the helpful mutation displaced those without.)

The very meaning of the term *evolution,* then, was in doubt. Hays said the prosecution claimed "that Professor Scopes taught and that evolution teaches that man has descended from a monkey. If Professor Scopes taught that, he would not be violating this law" against teaching man had descended from a "lower order." He explained that Carl Linnaeus, who developed the scientific method of animal classification a century before Darwin, was the one who grouped man, monkeys, apes, and lemurs into one zoological cluster, or order, he called primates. "To prove that man was descended from a monkey would not prove that man was descended from a lower order of animals, because they are all in the same order of animals."

After Hays's lengthy presentation Sue Hicks countered that testifying before the experts meant Scopes would be tried by a panel of experts rather than by a jury of his peers. An expert witness, "when asked the hypothetical question as to whether or not what Professor Scopes taught denies the story of the divine creation as taught in the Bible, is absolutely usurping the place of the jury."

As time approached for the noon recess, the temperature continued its rise and the lawyers worked mightily to keep their emotions under control. The tension was never far below the surface. Ben McKenzie suddenly asked Hays, "Do you believe in the story of divine creation?" Hays snapped, "That is none of your business." McKenzie fired back, "Then don't ask me any more impertinent questions."

At a quarter to noon, Judge Raulston announced that "the sheriff wants to put ceiling fans in during the noon hour" and recessed for lunch fifteen minutes early. Rumors circulated that early in the afternoon, William Jennings Bryan would speak at last, arguing for the prosecution on the motion to ban expert witnesses.

By the time court resumed at 1:30, the courtroom was packed shoulder to shoulder, judge's rule notwithstanding. As Philip Kinsley reported for the *Chicago Tribune,* "Word that the great Bryan was to speak made the courthouse a magnet, and long before the time set for the afternoon session of the Scopes trial the crowds filled the courtroom. Out under the cottonwoods, in a much cooler situation, the greater crowds gathered to hear the story from the brazen mouths of the loudspeakers. The whole town was one great sounding board of oratory."

Judge Raulston began by repeating his warning for everyone in the courtroom to be as quiet and still as possible, "especially have no applause." After a brief exchange with Darrow, the judge turned to the defense table and said, "Well, I believe Mr. Bryan then will speak next for the state."

As Bryan's name was spoken, the constant hum of a thousand people was momentarily stilled. The typewriters and telegraph keys all paused for an instant, leaving only the unfamiliar buzz of the new electric fans filling the vacuum of silence. Without coat, tie, or collar, the renowned populist and orator rose from the place where he had sat virtually silent and motionless through more than four days of testimony.

His face showed the crags and creases of his sixty-five years, his frame the consequences of an appetite as legendary as his voice. But his dark eyes—Mencken called them "magic" eyes—glistened with anticipation and the excitement of the moment.

CHAPTER 12

Malone Tops Bryan

FOR A WEEK the Scopes trial had swirled with arguments that were sometimes entertaining but almost exclusively beside the point. The constitutionality of the Butler Act and whether expert witnesses would testify were, to a waiting and anticipating world, warm-up acts to the main attraction. William Jennings Bryan had held his fire through both criticism and praise in the courtroom and in the press. He too was waiting—waiting for the strategic moment to strike.

The issue of expert witnesses cut to the heart of his reason for joining forces with the prosecution in the first place: what was the relationship between the law and the Bible? Was the truth of the Bible self-evident and absolute, or was it subject to interpretation and legal oversight?

Bryan began by explaining he had remained silent so far because the discussion had focused on state legal customs and rules of procedure. Now that they had come to the broader questions, he said he felt "justified in submitting my views on the case for the consideration of the court." He had been pegged as the "arch conspirator" in the case, "almost credited with leadership of the ignorance and bigotry," which "could alone inspire a law like this."

"Our position," he explained, speaking more to the gallery than to the judge, eventually turning his back on the court to face the audience, "is that the statute is sufficient. . . . It needs no interpretation." The law "says to teach that man is descended from any lower form of life" was illegal and that, referring to the defendant, "we have his own confession that he knew he was violating the statute."

In framing the argument at the beginning of his speech, Bryan made two essential points in his case that were not exactly true. First, the statute made it illegal to teach man's descent from "a lower order of animals" and not "a lower form of life." Bryan, and perhaps John Butler as well, overlooked or were unaware of the fact that in biology the word *order* has a special meaning as a level of classification.

Another point that Bryan addressed with a little smoke and fog was having the defendant's "own confession." John Scopes never took the stand, and the only account of his teaching came from Doc Robinson, who quoted Scopes as saying if he taught out of Hunter's biology text he "must have" taught evolution, and a couple of students whose testimonies were far from solid.

Bryan underscored the prosecution's contention that the court didn't need any experts to tell it what the law meant and Stewart's basic argument that a court trial "is not the place to try to prove that the law ought never to have been passed."

As he gained momentum, he began addressing his listeners as "my friends" in the style of his public presentations and orations, all but ignoring the judge until he caught himself and returned to addressing "your honor." He railed against a "minority" in Tennessee that would prevent the majority from teaching the Bible and instead force taxpayers to pay teachers who taught theories opposed to Scripture. Here he was returning to what John Washington Butler said was his original reason for proposing the law: as taxpayers his constituents had a right to influence the teaching for which they paid.

Bryan said that when the student Howard Morgan described what he testified was evolution, he was actually describing biological growth. "One trouble about evolution," Bryan said, "is that it has been used in so many different ways that people are confused about it." He attacked Hays's statement that monkeys and men were in "the same class." Hays interrupted to say he placed them in "the same order," opening a short discussion on biological classifications. After a moment Bryan exclaimed that whatever term Hays used, "it wouldn't make much difference because the answer would be the same." The crowd in the room laughed. At last they were getting the show they'd been waiting for.

Bryan displayed the evolutionary chart from Hunter's text, then read from the book, playing to the audience with his commentary. Reading that there were thirty-five hundred species of sponges, he added, "I am satisfied with some I have seen there must be more than thirty-five thousand sponges." He was interrupted repeatedly with laughter and applause. One notation in the record states "extended laughter."

Children taught this theory, Bryan sternly warned, would end up challenging the religious teaching of their parents: "The parents have a right to say that no teacher paid by their money shall rob their children of faith in God and send them back to their homes skeptical, infidels, or agnostics, or atheists. This doctrine that [defense attorneys] want taught, this doctrine that they would force upon the schools, where they will not let the Bible be read!"

Bryan then prepared to read from Darwin's *The Descent of Man,* but Dudley Field Malone stopped him, saying the book hadn't been entered into evidence. "Let me know if you want it, and it will go in," Bryan offered grandly. "I would be glad to have it go in," Malone quickly replied. Laughter rippled through the courtroom; the audience was lively but also fickle.

Bryan quickly regained control and read from *Descent,* commenting wryly that according to that book man was descended "not even from American monkeys but from old world monkeys." The crowd chuckled, safely back on Bryan's side. He went on to declare that, according to a scientist from London who spoke at the American Academy for the Advancement of Sciences in Toronto, "Today there is not a scientist in all the world who can trace one single species to any other, and yet they call us ignoramuses and bigots because we do not throw away our Bible and accept it as proved that out of two or three million species not a one is traceable to another."

In answer to a question from Judge Raulston, Bryan stated his belief that evolution could never account for the virgin birth of Jesus because "there is no place for the miracle in this train of evolution, and the Old Testament and the New are filled with miracles. . . . This doctrine . . . eliminates everything supernatural including the virgin birth and the resurrection."

By now Bryan had ventured far afield from his position that the Butler Act was simple and needed "no interpretation," continuing on in detail both about Darwinian evolution and the Bible. He then went further still, reading from Clarence Darrow's argument a year earlier in the sensational trial of classmates Nathan Leopold and Richard Loeb for the brutal murder of thirteen-year-old Bobby Franks.

Speaking of Leopold and his act, Darrow had asked the jury, "If this boy is to blame for this, where did he get it? Is there any blame attached because somebody took Nietzsche's philosophy seriously and fashioned his life on it? . . . Your honor, it is hardly fair to hang a nineteen-year-old boy for the philosophy that was taught him at the university." Darrow seemed to claim that natural forces beyond their control, analogous to popular Darwinism's natural selection and survival of the fittest, made Leopold and Loeb murderers.

Darrow objected to interjecting the Leopold and Loeb case into the Scopes trial, and the judge agreed. Bryan returned to his position that the members of the jury were expert enough on the Bible and didn't need a professor or scholar to tell them what the Scripture meant: "The one beauty about the Word of God is, it does not take an expert to understand it," Bryan stated, and that people could "know more about that Book by accepting Jesus and feeling in their hearts the sense of their sins forgiven than all of the skeptical outside Bible experts that could come in here to talk to the people of Tennessee."

He had been speaking for an hour, positioning his argument as heart versus smarty-pants brains. Now he built to his conclusion: "The facts are simple, the case is plain, and if those gentlemen [of the defense] want to enter upon a larger field of educational work on the subject of evolution, let us get through with this case and then convene a mock court if its purpose is to banish from the hearts of the people the Word of God as revealed."

To a thunderous roar of applause, the Great Commoner resumed his place at the prosecutors' table.

After a short recess Clarence Darrow spoke briefly in response to Bryan's quotation from the Leopold and Loeb trial. Bryan had read the record accurately, Darrow conceded, but hadn't read enough of it. Darrow added his own excerpt from the Chicago proceedings: "Even for the sake of saving the lives of my clients, I do not want to be dishonest and tell the court something I do not honestly think in this case. I do not believe that the universities are to blame. I do not think they should be held responsible. . . . It is the duty of the university, as I conceive it, to be the great storehouse of the wisdom of the ages, and to let students go there, and learn, and choose. I have no doubt but that it has meant the death of many; that we cannot help."

Bryan countered that Nietzsche, whose doctrines were the subject of the Leopold and Loeb testimony, himself became insane and tried to kill numerous people, including his parents. To that Darrow replied, "He didn't make half as many insane people as Jonathan Edwards." Bryan didn't respond further.

At last Malone rose to make the final argument for the defense on the motion to exclude expert testimony. "Every eye was on him before he said a single word," Scopes wrote, because for the first time in the trial Malone took off his coat. The fact that he alone had continued wearing his suit jacket day after sweltering day had made news already; now he carefully took it off, folded it, and laid it on the defense table. Then he half sat, half leaned on the table and addressed the court.

Malone allowed it was hard for him to distinguish between the various Bryans in this case: the lawyer, the propagandist, and Malone's "old chief and friend." Malone was an assistant secretary of state under Bryan and succeeded him as secretary when he resigned over his policy differences with President Wilson. "Mr. Bryan," he told Judge Raulston, "is not the only one who believes in the Bible" and should have no exclusive say over what the Word of God actually meant.

Malone acknowledged Bryan's popularity and conviction, his "enthusiasm, his vigor, his courage, his fighting ability these long years" but then declared that this trial "is not a conflict of personages; it is a conflict of ideas." Religion was "literal" and not to be changed or interpreted, while science was open and unfixed. "We have been told here that this was not a religious question," Malone said. "I defy anybody, after Mr. Bryan's speech, to believe that this was not a religious question."

Regarding the charge that he and Darrow were "foreigners," Malone reminded his listeners that "Mr. Bryan has offered his services from Miami, Florida," and that "it was only when Mr. Darrow and I heard that Mr. Bryan had offered his name and his reputation to the prosecution of this young teacher that we said, 'Well, we will offer our services to the defense.'"

The prosecution was trying to impose its theory of the law upon the defense and upon the court, Malone explained, and that was why the defense must be allowed to explain its theory of the law by using its expert witnesses. The facts were never in question. "We maintain our right to present our own defense, and present our own theory of our defense, and to present our own theory of this law, because we maintain, your honor, that if everything that the state has said in its testimony be true—and we admit it is true—that under this law the defendant Scopes has not violated that statute. Haven't we the right to prove it by our witnesses if that is our theory?"

Malone's voice was booming now, filling the room and captivating his audience. They had expected to be mesmerized by Bryan, but they hadn't anticipated such an impassioned and well-delivered rejoinder. This was exciting because it was superb oratory, doubly exciting because it was a complete surprise.

"Mr. Bryan is not the only one who has spoken for the Bible. . . . There are other people in this country who have given their whole lives to God. Mr. Bryan, to my knowledge, with a very passionate spirit and enthusiasm, has given most of his life to politics. We believe—" Malone was cut off in mid-sentence by applause. He had criticized the Great Commoner and been cheered for it.

Malone went on at length about the two separate disciplines of theology and biology, assuring his listeners that no child would be endangered by hearing a fair argument on the issue of evolution. "Close no doors to their knowledge," he implored. "Make the distinction between theology and science. Let them have both." The distinction could not be articulated, he argued, without the defense witnesses testifying before the jury. "We have come in here for this duel," he said, "but does the opposition mean by duel that our defendant shall be strapped to a board and that they alone shall carry the sword?"

That was no duel, Malone insisted. "Moreover it isn't going to be a duel. There is never a duel with the truth. . . . The truth does not need the law. The truth does not need the forces of government. The truth does not need Mr. Bryan. The truth is imperishable, eternal and immortal and needs no human agency to support it." A few minutes more and Malone finished his argument. The trial record noted "profound and continued applause."

As Scopes remembered the moment, "The courtroom went wild when Malone finished. The heavy applause he had received during the speech was nothing compared to the crowd's reaction now at the end. The judge futilely called for order. The Chattanooga policeman applauded too, pounding a table with a night stick that must have been loaded with lead; he split the table top and when another officer dashed up to help restore order he shouted back, 'I'm not trying to restore order. Hell, I'm cheering!'" Looking back at the trial more than forty years later, Scopes called Malone's rebuttal "the most dramatic event I have ever attended in my life."

Malone had requested that Darrow let him answer Bryan's argument, which Darrow had agreed to. Now Darrow spoke to insist once more that the story of creation in the Bible was not necessarily in conflict with evolutionary theory. Tom Stewart challenged Darrow's statement, asserting he didn't believe he "came from the same cell with the monkey and the ass," and steered the court's attention back to the Butler Act. Whatever the experts thought was irrelevant, he said, because "in the wording of this act the legislature itself construed this instrument according to their intention."

Caught up in the moment, Stewart shouted that it didn't matter what the scientists said: "I don't care. The law says you cannot teach [evolution]. . . . When science strikes upon that which man's eternal hope is founded, then I say the foundation of man's civilization is about to crumble. Shut the door to science when science sets a canker on the soul of a child." Stewart too drew applause from the captivated crowd, but he was furthering the image of a closed-eyes, closed-ears fundamentalism that emphasized heart and minimized the importance of mind.

The discussion continued, but, as Scopes observed, "there was no hope of having court any more that day. Malone's speech had left an electricity in the air and anything that followed was sure to be anticlimactic." Judge Raulston adjourned until the next morning to consider his decision on the admissibility of expert testimony.

The courtroom emptied until only Bryan, Malone, and Scopes were left. Bryan sat alone in a rocking chair beside the prosecution table, fanning himself intermittently and staring at a spot in front of him. Without turning his head, Bryan said to his old State Department subordinate, "Dudley, that was the greatest speech I have ever heard." Malone responded, "Thank you, Mr. Bryan. I am sorry it was I who had to make it."

It seemed to John Scopes that the townspeople were shocked and stunned by such a strong showing from Malone and "seeing their infallible hero cut to pieces," as well as by the well-reasoned defense argument that the Bible and evolution could peacefully coexist. Syndicated reporter Raymond Clapper captured the tone of the day in the opening sentence of his dispatch: "The Goliath of the fundamentalists ventured forth to stop the introduction of scientific testimony in the Scopes evolution trial today, but he was met by a missile of unexpected force from the sling of Dudley Field Malone of New York, who stirred even these loyal partisans of the idol Bryan to applause."

The *New York Times* deemed the day's proceedings "the greatest debate on science and religion in recent years" and published the full text of Bryan's and Malone's speeches, sometimes using as many as five telegraph operators simultaneously in order to meet press deadlines. The *Nashville Banner* reported, "Weary telegraphers worked until the morning hours to give the country the story of that eventful session. The big hour has gone into history, and all prophesies that the trial of the Rhea County schoolteacher would rank with that of Galileo are well nigh fulfilled."

H. L. Mencken cheered Malone's success:

> It was a great day for Ireland. And for the defense. For Malone not only out-yelled Bryan, he also plainly out-generaled and out-argued him. His speech, indeed, was one of the best presentations of the case against the fundamentalist rubbish that I have ever heard. It was simple in structure, it was clear in reasoning, and at its high points it was overwhelmingly eloquent. It was not long, but it covered the whole ground and it let off many a gaudy skyrocket, and so it conquered even the fundamentalists. At its end they gave it a tremendous cheer—a cheer at least four times as hearty as that given to Bryan.

Malone's spirited defense against Bryan that hot Thursday afternoon was, to Scopes, the turning point in the trial. "Bryan was never the same afterward," he believed, because "Dudley Field Malone had shattered his former chief's unbounded optimism." Soon Mencken was on his way back to Baltimore, having written in his last dispatch from Dayton, "All that remains of the great cause of the State of Tennessee against the infidel Scopes is the formal business of bumping off the defendant. There may be some legal jousting on Monday and some gaudy oratory on Tuesday, but the main battle is over, with Genesis completely triumphant."

The Sage of Baltimore was only partly right.

CHAPTER 13

Heating Up

THE COURT SESSION on Friday, July 17, was the shortest of the trial, convening at 9 AM and adjourning at 10:30. In that hour and a half, the stage was set, as the defense expected it to be, for a virtually certain finding that John Thomas Scopes was guilty.

After the customary opening prayer, Judge Raulston began immediately reading his ruling on Attorney General Tom Stewart's motion to exclude the defendant's expert witnesses from testifying. Dissecting the wording of the Butler Act, Raulston explained his view that the act interpreted itself: the crime of teaching against the story of biblical creation was specifically defined as teaching "that man descended from a lower order of animals." There was no ambiguity or uncertainty to explain, and "the evidence of experts would shed no light on the issues. Therefore, the court is content to sustain the motion of the attorney general to exclude the expert testimony."

Arthur Garfield Hays objected immediately, claiming the ruling was "a denial of justice" and "contrary to every element of Anglo-Saxon procedure and jurisprudence."

Attorney General Stewart then rose to take exception to the nature of the defense's objections, calling it "a reflection on the court."

"Well it don't hurt this court," Judge Raulston affirmed.

Darrow, already thinking past the current events to his appeal, chimed in, "There's no danger of it hurting us. . . . The state of Tennessee don't rule the world yet."

Determined nevertheless to fight to the last, Hays again asked whether the court would not want to hear the defense evidence in some form. When Raulston seemed interested in other options, Stewart suggested instead that the defense file affidavits of expert evidence. In that way the scientists' remarks would be in the record for the appeal, and the continual cycle of argument about expert testimony would be broken. Then Bryan spoke for the first time of the day, asking whether the scientists could be cross-examined about their statements.

Darrow showed fury at the request. As seriously hampered as his defense was now, he would be lucky to get any expert testimony at all into the record, even for information alone. He considered the idea that Bryan might cross-examine them an affront; that should be allowed only if the court permitted the statements as testimony. Speaking merely on a point of information shouldn't expose his experts to hostile questions from the prosecution.

The great Chicago attorney appeared to have reached the breaking point. His experts had been cooling their heels at the old mine company mansion for a solid week, and now he was faced with the prospect of going back there and telling them the judge had ruled they would not be allowed to testify. Turning to Bryan, he said, "Counsel well knows what the judgment and verdict in this case will be. We have a right to present our case to another court and that is all we are after." Then turning to Judge Raulston, "And they have no right whatever to cross-examine any witness when we are offering simply to show what we expect to prove."

Raulston asked Darrow whether such cross-examination weren't "an effort to ascertain the truth."

"No," Darrow shot back, "it is an effort to show prejudice, nothing else." The courtroom filled with laughter. "Has there been any effort to ascertain the truth in this case? Why not bring the jury and let us prove it?"

Up to this point in the trial, the jury had been seated a total of three hours or less; some eyewitnesses estimated the time at only an hour.

"Courts are a mockery when—" the judge began.

"They are often that, your honor," Darrow interjected sarcastically.

". . . they permit cross-examination for the purpose of creating prejudice. . . . Always expect this court to rule correctly."

"No, sir, we do not." More laughter in the court. "Otherwise we should not be taking exceptions here, your honor. We expect to protect our rights in some other court. Now that is plain enough, isn't it? Then we will make statements of what we expect to prove. Can we have the rest of the day to draft them?"

"I would not say—"

"If your honor takes a half day to write an opinion—"

"I have not taken—!"

"We want to make statements here of what we expect to prove. I do not understand why every request of the state and every suggestion of the prosecution should meet with an endless waste of time, and a bare suggestion of anything that is perfectly competent on our part should be immediately overruled."

"I hope you do not mean to reflect upon the court?"

Darrow hunched his shoulders and looked out the window. "Well, your honor has the right to hope."

Even in the passion of the moment, Darrow must have realized he'd gone too far, though the gallery clearly loved the show. In his column describing the moment, H. L. Mencken wrote that Darrow's commentary brought down "a metaphorical custard pie upon the occiput of the learned jurist" Raulston. The room waited for a reaction from the judge, but he didn't challenge the famous attorney. At least not now.

The bickering then began between the defense and prosecution about how the affidavits would be presented. After a few more minutes, the judge agreed to adjourn until Monday when he would consider the issue.

After the session was ended, photographers crowded around the judge's bench for the now-routine picture session. Raulston and Bryan stood together, and the judge asked Darrow and Malone to join them. Darrow declined; Malone said, "No thank you, your honor. We have had our pictures taken together enough."

Thinking the trial was finished for all practical purposes and that Scopes was bound to be convicted, many of the reporters, including Mencken, left town over the weekend. Mencken's acerbic commentary had angered many of the locals who saw the trial as a chance for Dayton to shine bright in the spotlight of world affairs and resented his harsh characterizations. The local sheriff claimed he had already squelched one plot to run the columnist out of town but wasn't sure he'd be successful in foiling another attempt. Whether he was ready to leave or not, Mencken chose the nonconfrontational route and headed north. For him and the rest, the party seemed over, and they were more than ready to catch the first train back to New York or Chicago or St. Louis.

Over the weekend the two sides continued their argument in the press, releasing statements to bolster their points of view. Clarence Darrow had come to Dayton in the hopes of a public showdown with Bryan. Now it looked like the two would never have the confrontation he expected. At least he could continue his case in the press, assailing the one-sidedness in the proceedings: "We know that in this state, under the surroundings and conditions of the trial, Mr. Scopes was condemned from the start. We are now interested in two things: that a higher court shall pass upon this case, and that, in other states, those who wish to pursue the truth shall be left free to think and investigate and teach and learn.

"Before the trial of this case, I had no idea that there was only one interpreter of religion in the world. Christianity has had in its ranks thousands of able and intelligent men in all of the countries of the world, but these were all set aside and Mr. Bryan is to be the one and only judge of what the Bible and Christianity mean."

Admitting he himself was an agnostic, Darrow continued, "It is hard to understand how an intelligent man can believe that a photograph of a human being needs only to be enlarged to give us a picture of God. On this subject I am not agnostic; I do not believe it. As to the first cause, and the power that is at the heart of the universe, it seems to me that most men must confess that they do not know."

Bryan on the other hand announced the Scopes trial had uncovered a conspiracy against biblical Christianity. "The evolutionists bring their doctrine before the public in a jeweled case and praise it as if it were a sacred thing. They do not exhibit, as Darwin did, its bloody purpose; they do not boast that barbarism is its only true expression." He added that Clarence Darrow represented "the most militant anti-Christian sentiment in the country."

Many of the locals, unaware of the court schedule and expecting another session on Saturday, came to town in anticipation, lingered a little while, and went back home. Groups of reporters attended dinners held in their honor in Chattanooga or went on tours of the Smoky Mountains, a vast wilderness nearby which would be preserved the following year as a national park with the help of a $5 million grant from John D. Rockefeller.

Neither Bryan nor Darrow remained in Dayton that weekend. Bryan spoke at a huge open-air church gathering at Pikeville in the beautiful Sequatchie Valley, where he compared evolution to a stagnant pool, "the center of disease and death," and biblical creation to a flowing spring, "giving forth all the time that which refreshes and invigorates." Darrow gave a lecture on Tolstoy to the Young Men's Hebrew Association in Chattanooga. Arthur Garfield Hays stayed at the defense's mansion headquarters, furiously preparing affidavits from the scientists totaling sixty thousand words, some of which would be read into the trial record on Monday. John Scopes followed his usual Sunday routine of church in the morning and a swim in the mountains in the afternoon.

Bryan's arrival in Dayton had been accompanied by loudspeaker trucks promoting real estate in Florida. With his visit drawing toward a close, he circulated brochures advertising a two-month tour to the Holy Land:

> Your imagination can readily visualize and your judgment evaluate the experience of listening to Mr. Bryan at the birthplace of the prince of peace, or on Good Friday in the Garden of Gethsemane; at Easter dawn by the garden tomb, and on Easter afternoon as he reviews the Great Commission on the

> Mount of Olives. The plan is to reserve an entire steamer, taking preliminary cruises around the Mediterranean. . . . It is a fitting climax to the career of Mr. Bryan that after his years of strenuous devotion to his country and to great moral cause he should now lead the hearts of Christian people personally to the Holy Land and share with them . . . his wide experience of life, the ripened maturity of his thoughts, and the inspiration of his religious convictions.

Following the customary prayer at the beginning of Monday's session, the trial entered its seventh day. As the first order of business, Judge Raulston declared that on the previous Friday "contempt and insult were expressed in this court, for the court and its orders and decrees." He then read from the record Darrow's outburst at the end of the session. Raulston found Darrow in contempt of court, ordered him to appear to answer the charges the next morning, and set his bond at $5,000, which a lawyer in the gallery from Chattanooga volunteered to arrange.

The business of the court moved on to a motion by Arthur Garfield Hays to read a message from the Tennessee governor to the legislature when the Butler Act was passed, which said in part, "It will be seen that this bill does not require any particular theory or interpretation of the Bible regarding man's creation to be taught in the public schools. . . . Therefore it will not put our teachers in jeopardy. Probably the law will never be applied." Tom Stewart objected. Then Hays began reading from *Biology and Human Welfare,* the biology textbook approved in Tennessee since the Butler Act was passed. The text referred to Charles Darwin as one "to whom the world owes a great part of its modern progress in biology" and included discussions of man as one of the primates. Stewart objected to that, too.

Then the court considered the business of the expert affidavits, which Hays prepared to read into the record. Tom Stewart wanted them submitted in written form, but Hays wanted excerpts from them read aloud. Stewart countered that reading aloud amounted to trying the case in the press. Hays insisted the defense had the right to present the statements in whatever way they wanted. Stewart said the defense plan was to get the expert testimony in front of the judge in order to convince him to reverse himself and allow the testimony in open court. Hays answered that the affidavits were specifically for the appeal.

In the end Judge Raulston gave the defense an hour to read summary statements into the record. First, Hays read from an affidavit by Walter C. Whitaker, rector of St. John's Episcopal Church in Knoxville, who swore that after thirty years of preaching he was "unable to see any contradiction between evolution and Christianity." Furthermore, "the man has never lived who took every word of the Bible literally. . . . When David said, 'The little hills skipped like rams,' he never expected what he wrote to be taken literally."

The next statement, from Dr. Shailer Matthews, dean of the divinity school at the University of Chicago, said that "a correct understanding of Genesis shows that its account of creation is no more denied by evolution than it is by the laws of light, electricity, and gravitation." This was followed by statements from Dr. Fay Cooper Cole, an anthropologist at the University of Chicago, Kirtley F. Mather, chairman of the geology department at Harvard, and Winterton C. Curtis, a zoologist at the University of Missouri.

Hays was interrupted in his reading by the noon recess. When court resumed at 1:30, Attorney General Stewart asked the court to hear a statement from Mr. Darrow. Darrow rose to offer an apology to the court for his conduct on Friday. In his forty-seven years of practice, he said, this was the first time he had ever been held in contempt. "I do think," he said, "that I went further than I should have gone. . . . One thing snapped out after another. . . . Personally, I don't think it constitutes a contempt, but I am quite certain that the remark should not have been made and the court could not help taking notice of it and I am sorry that I made it ever since I got time to read it [in the transcript] and I want to apologize to the court for it."

The spectators applauded, and Judge Raulston, citing Jesus Christ who "taught that it was godly to forgive," accepted Darrow's apology. Doubtless going further than Darrow would have liked, the judge went on to say he was speaking for all of Tennessee in saying to Darrow "that we forgive him and we forget it and we commend him to go back home and learn in his heart the words of the Man who said, 'If you thirst, come unto Me and I will give thee life.'" Now it was Judge Raulston's turn to bask in the approving applause that filled the room.

After the applause died down, the judge said, "I think the court should adjourn downstairs. I am afraid of the building. The court will convene down in the yard." Over the years there would be numerous versions of a story that the judge moved the trial outside because he was afraid the floor of the courtroom would collapse. True, he had repeatedly warned the spectators not to get excited or applaud. In *Summer for the Gods,* Edward J. Larson writes, "A rumor spread that cracks had appeared in the ceiling." In "World's Most Famous Court Trial," Richard M. Cornelius reports, "Judge Raulston inspected cracks in the first-floor ceiling caused by the weight of the crowd upstairs." Ray Ginger writes in *Six Days or Forever,* "Judge Raulston announced that cracks had developed in the ceiling of the room below the courtroom. He feared that large crowds might collapse the floor." In the official transcript the judge says only, "I think the court should adjourn downstairs. I am afraid of the building."

John Scopes flatly insisted that the courthouse was sound: "Even the judge, who had an electric fan that the rest of us didn't share, couldn't stand the man-killing heat, which had not let up. There was a rumor that cracks had appeared in the first-floor ceiling from the weight of the people upstairs in the courtroom. It made a good story; the fact was otherwise: It was the extreme heat that shifted the court."

The court reconvened on the north lawn of the courthouse square. A platform with a railing had been built next to the courthouse wall for public speakers (during July 4 festivities), and that area became the judge's bench and witness stand. The defense and prosecution placed their tables on the grass just in front of the platform. Behind them were a few rows of chairs. Behind that spectators stood or sat on the grass; in the outermost circle people sat on car hoods or stood on their running boards. There was more fresh air than in the courtroom but also much more sun. People shielded the right side of their faces from the afternoon glare with one hand and fanned with the other.

Because of the crush upstairs, many Dayton parents had not allowed their children in the courtroom—not because of what they might hear but because they might get injured in the crowd. Monday afternoon more children watched. The older ones knew Professor Scopes as a teacher, coach, and friend; the younger ones were drawn by the food and candy vendors and by the promise of hearing a celebrity like William Jennings Bryan.

Only a few reporters were left, perched on chairs or standing here and there on the lawn. Of the number that stayed through the weekend exodus, a lot of them had taken the afternoon off. Other than the usual legal skirmishing, all that seemed likely to happen was Arthur Garfield Hays continuing to read boring expert testimony into the record. All but a handful were out swimming or drinking somewhere.

Hays continued with testimony from Rabbi Dr. Herman Rosenwasser on inconsistencies among various Bible translations, other letters and statements, and a summary of the defense argument in favor of including expert testimony. He then filed his thick sheaf of affidavits collected at the mansion over the weekend to complement the verbal summaries he had just spent more than two hours reading.

At last the judge was ready to send for the jury when Darrow stopped him to request a large sign saying "Read Your Bible" be removed from the courthouse wall. Stewart objected and another legal tiff began. The judge declared he had "no purpose except to give both sides a fair trial" and that if anyone thought the sign was irritating or might influence the jury, he would have it removed. The sign came down, and the jury was called. But Hays asked Judge Raulston to hold off on the jury yet again while he entered into evidence differences among the Genesis account in the King James, Catholic Vulgate, and Hebrew Scriptures. Hoping to have front-row seats for the trial of the century, the members of the jury had been excluded from virtually all of it.

Attorney General Stewart objected to any testimony about translations, and Hays abandoned that line of attack. The line he picked up next led to the most famous, and one of the most misrepresented, episodes in the Scopes trial and one of the most legendary episodes in American legal history. Hays had done everything within his power to get testimony on the record that proved not every Christian believed teaching the Bible and teaching evolution were mutually exclusive. But Tom Stewart and Judge Raulston had thwarted him at every turn.

Hays turned to Scopes and said, "Hell is going to pop now!" The sun shined bright on the two tables of lawyers, casting sharp shadows on the grass. A soft breeze rustled the leaves of the oaks and maples nearby.

"The defense desires to call Mr. Bryan as a witness."

The little knot of reporters looked up from their pads, suddenly mighty glad they'd chosen not to go swimming that afternoon.

CHAPTER 14

The Evolution War

WE'RE AT THE POINT in the trial where Bryan was about to risk his reputation in an all-out assault on Darwinism. But let's stop for a moment to ask, "Why was the evolution debate so important to William Jennings Bryan and many others in the 1920s?" Clearly Bryan opposed Darwinism because it challenged the biblical claims that the universe and everything in it were created by God. Yet for years, including the span encompassing all three of his presidential campaigns, Bryan had essentially left the evolutionists alone to their theories. Early in the century he had shared the optimism of the times. Something happened to make more people feel that life was going awry, and that something was World War I and new problems in the war's aftermath as people saw modern life as empty and hopeless.

World War I, with its dependence on science, particularly affected Bryan. He observed, "The same science that manufactured poisonous gasses to suffocate soldiers is preaching that man has a brute ancestry and eliminating the miraculous and the supernatural from the Bible." In his book *The Creationists,* Ronald L. Numbers comments, "By substituting the law of the jungle for the teaching of Christ, [science] threatened the principles he valued most: democracy and Christianity." Books such as *Headquarters Nights* by Vernon L. Kellogg and *Science of Power* by Benjamin Kidd connected Darwinism to a German preoccupation with genetic purity and domination of "inferior" races (the same way Hunter's *A Civic Biology* connected Darwinism with eugenics).

Bryan also expressed concern about what Numbers called the "epidemic of unbelief that was sweeping the country." College students, it seemed, were being driven away from believing in the Bible by the tenets of evolution. As Bryan's wife wrote of him, "He became convinced that the teaching of evolution as a fact instead of a theory caused the students to lose faith in the Bible, first, in the story of creation, and later in other doctrines, which underlie the Christian religion."

As the Scopes trial began, one student who was losing faith was Philip Wentworth, who entered Harvard as a freshman in 1924. He later wrote in a 1932 issue of the *Atlantic Monthly* ("What College Did to My Religion") that he was unprepared for "the intellectual chemistry which has produced this wholesale apostasy of the younger generation." (In relating Wentworth's story in his year 2000 book *The Wedge of Truth,* Phillip Johnson—more about him in chapters 22–25—comments, "Of course that chemistry has produced the same apostasy for many generations before Wentworth's time and for many thereafter. So when I tell Wentworth's story . . . I am telling you a story that is representative of the experience of an entire culture of educated people over more than a century.")

Wentworth, who grew up in a small Midwestern town, decided to enter the ministry and to prepare himself by entering Harvard. His pastor advised against it, despite the school's Puritan beginnings, warning that it had become a place of false doctrine. Wentworth declined the minister's advice and wrote in the *Atlantic* about what he had learned:

> All things, it seemed, were subject to the laws of nature. This concept supplied my mind with a wholly new pattern into which my religious beliefs refused to fit. In such an orderly universe there seemed to be no place for a wonder-working God. . . .

> Then I began to marvel at the disingenuousness of the human mind when, unable to imagine how the world began, but demanding some explanation of the inexplicable, it can arbitrarily select three letters from the alphabet and call g-o-d an answer.

Wentworth had some reservations about the teaching he had accepted:

> The really serious dangers of skepticism become apparent when a student rejects the supernatural part of his religion and concludes that there are no valid reasons left for decent conduct. . . . In so far as the colleges destroy religious faith without substituting a vital philosophy to take its place, they are turning loose upon the world young barbarians who have been freed from the discipline of the Church before they have learned how to discipline themselves. Perhaps this was what one of my least orthodox Harvard professors had in mind when he once said: "There are only a few men in the world who have earned the right not to be Christians."

In 1921 Bryan delivered a lecture titled "The Menace of Darwinism," which became one of his most popular presentations. Bryan claimed that a little cluster of elite scientists had no right "to establish an oligarchy over the forty million American Christians." To the claim that creationism was intellectually lowbrow, Bryan responded, "Commit your case to the people. Forget, if need be, the highbrows both in the political and college world, and carry this cause to the people. They are the final and efficiently corrective power."

Two fundamentalists, J. Frank Norris and T. T. Martin, joined Bryan in whipping up public opposition to evolution theory. Though he was never as famous as Bryan, Martin was a tireless and fiercely loyal creationist who vowed to banish evolution from America's classrooms. His book *Hell and the High Schools,* published in 1923, made again a connection between the threat of Darwinism and the evil of German nationalism during World War I: he wrote that Germans accused of poisoning wells in France and Belgium and feeding poisoned candy to children were nothing "compared to the text-book writers and publishers who are poisoning the books used in our schools. Next to the fall of Adam and Eve, evolution and the teaching of evolution in tax-supported schools is the greatest curse that ever fell upon this earth."

J. Frank Norris was at least as incendiary as Martin. *Christian Century* magazine in 1924 called him "probably the most belligerent fundamentalist now abroad in the land." Among many other targets he sharply criticized Baylor University professors who failed to meet his anti-Darwinist standards, forcing at least two to resign. Described by his acquaintances as "disturbed and dangerous," Norris beat a murder charge by successfully pleading self-defense.

The debate continued and was especially strong in church-affiliated institutions such as Baylor: one of the professors forced to resign had written in a textbook that the first man appeared on earth "somewhere between one hundred thousand and a million years ago." A special investigative committee unequivocally stated Baylor's official stance on evolution in its final report: "We do not believe in Darwinian evolution or any form of evolution that leaves God out as Creator."

The popular campaign against Darwinism by Bryan, Martin, and others soon left evolutionists on the defensive. When Baylor went looking for a new science professor in 1925, the university president, Samuel Palmer Brooks, told one applicant that the school would not hire any professor who "doubts God as the creator of the world or discounts the Bible as God's revelation to man." The year before, a professor at Furman University in South Carolina was forced to resign after he was quoted as believing in evolution. In his resignation letter he wrote, "It is utterly foolish for a man to talk about teaching biology and not teaching evolution."

Many science textbook writers agreed. Hunter's *Biology* presented evolution as a fact, a typical approach of its time. Others supported the concept even more strongly. *Outlines of General Zoology,* published in 1924, boldly stated, "There is no rival hypothesis to evolution, except the out-worn and completely refuted one of special creation, now retained only by the ignorant, dogmatic, and the prejudiced."

The Scopes trial intensified the argument and gave both sides an international audience for their views, though it probably didn't change many people's minds. In a pattern that would be repeated innumerable times through the years, the scientists branded the creationists as uneducated religious fanatics, the creationists condemned the evolutionists as hell-bound threats to biblical truth, and many observers looked for a middle ground that acknowledged both a divine Creator and a belief that Darwinian evolution played some role in the creative process.

As the Scopes trial was beginning, evolution war was raging on several fronts. In 1919 William Bell Riley, pastor of the First Baptist Church in Minneapolis, founded the World's Christian Fundamentals Association. Within a few years the WCFA had focused on combating evolution and to that end formed a textbook committee to find and promote texts with creationist positions. A committee report of 1928 stated, "One of the greatest needs of the day is suitable textbooks on the physical and biological sciences, written by authors who are not obsessed with theories that are harmful to the young people of our schools," or as Bryan put it, "any text on biology which does not begin with monkeys."

Another skirmish was over exactly what Darwinian evolution was and what proof Darwin had to validate his ideas. These points too would recur again and again in the years ahead. In the Scopes case we saw that neither the Butler Act outlawing Darwinian theory in public schools nor the indictment against Scopes even included the word *evolution.* Expert witness and lawyers for both sides argued over what a "lower order of animals" meant. Publicists in Dayton, political cartoonists, reporters, essayists, pundits, and historians labeled it the Monkey Trial before the first day of testimony, yet prosecutor Thomas Stewart insisted that the whole business had nothing whatever to do with what evolution was, whether it was true, or whether it was compatible with the biblical account of creation. The passage of time was multiplying the confusion over the definition of creationism rather than resolving it.

In 1921 the American Association for the Advancement of Science had hosted a speech by the British biologist William Bateson, who insisted that science had not yet discovered "the actual mode and process of evolution." But what seemed a victory for creationists was short-lived; the AAAS swiftly issued a statement saying that "the evidences in favor of the evolution of man are sufficient to convince every scientist of note in the world." And so the debate continued, with neither side convincing the other, though creationism held onto its gains in the marketplace of ideas. Whereas the topic had been more or less ignored before the end of World War I and the Scopes trial, it became a hotly debated matter, sometimes couched in terms of religious dogma versus academic freedom.

Creationists developed several theories to explain the apparent conflict between the fossil record and other scientific evidence, which indicated an earth many millions of years old, and the biblical account of creation, which—according to the simplest reading of Genesis—took only six days and happened only a few thousand years ago. One issue that came up during the Scopes trial was how long a biblical "day" of creation actually was. Strict creationists such as James Bole at Wheaton College believed God created the earth in six literal days, though he admitted that "from the point of view of specialized knowledge it would seem that the greater authority rested with the evolutionists." Like other creationists he took comfort in the fact that the proof of evolution was circumstantial: "The evolutionist has faith in his hypothesis; the Christian has faith in his God."

The idea of creation taking place only thousands of years ago traced back to a seventeenth-century Anglican bishop named James Ussher. Calculating from the lives of Adam, Moses, and other Old Testament figures, Bishop Ussher figured creation took place in 4004 BC.

C. I. Scofield, whose edition of the Holy Bible, originally published in 1909, is still widely used, believed in the literal biblical account of creation but added a time gap between Genesis 1:1 and 1:2. Scofield accepted Bishop Ussher's calculations placing creation at 4004 BC, then explained in an annotation that the creation of heaven and earth "refers to the dateless past, and gives scope for all the geological ages." The description in the next verse of the earth as "without form, and void" indicated some sort of "cataclysmic change."

Scofield's note on the description of grass, herbs, and fruit trees in Genesis 1:11 read: "It is by no means necessary to suppose that the life-germ of seeds perished in the catastrophic judgment which overthrew the primitive order. With the restoration of dry land and light the earth would 'bring forth' as described. It was *animal* life which perished, the traces of which remain as fossils. Relegate fossils to the primitive creation and no conflict of science with the Genesis cosmogony remains."

Some adhered to the "six literal days" and "Genesis gap" schools but others, including William Jennings Bryan, believed biblical "days" could have been long periods of time; some believed they could have been millions of years each. Again the creationists were doing their best to conform a Bible-based viewpoint with scientific evidence that showed life evolving over eons.

One of the most famous public evolution debates of the late 1920s was between two creationists—W. B. Riley, the WCFA founder who thought the days in Genesis stood for geological ages, and Harry Rimmer, a Presbyterian minister from California, an energetic speaker and tireless self-promoter who believed creation days were twenty-four hours long but that there was a gap in the record as Scofield suggested. The two faced off at a summer Bible conference near Minneapolis, where in Rimmer's words "a buster of a crowd" filled the hall, stood in the aisles, sat on the platform with the speakers, and stood outside looking through the doors and windows.

"We sure skinned each other without mercy whenever there was a good opening and had a swell time," Rimmer recalled. When the crowd voted on the winner, Rimmer won by a five-to-one margin even though Riley was the host.

One of the scientists Bryan quoted in the Scopes trial was George McCready Price, a Canadian churchman and teacher who spent most of his life in the United States and believed the fossil record actually proved the creationists' case. (Bryan had invited Price to testify as an expert witness for the prosecution, but Price was teaching in England at the time.) Rather than arguing about natural selection and new species, Price based his argument on the observation that rocks were formed in layers but that the layers were twisted and overturned (in mountain ranges, for example) to the point where it was impossible to tell which layer had come first. If therefore the fossil time line wasn't reliable, the whole evolutionary argument fell apart, and creationists didn't have to stretch and strain to conform their thinking to the geological evidence.

To Price, geology confirmed the Genesis account of a catastrophic flood and rendered the fossil-based claims of the evolutionists worthless: the flood event had not only covered the ground but had folded and overturned the ground too. As he saw the situation, it did "not take a Solomon to see that the theory of organic evolution becomes nonsense if the flood theory is regarded as true."

Another scientist with unassailable international credentials who doubted Darwin was Albert Fleischmann, a zoologist who taught at the University of Erlangen in Bavaria. Long a critic of evolution, Fleischmann wrote in 1933 that a genealogical tree (such as the one in Hunter's *Biology*) was a "fascinating dream." Regarding Darwin's key claim in *Origin of Species* that natural selection eventually forms new and distinct species classifications, Fleischmann declared, "No one can demonstrate that the limits of a species have ever been passed. These are the Rubicons which evolutionists cannot cross."

Let's follow this historical thread before returning to the trial. Through the 1940s popular debate about evolution in America was rare. In 1941 a small group of evangelical scientists and educators founded the American Scientific Affiliation to promote a Christian worldview in science and religion. Over the years the consensus of the group steadily shifted from creationism to include theistic evolution, which claims that evolution was a means used by God to create the world.

At its founding, all members of the ASA had to pledge that they believed "the whole Bible as originally given to be the inspired word of God" and that God was "the Creator and Sustainer of the physical world." By 1957 one of its members spoke for many when he wrote, "I, an evangelical Christian, can accept the basic concepts of evolution. . . . I believe in creation, and simply affirm that in the light of the evidence now available, I think some evolution—that is, development of present-day forms by differentiation of previously existing forms—the most likely way God accomplished much of His Creation."

These men argued back and forth among themselves and with other scientists and academics about the flood, Noah, the Genesis gap, the fossil record, and other aspects of creation theory, but nothing captured the public's attention with anything like the fervor of the Scopes trial. The closest the controversy came to exciting the man or woman on the street was an experiment that claimed to prove life could have begun spontaneously in the antediluvian swamps.

In 1953 Stanley Miller, a graduate student at the University of Chicago, devised an experiment while working in the laboratory of Harold Urey, a chemist and Nobel laureate who had discovered deuterium and played a key role in developing the atomic bomb. The Miller-Urey experiment supposedly reproduced the prehistoric conditions that yielded the first life-forms.

Miller sent an electric spark, representing natural ultraviolet light, through a chamber filled with gases including hydrogen, ammonia, and water vapor thought to simulate the ancient earth's atmosphere. The electrical reaction produced small amounts of amino acids, the components of proteins sometimes called "the building blocks of life." According to one standard reference book of the time, this experiment "conclusively demonstrated" that a prehistoric chemical reaction could have produced amino acids, sugars, and other organic materials that eventually, through "spontaneous self-assembly" and other events over a billion years or so, began the process of life on earth.

Other advancements of the 1950s seemed to bolster the evolutionist cause. Nuclear science and molecular biology brought more of nature's secrets than ever into view, bolstering the Newtonian theory that mechanical, physical explanations worked for every aspect of life. Anyone could open a textbook and see electron microscope photos of the tiny machinery of creation for himself.

After the Scopes conviction, change came quickly to the world of science textbooks. In "How the Scopes Trial Changed Biology Textbooks," Randy Moore, a biology professor and editor of the *American Biology Teacher* magazine, notes that "textbook publishers and school boards throughout the country became reluctant to deal with evolution" following the high-profile trial in Dayton. "Simultaneously, the amount of evolution taught in public schools decreased dramatically, and virtually all publishers removed Darwin's ideas about evolution as the unifying theme of life from their biology books. Within a few months after Scopes's trial, Texas Governor Miriam Ferguson, the first female governor in the South, ordered her state's textbook commission to cut out (with scissors) the pages containing discussions of the theory of evolution from its high school biology textbooks."

Moore also reports that George Hunter, fearing sales of his popular text would evaporate, quickly produced a new edition which the publisher named *New Civic Biology.* He deleted the text and charts on evolution and referred to the "development" of species rather than "evolution." Another popular book titled *Biology for Beginners* was reissued with the frontispiece photo of Darwin replaced with a chart of the digestive system. By the 1930s, Moore writes, "Books that stressed evolution either sold poorly or became extinct. By 1940, most high school biology teachers did not include evolution in their courses."

Culling evolution out of science classes may have pleased parents and school boards, but it made scientists fume. Moore quotes one biologist who said in 1941, reflecting sentiments from some of the Scopes witnesses almost a generation before, that "biology is still pursued by long shadows from the middle ages, shadows screening from our people what our science has learned of human origins . . . a science sabotaged because its central and binding principle displaces a hallowed myth."

Moore points out that the best-selling biology text of the 1930s, *Dynamic Biology,* by Baker and Mills, did not contain the word *evolution* or anything about the fossil record of man and stated that Darwin's theory was "no longer generally accepted." A 1949 text treaded extremely lightly on the topic and then followed quickly with a reference to biblical creation: "Later one-celled green plants must have come into existence and then one-celled animals, which feed on the green plants and bacteria. As you see, if you turn to the first chapter of Genesis, this is the order of Creation."

Moore writes, "As the 1950s came to a close, there was no evidence in textbooks that evolution was regarded as a major concept in biology." But just over the horizon, two forces were poised to cause a radical change in the way textbooks were written and transform once again the whole evolution debate. One was in outer space, the other on Broadway.

CHAPTER 15
Inherit the Wind

ON OCTOBER 4, 1957, the Soviet Union launched *Sputnik*, the world's first artificial satellite. The name was Russian for "traveling companion," but few Americans saw any signs of companionship in the gesture. The Cold War was in full swing; the Soviets controlled all of Eastern Europe, and Communism seemed to be spreading across the world. Now they also had a presence in outer space, and there was no telling what they might send up next: a spy camera? a death ray?

Shocked into action, America's leaders set a goal for the country's education system to retake the lead in science from the Communists. One result of their resolve was the National Defense Education Act, signed into law the next year, which funded the development of new state-of-the-art science textbooks. The authors of the biology books the Act produced were leaders in their fields who cared little for the popular rejection of evolution. Reading through the books his work was slated to replace, one contributor exclaimed with enthusiastic overstatement, "One hundred years without Darwin is enough."

Within a decade evolution, all but absent from the most popular texts through the 1930s, '40s and '50s, became in Randy Moore's words, "the unifying theme of biology." From being unacceptable, or at best mentioned only in passing, Darwinian theory resumed its place as the dominant explanation for the origins of life. Opposition faded away, and a new generation of students learned, as their grandparents had, that Charles Darwin was the father of evolutionary biology.

Another event closer to home made an even bigger impact on the reemergence of Darwinism. In fact, this event did more to define the evolution debate in popular terms than the Scopes trial itself, and its influence continues today. On April 21, 1955, the curtain rose at the National Theater in New York City on a new play by Jerome Lawrence and Robert E. Lee called *Inherit the Wind.* First written in 1951 and previewed in Dallas three months before its New York opening, *Inherit the Wind* is the story of an idyllic young teacher named Bertram Cates, who was arrested and jailed in Hillsboro, Tennessee, for teaching evolution in the local school. He is prosecuted by the legendary Matthew Harrison Brady, three-time presidential candidate and wildly popular fundamentalist orator; he is defended by Henry Drummond, renowned lawyer, unrepentant evolutionist, and Brady's ideological opposite.

In the published text of their play, Lawrence and Lee added a note that said in part, "*Inherit the Wind* is not history. The events which took place in Dayton, Tennessee, during the scorching July of 1925 are clearly the genesis of this play. It has, however, an exodus entirely its own. Only a handful of phrases have been taken from the actual transcript of the famous Scopes Trial. Some of the characters of the play are related to the colorful figures in that battle of giants; but they have a life and language of their own. . . . *Inherit the Wind* does not pretend to be journalism. It is theater."

Despite this clear disclaimer, generations of viewers came to see the play as a historic account of the Scopes trial. This gave popular culture a highly distorted view of the facts. In the play the Scopes character, Cates, purposely breaks the law because he thinks ignoring evolution theory is wrong; the real Scopes didn't care much either way, was concerned more with freedom of thought and speech than the issue of religion, and almost certainly never taught evolution anyway. Brady, the Bryan character, appears as a puffed-up grandstander who fails to defend his faith and dies a broken and defeated shell as a result; Bryan in the flesh was calm, confident, and articulate on the witness stand. The Darrow character, Drummond, is a profane, acerbic figure who systematically destroys Brady on the stand; the real Darrow was more professional and controlled and certainly didn't achieve the degree of success with his witness that Drummond achieved onstage.

Equally important, perhaps more so, to the historical impact of the play is the way Lawrence and Lee used the townspeople in their script to tell the audience what to think of the Bryan and Darrow stand-ins and what to think of the townspeople themselves. The opening stage direction reads, "It is important to the concept of the play that the town is visible always, looming there, as much on trial as the individual defendant. The crowd is equally important throughout, so that the court becomes a cockpit, an arena, with the active spectators on all sides of it."

When Bryan and Darrow arrived in Dayton, the townspeople and visitors turned out to see them both; both were guests at their respective welcoming banquets. During the trial the speaker the crowd appreciated most was probably Dudley Field Malone, who spoke so stirringly for the defense in response to Bryan's remarks for the prosecution. It was Malone's great monologue, not anything Darrow said before or after, that challenged Bryan most strongly. During Darrow's famous examination of Bryan on the stand, the crowd responded to both men's zingers.

In the play on the other hand, the people are strongly with the Bryan figure at the beginning and turn completely against him at the end. The playwrights show popular opinion making a U-turn away from creationism and embracing the voice of reason and learning and the future—from the character who earlier in the action is branded by a petrified young girl as "the Devil."

The townspeople themselves start out as seemingly gullible, simplistic, fundamentalist yokels who get all lathered up at a camp meeting and think Bert Cates will burn in hell for teaching evolution. They blindly idolize Brady until he falters under Drummond's questioning, then turn heartlessly against him.

This portrayal reinforced the image H. L. Mencken had planted in the minds of America with his scathing reports of idiot rubes in

Tennessee who were too eaten up with wild religious fervor to realize how little they knew and how backward they were. For example, in his second column from Dayton, on July 10, Mencken described the fundamentalist pastor T. T. Martin of Blue Mountain, Mississippi, who

> hired a room and stocked it with pamphlets bearing such titles as "Evolution a Menace," "Hell and the High Schools," and "God or Gorilla," and addresses connoisseurs of scientific fallacy every night on a lot behind the Courthouse. . . .
>
> The courthouse is surrounded by a large lawn, and it is peppered day and night with evangelists. . . . I have listened to twenty of them and had private discourse with a dozen, and I have yet to find one who doubted so much as the typographical errors in Holy Writ. . . . Most of the participants in such recondite combats, of course, are yokels from the hills, where no sound is heard after sundown save the roar of the catamount and the wailing of departed spirits, and a man thus has time to ponder the divine mysteries. But it is an amazing thing that the more polished classes also participate actively.

Most newspapers around the country printed the whole courtroom transcript every day. The truth was there on the page for anyone who wanted it, but Mencken was shorter and a lot more entertaining. Fairly or not, he pegged the creationists as wild-eyed fundamentalists who mistakenly thought they understood the Bible and thus couldn't understand or accept true science.

Inherit the Wind built on Mencken's stereotypes. It solidified the image of anyone who believed in creationism as a pitiful Bible-thumping backwoods buffoon. It cast evolutionists as the educated, modern, forward-thinking, level-headed people ready to rescue the culture from its dull-witted opponents. *Inherit the Wind* was to creation science what the *Hindenburg* was to Zeppelin travel: a famous event that dramatically misled the public and permanently overwhelmed the truth.

Lawrence and Lee, as they freely admitted, never intended to be true to history. What they did set out to do, they later explained, was to use the Scopes story as a frame for a cautionary tale of their own about the dangers of McCarthyism. In 1950 Senator Joseph McCarthy, a Republican from Wisconsin, accused the U.S. State Department and later the military of employing Communist sympathizers. His Senate hearings and the accusations they generated set off a flurry of charges and countercharges and produced lists of people accused of treason. In 1954 the United States outlawed the American Communist Party, and McCarthy targeted the entertainment industry, demanding the names of party members and blacklisting anyone who refused to cooperate.

In *Inherit the Wind,* first drafted the year after Senator McCarthy came on the national scene, Lawrence and Lee set out to show the dangers of thought control and curbing free speech, no matter how noble the intention. Religious dogma threatening the advancement of science and learning was a metaphor for governmental overreaction to the perceived threat of Communism that itself threatened traditional American ideals of free thought and free speech.

Other writers used similar theatrical metaphors to warn their countrymen of McCarthyism's dangers. During the early 1950s when Lawrence and Lee were at work on their script, Pulitzer Prize-winning playwright Arthur Miller wrote *The Crucible,* based on the Salem witchcraft trials of 1692. While there were ties to the facts of history (more direct ties than in *Inherit the Wind*), Miller's underlying purpose was to showcase the dangers in restricting freedom of thought. Miller himself was accused by McCarthy of being a Communist, though the charges were later dropped as McCarthy's credibility faded.

With Broadway stars Ed Begley and Paul Muni as Brady and Drummond and newcomer Tony Randall as reporter E. K. Hornbeck (the fictional H. L. Mencken), *Inherit the Wind* was a hit. Muni, already an Oscar winner in Hollywood, won a Tony Award in 1956 for his stage interpretation of Drummond.

The popularity of the play further cemented its fictionalized account of the Scopes trial as historical fact in the public consciousness: Brady/Bryan was a fanatical buffoon; Drummond/Darrow was a secular savior who rescued the world from the countrified imbecility of religious hard-liners; fundamentalist Christians were uneducated impressionable dimwits; and evolutionists were educated, sane, and our only hope for the future.

When Stanley Kramer decided to produce a Hollywood film version of the stage production, the power of its impression increased exponentially: thousands of people saw the play; millions would see the movie. Kramer cast Spencer Tracy as Henry Drummond and Frederic March as Matthew Harrison Brady, both top box-office draws who had already won two Oscars apiece. Gene Kelly, playing against type, portrayed E. K. Hornbeck.

Far more than the play, the movie presented itself as a slice of popular American history: there was no opening disclaimer that it didn't "pretend to be journalism." *Life* magazine declared it representative of the facts: "The movie is fiction but still a fair picture of the furies that drove [William Jennings Bryan] when, in 1925, he prosecuted John T. Scopes for teaching evolution in defiance of the oldtime religion and the Tennessee legislature." *Newsweek* reported, "*Wind*, as most people should know by now, is based on the actual trial of John Scopes . . . for teaching Darwin's 'godless' theory of the evolution of man from ape."

Some viewers took a more careful look at the film. In his review for the *New Yorker*, Brendan Gill wrote with rare perception of the difficult balancing act between fact and fiction:

> The picture, like the play from which it was taken, tries to be two radically different things at once and, of course, succeeds in being neither. . . . Every effort is made to engage our interest by identifying its action and characters with the events and personages of the famous Scopes 'monkey' trial . . . ; that goal accomplished, every effort is made to hold our interest by acts of melodramatic license that flagrantly alter the nature of those events and personages. From one moment to the next, we can never be sure whether we are in history or out of it. . . .
>
> *Was* Bryan a Brady? *Was* Darrow a Drummond? For that matter, was H. L. Mencken really anything like the tiresomely brash, cheesy-epigram-uttering newspaperman called, in the picture, E. K. Hornbeck? Dear Lord, I hope not.

Kramer organized a premiere in Dayton and invited anyone connected with the story as a special guest. For one night at least, the small East Tennessee town was famous again because thirty-five years before George Rappleyea had seen opportunity in an ad in the Chattanooga paper looking for a schoolteacher willing to test the Butler Act.

To handle the crowd, the celebration took place at a local drive-in. Kramer attended the festivities, and after the screening he asked various guests how they liked it. They didn't. The movie portrayed the townspeople as a shallow, bigoted mob ready to destroy the Scopes character. Few of them had ever seen a Broadway play, but now they sat face-to-face with a distorted picture of themselves that the whole world would watch. Eloise Reed, who attended the trial the day Bryan examined Darrow on the stand, was sitting on a couch at the reception when Kramer sat down beside her and introduced himself.

"How did you like it?" he asked.

"I didn't like it at all," she answered and proceeded to tell him why. After she finished her critique, the Hollywood figure thanked her, stood up, and left without another word.

Kramer met resistance early on from historical figures in the Scopes trial who took issue with his presentation of the facts. By all accounts Attorney General Thomas Stewart was the man who charted the course for the prosecution and was the only local figure on either side universally praised for his work, even for a while by Mencken. He went on to a successful career in law and public life, including service as a United States senator in the 1940s. During the preproduction phase of the film, Kramer contacted Stewart and asked him to be a consultant on the project. Stewart wanted nothing to do with Hollywood and declined the offer.

Kramer warned him that if he didn't help, Kramer would brand him in the movie as a country bumpkin who was nothing but local window dressing for Bryan/Brady's leadership and legal genius. Stewart held fast. Kramer was true to his word.

The movie was a success, bringing Spencer Tracy another Oscar nomination and exposing a new generation to the Hollywood version of the history of the creation/evolution debate which came down with all its enlightened liberalism against creation. Kramer proudly told an interviewer that a group of high school students in Berlin voted it their favorite picture at a film festival. When Kramer spoke to the students and said their vote meant "they believed the mistakes of the past could be rectified," it "brought down the house," he recalled. Kramer believed that in addition to a cautionary tale about the dangers of McCarthyism, *Inherit the Wind* was also a story of hope for people, like the Germans, who once suffered at the hands of a government with a hammerlock on freedom of thought. "The one thing we've got to sell overseas," Kramer said, "is personal liberty."

So from science to religion to legal precedent, the movie, at least in the eyes of its director, shifted the discussion to "personal liberty": evolution encouraged it, biblical creationism didn't. The real Bryan was more right than he could have imagined in 1925 when he wrote, "The evolutionists have not been honest with the public. Christians who have allowed themselves to be deceived into believing that evolution is a beneficent, or even a rational, process have been associating with those who either do not understand its implications or dare not avow their knowledge of these implications."

In an article for *First Things* published in 1997, educator and academician Carol Iannone incisively summed up *Inherit the Wind* as history:

> While it stands nominally for tolerance, latitude, and freedom of thought, the play is full of the self-righteous certainty that it deplores in the fundamentalist camp. Some critics have detected the play's sanctimonious tone—"bigotry in reverse," as Andrew Sarris called it—even while appreciating its dramatic quality and well-written leading roles. The play reveals a great deal about a mentality that demands open-mindedness and excoriates dogmatism, only to advance its own certainties more insistently—that promotes tolerance and intellectual integrity but stoops to vilifying the opposition, falsifying reality, and distorting history in the service of its agenda. . . .
>
> The truth is not that Bryan was wrong about the dangers of the philosophical materialism that Darwin presupposes but

that he was right, not that he was a once great man disfigured by fear of the future but that he was one of the few to see where a future devoid of the transcendent would lead.

CHAPTER 16
Establishing Atheism

HOLLYWOOD'S TAKE ON EVOLUTION in *Inherit the Wind* came at the high-water mark of Darwinian influence on popular American culture. In academic circles the comparable event was the Darwin Centennial, sponsored ironically over Thanksgiving weekend in 1959 by the University of Chicago to mark a century since *The Origin of Species* was published. Charles Galton Darwin, grandson of the evolutionist, spoke, as did Sir Julian Huxley, grandson of one of Darwin's earliest and most enthusiastic supporters, Thomas Huxley.

As described in a feature the following February in the *Christian Century*, the two main points of agreement during the festivities were: "(1) Evolution is a demonstrated fact and is basic to the interpretation of nature's processes. It is no longer considered by scientists to be theoretical. (2) Sir Julian Huxley's interpretation of the philosophical significance of evolution was generally seen as providing the center of synthesis; around themselves other views arranged themselves like planes in a crystal."

Speaking on Thanksgiving Day, Huxley entitled his remarks "The Evolutionary Vision." He confidently proclaimed that science at the mid-point of the twentieth century was omniscient, that the universe had evolved and was not created, and that there was no "cosmic helper" for mankind to fall back on or appeal to: "Religions are destined to disappear." That statement, the *Christian Century* reported, "touched off a barrage of public protests" and not just from religious conservatives.

Huxley envisioned a modern theological age unburdened by the guilt or humility of a supreme being that was a logical continuation of the evolution process. He explained:

> Could the early amphibians have been gifted with imagination they might have seen before them the possibilities of walking, running, or even of flying above the earth . . . and the inevitability of an upsurge of mind to new levels of performance. So with ourselves.

Huxley orated on:

> Our feet still drag in the biological mud even though we can lift our heads into the conscious air. [Man must stop] creeping for shelter into the arms of a divinized father-figure whom he has himself created and trying to escape responsibility by sheltering under the umbrella of divine authority. . . . In the evolutionary pattern of thought there is no longer either need or room for the supernatural. The earth was not created, it evolved. So did all the animals and plants that inhabit it, including our human selves, mind and soul as well as brain and body. So did religion.

Five years later, in his seventy-seventh year, Huxley published an essay titled "The New Divinity" that further refined his position. He wrote of a "new vision" that integrated "the fantastic diversity of the world into a single framework, the pattern of all-embracing evolutionary process. . . . There is no separate supernatural realm: all phenomena are part of one natural process of evolution. There is no basic cleavage between science and religion; they are both organs of evolving humanity."

Huxley continued:

> God is a hypothesis constructed by man to help him understand what existence is all about. The God hypothesis asserts the existence of some sort of supernatural personal or superpersonal being, exerting some kind of purposeful power over the universe and its destiny. To say that God is ultimate reality is just semantic cheating, as well as being so vague as to become effectively meaningless. . . . Today the God hypothesis has ceased to be scientifically tenable, has lost its explanatory value and is becoming an intellectual and moral burden to our thought. It no longer convinces or comforts, and its abandonment often brings a deep sense of relief.

Huxley granted that mankind needed an element of divinity in its existence and proposed "divinity without God." Divinity, he explained, was "the chief raw material out of which gods have been fashioned. Today we must melt down the gods and refashion the material into new and effective organs of religion, enabling man to exist freely and fully on the spiritual level as well as on the material." God, then, was a manifestation of the human imagination. So we might as well make him something we like, something that makes us feel good.

By the time "The New Divinity" was published in 1964, American culture and morality were undergoing their most dramatic changes in history. President John F. Kennedy was assassinated the previous November. Civil rights protests were gathering steam. Birth control pills were revolutionizing intimate relationships and public morals. First Elvis Presley and then the Beatles transformed popular music. In 1964 lighthearted *My Fair Lady* won the Academy Award for best picture; two years later grit, social commentary, and harsh realism had come to Hollywood to stay in films like *In the Heat of the Night* and *Guess Who's Coming to Dinner?* (turning the spotlight on race relations), *The Graduate* (seduction and adultery), and *Bonnie and Clyde* (romanticization of lawlessness and murder).

During the time these historic changes were transforming the nation, the U.S. Supreme Court reversed nearly two hundred years of tradition and precedent: instead of courts around the country requiring that Christian teaching be protected and encouraging that it be taught, they suddenly required schools to forbid it. On the foundational point of law in the Scopes case—Tennessee schools should teach what the Bible taught—the court and the country did a complete about-face.

On November 11, 1620, before the first Pilgrim set foot on dry land and while the *Mayflower* was anchored off the coast of the New World, those brave settlers drew up the Mayflower Compact as a temporary set of rules to live by. They stated they had come to America first of all "for the Glory of God, and Advancement of the Christian Faith." From that time through the 1950s, American institutions and a Christian culture were inseparable: while the First Amendment guaranteed the government would never officially support a specific religion or force it on anyone, tradition and the interpretation of the law held that the government could and should encourage faith in God. The national motto, after all, was and is "In God We Trust." Christianity was by far the most popular and common expression of that faith.

On June 17, 1963, the U.S. Supreme Court ruled 8–1 in its final deliberation of the case that public schools could not require children to recite a prayer or listen to a Bible reading in class. Parents in Maryland and Pennsylvania had complained about it, and the resulting lawsuit eventually put an end to the practice in all fifty states. Prayer proponents suggested the offended students excuse themselves from the classroom, but the court ruled that children might be afraid to speak up.

In a letter to *Life* magazine, Madalyn Murray—who as Madalyn Murray O'Hair soon became a prominent atheism activist—boldly identified herself and her cause:

> I am that Maryland atheist [responsible for the state suit leading to the Supreme Court ban]. . . . We find the Bible to be nauseating, historically inaccurate, replete with the ravings of madmen. We find God to be sadistic, brutal, and a representation of hatred, vengeance. We find the Lord's Prayer to be that muttered by worms groveling for meager existence in a traumatic, paranoid world. The business of the public schools, where attendance is compulsory, is to prepare

> children to face the problems on earth, not to prepare for heaven—which is a delusional dream of the unsophisticated minds of the ill-educated clergy.

The Supreme Court ruling, while it mentioned in passing the phrase "under God" in the Pledge of Allegiance and the Gettysburg Address (still allowed) and Christmas carols (eventually outlawed), did not mention teaching about the origins of life. The court allowed for teaching the Bible as "the history of religion and its place in the advancement of civilization" but no "religious exercises."

Biblical creationism was already under fire for being too "unscientific." Now in the eyes of its detractors, it was patently illegal. The scientific establishment, securely in control of science curriculum once more and strongly opposed to the idea of a supernatural Creator, suddenly had a powerful new tool for ridding the landscape of this tenacious and inconvenient figure.

A few brave pro-creation voices sounded in the wilderness. In 1961 John C. Whitcomb Jr. and Henry M. Morris published *The Genesis Flood,* which not only bolstered the creationist position but argued that humans and dinosaurs could have lived at the same time before Noah built the ark. The book eventually sold over 200,000 copies, but it divided creationists against themselves. People who believed the biblical account of the flood loved it, but other Christians, according to one commentator, "denounced it as a travesty on geology that threatened to return Christian science to the Dark Ages."

Whitcomb and Morris compellingly argued for "literal creationism," as opposed to the Genesis gap theory or the idea that biblical days could have been millions of years long. Popular as the book was, it had a rough go in academic circles because scientists refused to accept the Bible as proof of anything. Whitcomb and Morris took the literal truth of the Bible as a starting point; for people who didn't, *The Genesis Flood* was a fantasy.

The assault on religion in public life continued unchecked so that by the end of the 1970s Christians at every level of society were in full retreat from defending a role for God in public life. The government that had once embraced religious observances in general, and

Christianity in particular, as something essential and good seemed transformed into a force dedicated to stamping out every vestige of religious symbolism and practice. Christmas school vacations became "winter breaks." The origin and purpose of Thanksgiving as a day of prayer and feasting in humble thanks for God's blessings on the country were completely glossed over in the public arena. In 1980 the Supreme Court ruled that posting the Ten Commandments as a religious text in public schools was unconstitutional.

Though clearly the legal current was strong against religion, polls continued to indicate that 80–90 percent of Americans considered themselves Christians. In several states, particularly in the more traditional South, legislators reintroduced (or tried to safeguard) provisions that at least echoed the traditional recognition of religion.

In 1981 the Alabama legislature passed a bill authorizing a daily moment of silence for "meditation or voluntary prayer" in public classrooms. In 1985 the U.S. Supreme Court ruled it unconstitutional, yet the practice eventually survived in modified form. (Numerous other states had similar laws; student-led prayer eventually survived a constitutional test.)

Also in 1981 Louisiana passed a law that was in many ways what supporters of the 1925 Butler Act in Tennessee may have intended to do. The Louisiana statute required state schools to teach creationism as an alternative theory to evolution. Much of the original objection to evolution in Rhea County, Tennessee, was that taxpayers didn't want it taught as the only option. The effect of the Louisiana law was to say Darwinian evolution was not the only valid explanation for the origins of life and that students had to be taught it was a hypothesis, not an unassailable fact.

It didn't take long for opponents to attack the law. As happened with the Scopes case, the preferred battleground was the courtroom. Also like Scopes, and like virtually all the cases challenging religion in public life in the sixty years since the Dayton trial, the American Civil Liberties Union was in the forefront, in the headlines, and footing the bill through a series of lawsuits and appeals. When the Louisiana case finally went to the U.S. Supreme Court, seventy-two Nobel Prize-winning scientists filed a friend-of-the-court brief opposing creationist teaching in public schools.

The case was tried in Washington on December 10, 1986. State Attorney General Wendell Bird argued that, seen in context, creation science was science and not religion. Bird claimed that the statute met the three-part legal test for laws with religious connotations: it had a secular legislative purpose, neither advanced nor inhibited religion, and did not "foster an excessive entanglement" with religion. He also argued that creation science "did not necessarily involve a Supreme Being." The ACLU countered that creation science was Genesis in disguise.

On June 19, 1987, the court ruled the Louisiana law unconstitutional. In his majority opinion Justice William Brennan wrote that the law was enacted "to serve a religious purpose." Chief Justice William Rehnquist and Justice Antonin Scalia dissented, declaring that Louisianans were entitled "to have whatever scientific evidence there may be against evolution presented in their schools" as "a secular matter." But Justice Brennan saw a "discriminatory preference for the teaching of creation science and against the teaching of evolution" in the statute; the court's 7–2 decision brought the battle to a close.

As the Louisiana case was working its way through the courts, a science professor at Oxford University put the final touches on a book, *The Blind Watchmaker: Why the Evidence of Evolution Reveals a Universe without Design*, that explained Darwinian evolution in an accessible and engaging new way. In the first line of the preface, author Richard Dawkins confidently explained, "This book is written in the conviction that our own existence once presented the greatest of all mysteries, but that it is a mystery no longer because it is solved."

Dawkins's title was homage to the 1802 William Paley treatise (discussed in chapter 8) that compared complex life on Earth to a watch found on the ground and concluded that the watch mandated a watchmaker. Dawkins admired Paley's thinking but disagreed with his conclusion. He wrote that the watchmaker argument was "made with passionate sincerity" and took "the best biological scholarship of his day" into account. "But it is wrong," Dawkins concluded. "All appearances to the contrary, the only watchmaker in nature is the blind force of physics."

Later in the book Dawkins explained, "Natural selection is the blind watchmaker, blind because it does not see ahead, does not plan consequences, has no purpose in view. Yet the living results of natural selection overwhelmingly impress us with the appearance of design as if by a master watchmaker, impress us with the illusion of design and planning. The purpose of this book is to resolve this paradox to the satisfaction of the reader, and . . . to impress the reader with the power of the illusion of design."

The Blind Watchmaker won the Heinemann Prize from the Royal Society of Literature and the *Los Angeles Times* Book Award. The London *Times* called it "brilliant exposition" and "popular science at its best" with plenty of "sidesweeps" to "creationists, erring colleagues, misguided interlopers from other sciences, and the media that gleefully misreport their muddleheaded musings." The *New York Times* declared of Dawkins, "He succeeds admirably in showing how natural selection allows biologists to dispense with such notions as purpose and design and he does so in a manner readily intelligible to the modern reader."

One gap that Dawkins himself noted in his circle of admirers was "backwoodsmen" in the United States—deftly touching on the *Inherit the Wind* stereotype—"anti-evolution propagandists [who] are always religiously motivated." Again and again, ever since 1925, anti-Darwinists have been handicapped by their association with fundamentalist Christianity. That association was indelibly etched on a day in Dayton when William Jennings Bryan took the stand. Now that we've seen the importance through the decades of that day, let's examine exactly what happened.

CHAPTER 17

The Main Event

HAYS'S MOTION on Monday, July 20, to put prosecuting attorney Bryan on the stand for the defense was not something that came on the spur of the moment. Over the weekend Clarence Darrow had told Charles Francis Potter, the Unitarian minister who had accompanied Hays and Malone from New York, that despite Judge Raulston's opposition he was going to put a Bible expert on the stand. "A greater expert than you," he explained, "greatest in the world—he thinks." When Potter solved the riddle and excitedly congratulated him on the idea of putting Bryan on the stand, Darrow warned him to keep it to himself: "Too many reporters around here."

Sunday night Darrow rehearsed his questioning with Kirtley Mather, the Harvard geologist (and also a Baptist), portraying Bryan. To outline his inquiry Darrow used a series of questions in a public letter he'd written Bryan two years before in the *Chicago Tribune*. At least some of the pressmen knew something was up. A page-one story in the *Nashville Banner* reported, "Rumors go about that the defense is preparing to spring a coup d'etat." Meanwhile, thinking the trial was over except for legal formalities, Tom Stewart proclaimed a "glorious victory" for the prosecution, and William Jennings Bryan Jr. was already on his way back to Los Angeles.

Why did Bryan agree to be examined? One possibility: a week earlier, responding to news that Columbia University proposed to bar Tennessee public school students who didn't get a Darwinian education, superintendent Walter White had proposed the founding of a Bryan University in Dayton. By the next Sunday a Florida philanthropist named George F. Washburn pledged $10,000 to the project, calling it "a psychological moment to establish a Fundamentalist university." Bryan was already contemplating a speaking tour on creationism; news of the school and its founding gift must have made him all the more eager to jump at the unexpected chance to expand on his beliefs as a witness for the defense.

One certainty: When Hays called Bryan to the stand the rest of the prosecution team was unified in its objection. As Scopes remembered the moment, "All the lawyers leaped to their feet at once." Ben McKenzie said "calling a lawyer who represents a client" to the stand was unnecessary. Edward J. Larson writes in *Summer for the Gods* that "Stewart seethed with anger," and Scopes adds that the attorney general, "fast on the trigger, objected and gave the judge his cue. Raulston probably would have ruled with Stewart, had Bryan himself not been on his feet, *demanding* his right to testify."

According to the transcript, Stewart was silent at first, and Bryan's worry was not what he might say about the Bible but rather making sure he would have an equal chance to question the defense: "If your honor please, I insist that Mr. Darrow can be put on the stand, and Mr. Malone and Mr. Hays." The judge replied, "Call anybody you desire. Ask them any questions you wish."

Judge Raulston allowed Bryan to testify for the defense. Dressed in a white shirt but without coat, collar (they were separate from the shirts in those days), or tie, wearing his familiar suspenders and steadily working his palm-frond fan, Bryan took a chair near the middle of the outdoor platform. Darrow, also without coat or tie, stepped up onto the platform beside the witness chair to question him. The two shared the angled afternoon shadow of the courthouse, which also shaded a wedge of spectators.

At the startling news that Bryan was being examined as a defense witness, the crowd on the courthouse lawn quickly swelled. By one estimate five hundred spectators were in the room early that afternoon when Judge Raulston moved the trial outside. After Bryan took the stand, the audience grew until perhaps three thousand crowded the lawn and the sidewalks. Some perched on running boards or stood between the cars at the curb. The atmosphere quickly took on the feel of a country fair, as the *New York Times* described it, with "men, women, and children, and among them here and there a negro. Small boys went through the crowd selling bottled pop. Most of the men wore hats and smoked."

Darrow started out by establishing Bryan's credentials as a Bible expert, making particular note of his weekly syndicated Bible lessons; Bryan testified that he had studied the Bible for "about fifty years, or some time more than that."

Darrow moved quickly to the issue and the line of questioning that had been hamstrung by Raulston's ruling against expert testimony: "Do you claim that everything in the Bible should be literally interpreted?"

Bryan countered that everything in the Bible "should be accepted as it is given there," though some was "given illustratively," such as the description of a Christian as the salt of the earth.

Darrow asked if Bryan believed the biblical story of Jonah. "Yes, sir," he answered. "Let me add, one miracle is just as easy for me to believe as another. . . . A miracle is a thing performed beyond what man can perform."

Other similar questions followed in succession: "Do you believe Joshua made the sun stand still?" "How long ago was the flood?" "Where did Cain get his wife?" Each time Darrow fired a question, Bryan answered back at length and seemingly unruffled. Seated in the first row of chairs, Eloise Purser (later Eloise Reed), who had celebrated her thirteenth birthday the day before, thought Bryan's calmness seemed to agitate Darrow all the more. Bryan sat in the witness chair, still except for the fan he waved toward his face from time to time, while Darrow paced back and forth in animated fashion across the outdoor platform as he spoke.

Both men played to the gallery, and both were rewarded with applause more than once. When Darrow asked Bryan if he had an opinion whether the author of Joshua thought the sun went around the Earth, Bryan explained, "I believe he was inspired."

"Can you answer my question?" Darrow pressed.

"When you let me finish the statement," Bryan retorted.

"It is a simple question, but finish it."

"You cannot measure the length of my answer by the length of your question."

The courtyard burst into laughter.

"No, except that the answer be longer."

Laughter again.

From Attorney General Stewart's perspective, this whole exercise was a waste of time that only took them farther from the legal question at hand. Yet when he tried to cut Bryan's testimony short, both Bryan and the judge let the examination continue. Even so Stewart kept up his protests. When Darrow began to press Bryan on exactly when the biblical flood took place, the two got into a lively discussion about specific dates.

Stewart interrupted, saying, "I am objecting to his cross-examining his own witness." When Darrow argued that Bryan was a hostile witness, Bryan responded with anticipation of his later questioning of Darrow: "I want him to have all the latitude he wants. For I am going to have some latitude when he gets through."

"You can have latitude and longitude," Darrow quipped, evoking laughter once more from the crowd.

Bryan continued with his testimony, serene with the thought that he would later have the opportunity to expose Darrow. Stewart continued with his objections, claiming at last, "I have a public duty to perform, under my oath, and I ask the court to stop it. Mr. Darrow is making an effort to insult the gentleman on the witness stand."

Raulston had no intention of stopping the two jousting celebrities and spoke in terms of enforcing the agreed-upon arrangement: "To stop it now would not be just to Mr. Bryan. He wants to ask the other gentleman questions along the same line."

The two heavyweights sparred on. The crowd was captivated. The judge acted almost as a spectator, and Attorney General Stewart, right though he was to say none of this bore on the case (the jury was still absent), became quiet. Darrow kept trying to show that the Bible could not be taken literally, while Bryan continued to insist that the Scriptures were absolutely true even if they were indefinite.

"Would you say that the earth is only four thousand years old?" Darrow probed.

"Oh no," Bryan answered, "I think it is much older than that."

"How much?"

"I couldn't say."

"Do you say whether the Bible itself says it is older than that?"

"I don't think the Bible says itself whether it is older or not."

"Do you think the earth was made in six days?"

"Not six days of twenty-four hours."

"Doesn't it say so?"

"No, sir."

A little later: "Mr. Bryan, do you believe that the first woman was Eve?"

"Yes."

"Do you believe she was literally made out of Adam's rib?"

"I do."

"Did you ever discover where Cain got his wife?"

"No sir. I leave the agnostics to hunt for her."

At one point Stewart rose to ask what was the purpose of this whole examination. His colleague Bryan answered that the purpose was to "cast ridicule on everybody who believes in the Bible."

Darrow fired back, "We have the purpose of preventing bigots and ignoramuses from controlling the education of the United States, and you know it."

Dudley Field Malone weighed in, reviewing the accusation that Bryan was trying to get evidence in the record contesting the truth of the experts' affidavits. Bryan's eyes flashed dark in the afternoon sun as he answered: "I am not trying to get anything into the record. I am simply trying to protect the Word of God against the greatest atheist or agnostic in the United States." The transcript here notes "prolonged applause."

The enormous audience on the courthouse lawn admired Bryan's testimony; he was testifying and playing to the crowd at the same time. However, his listeners soon demonstrated that they enjoyed a clever joke or turn of phrase no matter who said it. Darrow read the passage from Genesis describing the moment after the fall of Adam and Eve when the serpent was condemned by God to crawl upon his belly. He asked Bryan if he believed serpents crawled because of God's curse.

"I believe that."

"Have you any idea how the snake went before that time?"

"No, sir."

"Do you know whether he walked on his tail or not?"

By the time he could answer, the audience was already laughing. Even Bryan's most ardent fans, caught up in the exuberance of the exchange, could laugh heartily at the mental image of a snake hopping along upright on the tip of his tail. "No, sir," he said, "I have no way of knowing."

The two went on until Darrow asked about the rainbow after the flood: "Do you believe in that?"

Bryan had had enough. "The only purpose Mr. Darrow has is to slur at the Bible, but I will answer his question." Darrow, for the first time, objected to the statement of his own witness. "I am [examining] you on your fool ideas that no intelligent Christian on earth believes!"

Judge Raulston saw the tension as a sign that the session had gone on long enough. He rapped his gavel. "Court is adjourned until nine o'clock tomorrow morning." With astonishing suddenness, the great debate was over. Though Bryan had given credible answers to every question he knew and honestly admitted those he didn't, the Great Commoner failed to land the knockout blow he doubtless expected to score when he took the stand. Darrow hadn't tripped up Bryan or tricked him into making extrabiblical claims, nor had he backed him into a corner. Recounting the afternoon almost eight decades later, eyewitness Eloise Reed insisted the audience never applauded Darrow

Dayton, Tennessee, showing the Rhea County Courthouse (left), site of the Scopes trial, and the smelting furnaces (center) built by English firm Titis Salt and Sons, Ltd. Iron mining and smelting once employed 5,000 people in the region; the company's bankruptcy eventually led the town to host the trial in hopes of reviving the local economy.

Downtown Dayton at the time of the trial. The Hotel Aqua boasted the area's finest lodging and was the site of welcoming banquets for both William Jennings Bryan and Clarence Darrow.

For the trial, the Rhea County Courthouse, still in use today, was spruced up with paint, new water fountains, restrooms, and telephones.

Kentucky native John Thomas Scopes had just graduated from college and planned to teach a year or two to save money for law school. He had been hired on short notice to coach high school football when the previous coach resigned unexpectedly.

Coach Scopes (top left) and his Rhea County High School squad. Because he was only a few years older than his students, he socialized more with them than other teachers did. After the trial the school board offered him a new contract, but he never taught again.

The real Rhea County High School was less imposing than the neoclassical version in *Inherit the Wind*, the fictional film that still defines the history of the Scopes trial for many people.

This reenactment of the meeting that hatched the Scopes trial was far more crowded than the actual event. Scopes (seated center), mine superintendent George Rappleyea (leaning over Scopes's shoulder), and druggist F. E. Robinson (standing far right) were among the original group. Scopes was doubtless dressed differently; he interrupted a game of tennis to attend.

Though notoriously disheveled and eccentric, law professor John R. Neal had a doctorate from Columbia and a brilliant legal mind. He was the first lawyer to volunteer help to Scopes.

William Jennings Bryan arriving in Dayton July 7, 1925, from his Florida estate. A three-time presidential candidate, Bryan was one of the most famous and popular orators in the country. His offer to prosecute Scopes ensured that the trial would be an international spectacle.

Bryan served as Secretary of State under President Woodrow Wilson until he resigned over differences with the president's policy toward Germany.

In Florida Bryan taught a weekly Sunday school class outdoors that often drew a crowd of 5,000. His skill as a orator enabled him to speak without straining to huge audiences and still be clearly heard.

Scopes and defense attorney Clarence Darrow pose for cameras while John R. Neal stands between them. Though contemplating retirement at 68, Darrow couldn't resist the opportunity to oppose Bryan on so high profile a case.

Lawyer Wallace Haggard, county judge Gordon McKenzie, John R. Neal, and George Rappleyea confer outside during a recess in the trial.

Robinson's Drug Store on Main Street became the town communications center during the trial. Updates were posted on the windows.

Revival preachers streamed into town to take advantage of the crowds and the heightened interest in religion. Visitors could hear three or four messages at once.

H. L. Mencken, correspondent for the *Baltimore Sun,* first encouraged Clarence Darrow to defend Scopes, saying, "Nobody gives a damn about that yap schoolteacher. The thing to do is to make a fool out of Bryan." With his trademark acerbic wit, he pronounced the trial nothing more than "the conspiracies of the inferior man against his betters," labeling anti-evolutionists as ignorant Bible-thumping yokels. His millions of readers ate it up, and the characterization has withstood eighty years of debate.

Attorney general Thomas Stewart, William Jennings Bryan Jr., and Bryan Sr. confer. Stewart led the prosecution and formulated a simple strategy based on the facts of the case that avoided discussion of Genesis, but Bryan lobbied forcefully to argue the Bible and religious faith.

Neal flanked by Darrow (right) and Darrow's law partner, Dudley Field Malone, who, among other business, had a lucrative practice in expensive French divorces for wealthy socialites. Malone was an Undersecretary of State under Bryan in the Wilson cabinet and became Secretary after Bryan resigned.

Eighteenth Circuit Court Judge John Raulston and his family. Accustomed to a docket of moonshiners and petty thieves, Judge Raulston basked in the celebrity of the Scopes trial.

John Scopes at his arraignment. Chicago radio station WGN paid $1,000 a day for one of the nation's first live broadcast hookups. Watching are Bryan (in bow tie behind Scopes) and defense counsel Malone (right bottom corner).

The jury is sworn in. Darrow was surprised that he was supposed to pick 12 men from a pool of only 17. Because of legal wrangling, jury members heard only about three hours of testimony in all.

Every available courtroom space was filled with spectators and newsreel cameramen standing on tables, in doorways, and seated on windowsills. The 90°+ temperatures reflected a region-wide heat wave.

Darrow in the thick of battle. Like Bryan he had removed his coat, collar, and tie to compensate for the blistering heat.

Malone addresses the jury and spectators, some of them spilling through the open door. Clearly this is not the moment of his famous rebuttal to Bryan, when for the first time in the trial he took off his coat.

The Sunday between the two weeks the trial took place, Bryan spoke on the north side of the courthouse from a platform built for July 4 festivities. The sign saying "Read Your BIBLE" became a point of contention days later when the trial moved outside to the same location.

Celebrities at Robinson's Drug Store included chimp Joe Mendi, who was reportedly insured for $100,000.

STEINWAY TUNNEL OPENED TO TRAFFIC

FINAL NIGHT EXTRA — NEW YORK JOURNAL — FINAL NIGHT EXTRA

MONKEY TRIAL LAWYERS FIGHT OVER PRAYER OPENING COURT

Thrill-Slayer Traced to Syracuse

CALLED AT HOME OF GIRL

Shepherd Fights for $1,000,000 Estate of McClintock

STEINWAY TUNNEL IS OPENED

Six Chief Figures in Evolution Case

These are the men whose activity has put the town of Dayton "on the map."

DARROW OBJECTS TO "TURNING COURT INTO A MEETING HOUSE"

DAYTON, Tenn., July 14.—A direct religious controversy was thrown into the Scopes case today when Clarence Darrow, leading defense counsel, formally objected to opening the trial with prayer.

MERCHANTS IN TRACTION RING, HYLAN'S REPLY

A typical headline from the trial. Newspapers around the world put the proceedings on the front page every day, and many printed the complete transcript.

Malone and attorney Herbert Hicks (behind Malone) listen to testimony. Hicks's brother Sue, named after their mother, who died giving him birth, was the "boy named Sue" of story and song.

A moment later Tom Stewart stands with Malone at far left. Hicks is joined by Gordon McKenzie and, behind them, Wallace Haggard. Seated front in profile is H. L. Mencken.

July 20, 1925, Darrow (right) called Bryan as an expert witness on the Bible when Judge Raulston refused to let other experts testify. The trial convened outside because of the unbearable heat, though persistent reports claimed that the weight of so many spectators was cracking the ceiling in the room below.

Bryan died in his sleep of a stroke five days after the trial. Though he had won the case and was energetically planning a nationwide speaking tour and a trip to the Holy Land, popular history has tenaciously attributed his death to grief over the Scopes controversy. His body lay in state in Dayton, then went to Washington by special train for burial in Arlington National Cemetery.

Famous though he already was, the impression that Bryan died a martyr's death defending biblical creationism made him even more of a popular hero. Among the honors accorded him was a larger than life statue sculpted by Gutzon Borglum, designer of Mt. Rushmore.

School superintendent Walter White (left), the official plaintiff in the Scopes case, and F. E. Robinson return in 1948 to the drug store table where the Scopes saga began.

John Scopes (right) attending the Dayton premiere of *Inherit the Wind* in 1960. For decades he shunned the limelight, working in the oil industry in South America, Texas, and Louisiana. Producer Stanley Kubrick convinced him to attend the premiere to promote the same educational and scientific principles he defended in 1925.

In 1955 *Inherit the Wind* became a Broadway hit starring Paul Muni (left) as the Darrow character, Henry Drummond, and Ed Begley as the Bryan-like Matthew Brady. Though the playwrights specifically described their work as fiction, reviewers and the public embraced it as history.

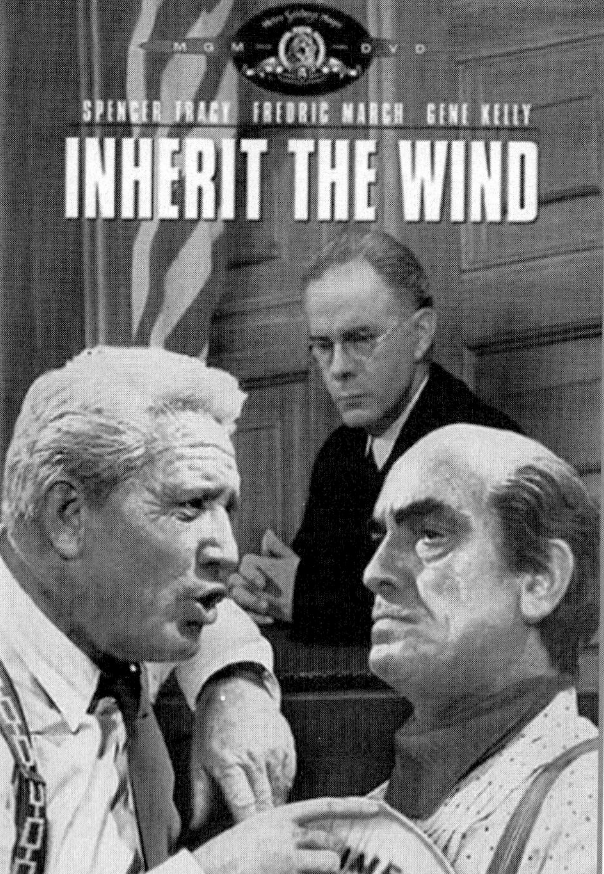

In 1960 *Inherit the Wind* was filmed starring Hollywood heavyweights Spencer Tracy and Fredric March, bringing this mythological retelling of the Scopes trial to millions.

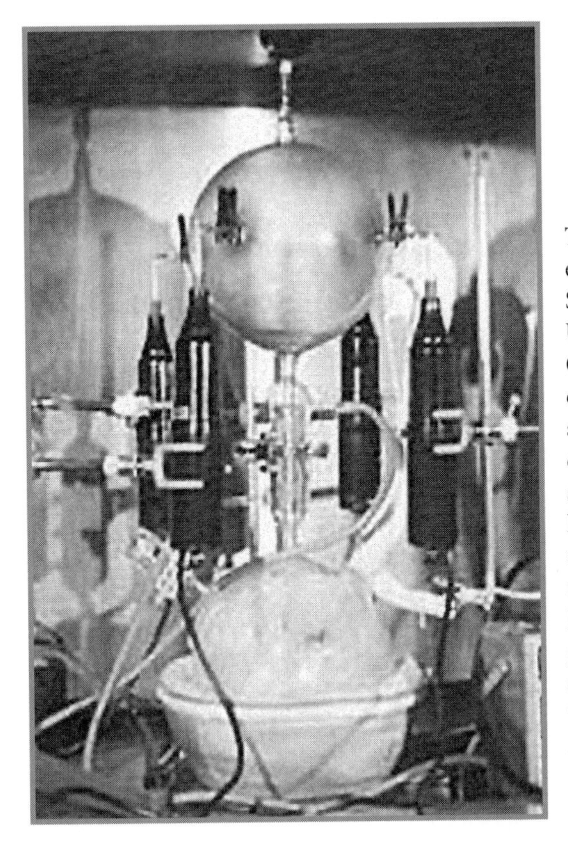

The Miller-Urey experiment. In 1953 Stanley Miller and Harold Urey of the University of Chicago developed an experiment that supposedly proved life could have begun spontaneously from non-living matter. Miller sent an electric spark, representing ultraviolet light, through a chamber of gasses representing the ancient earth's atmosphere. The spark produced amino acids, protein components sometimes called the "building blocks" of life.

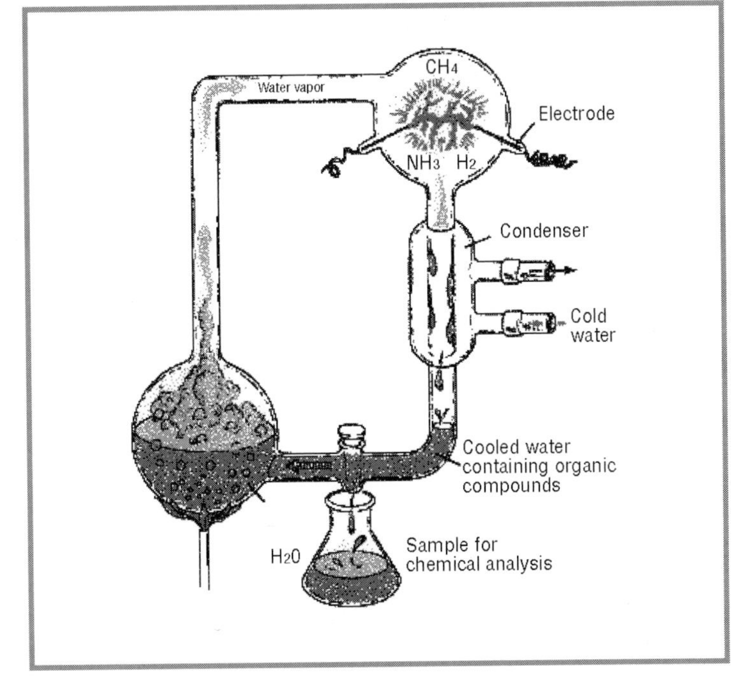

Phillip Johnson developed the theory of Intelligent Design after reading arguments supporting evolution. He was not a scientist but rather held an endowed chair at Berkeley in the School of Law. This position, he said, meant he had no reason to fear for his career or peer standing by opposing the "Mandarins of Science" who insisted that evolution was a proven fact. Unlike all previous positions against evolution, Intelligent Design theory does not depend on a Judeo-Christian God to refute Darwinism. Instead it holds only that no evolutionary mechanism can account for the appearance of new species. Intelligent Design is emerging as a viable and intellectually sound challenge to evolution that avoids the public and legal pitfalls of faith-based argument.

and that Bryan sat calmly and answered confidently while Darrow paced back and forth across the platform.

But Bryan holding his own seemed somehow insufficient. Accustomed to his flights to the oratorical heights before spellbound (and friendly) audiences, many of the thousands present no doubt saw Bryan on the defensive debating an articulate and informed opponent for the first time. Darrow was mobbed by excited onlookers who followed him off the lawn and down the street while Bryan was left alone. Malone's inspired peroration on Thursday had pierced Bryan's shell of invincibility; as John Scopes saw it, Dudley Field Malone "shattered his former chief's unfounded enthusiasm." Monday's direct questioning seemed to affect him less, but it was still a powerful follow-up punch delivered before a crowd of perhaps three thousand: mostly people who had expected a clear-cut Bryan victory in defending the Bible he said he'd studied for more than fifty years.

The few reporters who attended the afternoon session bolted back to their makeshift headquarters over Bailey's Hardware to file their stories. Each made five carbons of his story, then the carbon copies were rewritten enough so that the stories could be telegraphed to the various publications and wire services of the reporters playing hooky in Morgan Springs or cruising on the Tennessee River. At a reporter's invitation John Scopes even tried his hand at rewriting. "It was then," Scopes observed, "that I learned I wasn't cut out to be a journalist." Once the stories were all written, the writers who were present sent their own stories first, scooping their absent colleagues, then filed the rest.

Many newspapers printed the complete transcript of the afternoon's amazing session. Spectators had believed Bryan held the upper hand when it was all over, and many of them felt he had received more applause than Darrow overall. The Memphis *Commercial Appeal* called it a draw of sorts, insisting the testimony "was not a contest. Consequently there was no victory. Darrow succeeded in showing that Bryan knows little about the science of the world. Bryan succeeded in bearing witness bravely to the faith which he believes transcends all the learning of men."

The national press, however, declared Darrow the winner. The *New York Times* called Bryan's testimony "an absurdly pathetic performance, with a famous American the chief creator and butt of a crowd's rude laughter." Tom Stewart decided Monday night that if Bryan either returned to the stand himself or insisted on questioning Darrow as he had said he would, the judge would probably disallow it, and that if the judge didn't stop this reciprocal questioning the state would dismiss the case. Bryan chafed at the thought of foregoing his oratorical revenge but consented in the end.

Most commentators say either that Bryan accepted Stewart's strategic argument against returning lawyers to the stand or they omit any reason Bryan agreed to give up questioning the defense counsel. Ray Ginger, never shy with a hypothesis, reconstructs Bryan's reaction in *Six Days or Forever?* "That night Stewart went to Bryan and told him that he would not be allowed to return to the witness stand the next morning. Bryan protested bitterly; he wanted to recoup himself with his admirers. The two men quarreled vehemently and long. But Stewart held the trump cards: he was the official chief of the prosecution, and he knew John T. Raulston, and logic was on his side."

Tuesday, July 21, court reconvened in the courtroom rather than outside because it was raining. After the opening prayer Judge Raulston announced that all of Bryan's testimony as a witness would be expunged from the trial record. While acknowledging the defense's interest in building a record for appeal, the judge said, "I feel that the testimony of Mr. Bryan can shed no light upon any issues that will be pending before the higher courts."

Darrow rose to except to the ruling, but Raulston stood firm. The only way to get Bryan's testimony into the record would be for the higher court to issue a writ for it. Exasperated that this last-ditch effort at expert testimony had failed like all the rest, Darrow said, "Let me suggest this. . . . I think to save time we will ask the court to bring in the jury and instruct the jury to find the defendant guilty. We make no objection to that."

Stewart responded, "We are pleased to accept the suggestion of Mr. Darrow." This agreement, they would all soon see, meant that the defense would not make any closing statement; therefore, neither could the prosecution, which deprived Bryan of delivering the monumental summation of the case he had been working on in Florida before he even came to Dayton.

Stewart and Bryan had had different objectives from the beginning and displayed those differences here as the trial drew toward its close. When the defense suggested the jury find their client guilty, the attorney general quickly agreed; that was his objective. Bryan on the other hand felt deprived of his chance to finish defending the Bible and then to question his questioner. The court had denied him his objective, and so he would take his message beyond the court. Granted permission to address the bench, Bryan declared, "I shall have to trust to the justness of the press . . . not to the court, but to the press, in answer to the charge scattered broadcast over the world and I shall also avail myself of the opportunity to give to the press, not to the court, the questions that I would have asked had I been permitted to call the attorneys on the other side."

This indicates an honest disagreement between Stewart and Bryan, yet the two evidently kept cordial professional relations. Stewart never relinquished his lead role as attorney general but never seemed weary at Bryan's populist grandstanding as long as it could help win the case. When it became a liability, Stewart stepped in, and Bryan seemed to respect Stewart's position both then and throughout the trial.

At long last the jury came in, but even then the first several exchanges between the two sides were around the bench, out of public earshot, as they discussed the appeal. Then the judge declared a recess to dictate his charge to the jury. After court resumed, the charge was read into the record. Darrow addressed the jury briefly to explain why they had heard no evidence on behalf of the defendant.

> The court has held under the law that the evidence we had is not admissible, so all we can do is to take an exception and carry it to a higher court to see whether the evidence is admissible or not. . . . If you think my client taught that man descended from a lower order of animals, you will find him guilty, and you heard the testimony of the boys on that question. . . . We cannot argue to you gentlemen under the

> instructions given by the court—we cannot even explain to you that we think you should return a verdict of not guilty. We do not see how you could.

Attorney General Stewart then briefly revisited a portion of the judge's charge to the jury that explained, "If you are content with a $100 fine [the minimum for violating the Butler Act], then you may simply find the defendant guilty and leave the punishment to the court." Stewart thought it was always the jury's duty to fix the fine.

"There is no reason why the jury should not fix the minimum if you prefer," Judge Raulston said. "The practice, however, is for the court to impose the minimum."

This seemingly minor detail would become the basis for the appeal. The general statute held that all fines over $50 be assessed by the jury. Because Judge Raulston assessed the fine of $100 (the standard minimum for bootlegging, the circuit court's most frequent type of case), his ruling would later be thrown out.

The jury left for its deliberation. They were gone nine minutes, most of which were spent getting in and out of the crowded room. Huddled together in the hallway outside the courtroom, they took one poll, reached their unanimous verdict, and returned to their places inside.

"We have found for the state," the foreman announced, "found the defendant guilty." The judge had already announced the $100 fine before John R. Neal reminded him that the defendant had a right to be heard. At the invitation of Judge Raulston, John Thomas Scopes gave his only official testimony of the trial in less than a minute:

"Your honor, I feel that I have been convicted of violating an unjust statute. I will continue in the future, as I have in the past, to oppose this law in any way I can. Any other action would be in violation of my ideal of academic freedom, that is, to teach the truth as guaranteed in our constitution, of personal and religious freedom. I think the fine is unjust."

There was also the matter of bond for the appeal. Dudley Field Malone asked the judge what the bond would be. "Well, how much bail can Mr. Scopes make?" the judge asked. "We can arrange any amount your honor demands." The appearance bond was set at $500.

Malone announced that the bond would be paid by the Baltimore *Evening Sun*, Mencken's paper. (The ACLU subsequently paid the $100 fine plus Scopes's court costs of $327.77.) Then came a round of thanks: Malone thanked the people of Tennessee for their hospitality, a member of the press echoed those thanks on behalf of the reporters, and Gordon McKenzie accepted their thanks on behalf of everyone.

Bryan made some short closing remarks, noting the Scopes case had put Dayton on the world map because the stakes reached "into the future beyond the power of man to see." It was a little case, "but the world is interested because it raises an issue, and that issue will someday be settled right, whether it is settled on our side or the other side." Individuals were small, Bryan observed, "but causes go on forever, and we who participated in this case may congratulate ourselves that we have attached ourselves to a mighty issue."

Darrow also made a farewell statement and drew a laugh from the audience early on when he thanked Judge Raulston for not jailing him for contempt of court. He agreed with Bryan that Dayton was a small place where something big had happened, comparing it to "the place where the Magna Charta was wrested from the barons of England." Darrow continued, "I think this case will be remembered because it is the first case of this sort since we stopped trying people in America for witchcraft because we have done our best to turn back the tide that has sought to force itself upon this modern world, of testing every fact in science by a religious dictum."

Even George Rappleyea, who had remained in the background since turning the plaintiff's role over to Walter White, spoke, publicly thanking Bryan for his work "in spite of the criticisms he has had."

After a little further pontificating by the judge and a benediction, the matter of *Tennessee v. John Thomas Scopes* was officially adjourned.

CHAPTER 18

Journalistic Monkeys

"I WILL HAVE TO TRUST to the justness of the press," Bryan said when he was unable to put Darwin on the stand or give his prepared speech. That proved to be a futile hope, and we need to stop our narrative for a moment to document the extent of press bias against Bryan.

The background to bias begins in the late nineteenth century when major newspapers began regularly reporting that American society was a mess and that hope of social progress lay not with spiritual transformation but with scientific advance. For example, features in Joseph Pulitzer's *New York World* such as "Experimenting with an Electric Needle and an Ape's Brain" showed that scientific transformation of man's thought patterns was just around the corner.

From 1895 on William Randolph Hearst took Pulitzer's insights and spread them across the nation. Day after day Hearst's chain of newspapers provided an artful combination of sensation and hope. On the one hand, the present was tragedy, with headlines such as "He Murdered His Friends" or "He Ran Amuck with a Hatchet." Story after story: A woman beat a man senseless with a beer bottle and then stabbed her jailer with a hatpin. A maidservant poisoned her mistress's soup. A boy shot and killed his father, who was beating his mother. An eleven-year-old drank a bottle of acid because she did "not want to live." On the other hand, the future would be much better, thanks to science (actually, pseudoscience). The *San Francisco Examiner* reported that one professor had produced "solidified air." Another found out that what a woman eats determines the gender of her baby.

The journalistic muckrakers who became famous early in the twentieth century almost always assumed evolution and wrote out of a totally materialistic sensibility. The most famous muckraker, Lincoln Steffens, wrote that he began his quest as a student at the University of California during the 1880s, where professors "could not agree upon what was knowledge, nor upon what was good and what evil, nor why," but they knew that Darwin had nailed the origins of man. Once, discussing the biblical fall within the garden of Eden, he said the culprit was not Adam, or Eve, or even the snake: "It was, it is, the apple." Good people were changed by their surroundings and so were species. Upton Sinclair wrote of how all the leading muckrakers shared a belief in social evolution: "Races emerge from barbarism. They are joyous and proud and strong; they struggle and conquer, they toil and achieve."

The younger followers of Sinclair and Steffens absorbed such beliefs; the experience of one Scopes trial reporter, Raymond Clapper, shows the pattern. Clapper didn't write much explicitly about his own beliefs, but his wife Olive Clapper later drew a portrait of his pilgrim's regress. She first depicted how Raymond was a young Bible believer in 1912: "He led the Christian Endeavor meeting at the Presbyterian Church. He read the Bible lesson, announced the hymns we would sing, and opened the discussion."

Four years later, as both were ready to graduate from the University of Kansas, beliefs had changed: "We owed a lot all our lives to this great state-supported University. It gave us knowledge and confidence in our capacity to learn and to do. . . . We were beginning to question the rigid beliefs of our parents and needed a more reasonable belief. . . . We particularly enjoyed Dr. E. C. A. Smith of the Unitarian Church in Lawrence when he discussed evolution and religion."

By 1923, when the Clappers's first child was born, they were firm in their new faith: "We outlined and agreed upon certain fundamentals to be taught to our children. Chief among these was our attitude toward religion. We had long since discarded the orthodox teachings of our youth. We could not believe the Old Testament prophets, whose teachings no doubt fitted well the savage age in which they lived but suited our world no better than the Greek oracles. The story of Christ we thought was moving and beautiful but we could not accept the virgin birth or the resurrection."

Two years later it was not surprising that Ray Clapper told his editor that he just had to cover the Scopes trial because, as Olive Clapper recalled, her husband was certain that Bryan would show the world that "the whole case of fundamentalism [was] ridiculous. . . . Not even chains could have kept Ray from covering that famous trial. In his story of July 17, near the end of the trial, Ray wrote, 'Fundamentalist justice has plugged up the ears of this Tennessee mountain jury.' . . . And so it was. Unbelievable as the trial was to intelligent people, it did have value because the end result was greater enlightenment of people on the subject of evolution."

Journalists who descended on Dayton in 1925 had often gone through similar processes of theological change. They carried with them antipathy toward fundamentalist Christianity. Their newspapers were religiously committed to evolution. The *New York Times* editorialized that modern man needed "faith, even of a grain of mustard seed, in the evolution of life. . . . If man has evolved, it is inconceivable that the process should stop and leave him in his present imperfect state. Specific creation has no such promise for man. . . . No legislation should (or can) rob the people of their hope." The *Times* quoted Bernard Shaw's statement that "the world without the conception of evolution would be a world wherein men of strong mind could only despair," for their only hope would be in a God to whom such modernists would not pray.

Other newspapers featured more spokesmen for evolutionary beliefs. The *Chicago Tribune* gave front-page space to zoologist H. J. Muller's faith concerning man that "so far he has had only a short probationary period. He is just at the beginning of a great epic adventure in the course of world evolution." Belief in evolution had grown ever since Darwin had reinvigorated the age-old concept through his mid-nineteenth century writings, but World War I had given it new impetus. The great and terrible war so decimated hopes for peaceful progress of mankind that millions came to believe in one or other of two ways upward from misery: either God's grace or man's evolution.

Newspaper editors backed up their editorial rhetoric with strenuous effort. They dispatched more than one hundred reporters to the trial, and those reporters wired 165,000 words daily to their newspapers during the twelve days of extensive coverage in July 1925. The *New York Times* itself received an average of 10,000 words per day from its writers on the scene. In theory trial coverage was an opportunity to illuminate the theological bases on which both evolutionist and creationist superstructures were built. For instance, even a pro-evolution journalist at one point admitted that one creationist was "a sound logician." Another reporter wrote with amazement of a Tennessee mountain man who had, along with his old clothes and unpolished boots, a scholar's knowledge of Greek and the ability to make careful comparisons of New Testament translations.

In practice reporters described the story as one of pro-evolution intelligence versus antievolution stupidity. We've seen how the era's most famous journalist, H. L. Mencken, put aside his typical amusement with life to ride Paul Revere-like through the land with dire warnings about the trial: "Let no one mistake it for comedy, farcical though it may be in its details. It serves notice on the country that Neanderthal man is organizing in these forlorn backwaters of the land, led by a fanatic, rid of sense and devoid of conscience."

Mencken summarized his view of the debate's complexity by noting, "On the one side was bigotry, ignorance, hatred, superstition, every sort of blackness that the human mind is capable of. On the other side was sense." Other journalists from the Northeast and the urban Midwest shared that view. Nunnally Johnson, who covered the trial for the *Brooklyn Eagle* and then became a noted Hollywood screenwriter, remembered years later, "For the newspapermen it was a lark on a monstrous scale. . . . Being admirably cultivated fellows, they were all of course evolutionists and looked down on the local fundamentalists."

Westbrook Pegler, a secular conservative journalist who admired Mencken and imitated his coverage, noted years later that "the whole Blue Ridge country was ridiculed on religious grounds by an enormous claque of supercilious big town reporters." Pro-evolutionist L. Sprague de Camp wrote of the reporters, "most of them were city, men, hostile to [Bryan, whom they saw as] the leader of organized ignorance, the modern Torquemada," that heresy hunter who burned enemies at the stake.

Journalistic ridicule came from both liberal and conservative large-city newspapers. The liberal *New York Times* editorialized that the creationist position represented a "breakdown of the reasoning powers. It is seeming evidence that the human mind can go into deliquescence without falling into stark lunacy." The conservative *Chicago Tribune* sneered at fundamentalists looking for "horns and forked tails and the cloven hoofs." Two weeks before the trial began, the *Arkansas Gazette* noted, "These days a newspaper that does not contain a barbed thrust aimed directly or otherwise at Tennessee is fully as difficult to find as a needle in a haystack . . . or more to the point, a link in the chain of evolution."

Nor did coverage simply reflect journalistic preference for urban civilization over rural living conditions. When Mencken first arrived in Dayton, he was so surprised that he produced his only nonacidic description of Dayton, calling it "a country town full of charm and even beauty. . . . The two chief streets are paved from curb to curb. The stores carry good stocks and have a metropolitan air. . . . The Evolutionists and the Anti-Evolutionists seem to be on the best of terms and it is hard in a group to distinguish one from the other." Another reporter mentioned with surprise that a Dayton drugstore had gleaming counters and packaged goods similar to those available on Fifth Avenue.

The ridicule primarily reflected those reporters' outrage at fundamentalist theology, in part because their own cultures had only recently "outgrown" that theology. The *New York Times* noted at one point "a certain unexpectedness in the behavior and talk of the Dayton people. The unexpectedness comes from the absence in these Dayton people of any notable dissimilarity from the people elsewhere except in their belated clinging to a method of scriptural interpretation that not long ago was more than common in both North and South." The *Times* writer in those two sentences understood that the fundamentalist beliefs were far from bizarre; in fact, it was the newer method of scriptural interpretation that had been regarded as bizarre in Times Square as well as Tennessee only a short time before.

Many of the journalists in Dayton presented the trial as one about free speech. The *Chicago Tribune*'s Kinsley wrote that the Tennessee law, if upheld, would make every work on evolution "a book of evil tidings, to be studied in secret." That statement was nonsense, and Kinsley himself must have seen that hundreds of pro-evolution publications were on sale in Dayton. Even a drugstore had a stack of materials representing all positions. Remember that John Butler, the legislator who introduced the antievolution bill, told reporters, "I am not opposed to teaching of evolution, but I don't think it ought to be taught in state-supported schools," and he had a copy of Darwin's *The Origin of Species* for his teenage children to read.

With rare exceptions journalists turned the trial into a battle of intellectual freedom versus slavery. The *New York American* began one trial story with the sentence, "Tennessee today maintained its quarantine against learning." The battle pitted "rock-ribbed Tennessee" against "unfettered investigation by the human mind and the liberty of opinion which the Constitution makers preached." Reporters from the *New York Times* and the *Chicago Tribune* regularly attacked Christian faith and "this superheated religious atmosphere, this pathetic search for the 'eternal truth.'"

Columnist Bugs Baer wrote with lively viciousness. He depicted Scopes as an imprisoned martyr, "the witch who is to be burned by Dayton." Baer described Bryan's face as "a panorama of curdled egotism." The columnist predicted that a fundamentalist victory would turn "the dunce cap" into the "crown of office." Baer called residents of Dayton "treewise monkeys [who] see no logic, speak no logic and hear no logic." When William Jennings Bryan Jr. arrived from California for the trial, Baer wrote, "Junior is bound to be a chip off the old blockhead. . . . Like father, like son, and we don't like either."

Many reporters also turned the story into an account of smart versus stupid. One New York headline described the Dayton jurors this way: "Intelligence of Most Lowest Grade." It seemed that "all twelve are Protestant churchgoers. . . . Hickory-shirted, collarless, suspendered, tanned, raw-boned men are these. . . . The grade of intelligence as revealed by the attitudes and words of the twelve indicates to this observer that at least nine of the Scopes jurors had never used a four-syllable word in their lives until the term 'evolution' was crowded into the local vocabulary." One prospective juror even had "a homemade hair cut and ears like a loving cup."

Newspapers ran humorous comments about Dayton similar to today's ethnic jokes; the *New York Times,* though, worried that the situation was serious, and trumpeted of "Cranks and Freaks" in a front-page headline. The *Times* worried about the belief in creationism by "thousands of unregulated or ill-balanced minds" and portrayed as zombies the Tennesseans entering the courthouse: "All were sober-faced, tight-lipped, expressionless." The *Chicago Tribune* news service sometimes criticized antievolutionists more subtly: "At regular intervals loud, ringing tones from the courthouse steeple announce the hour to Dayton folk—and announce it consistently 35 minutes ahead of central standard time. This little town, object of scorn to residents of great cities, is far from being backward in counting the hours."

The typical major newspaper reporter did not provide accurate news coverage of the actual trial events. For example, as chapter 12 shows, William Jennings Bryan was bested by Dudley Malone on July 16, but he did not embarrass himself. Bryan stressed Darwinism's lack of scientific proof and emphasized its inability to answer questions about how life began, how man began, how one species actually changes into another, and so on. He pointed out the irreconcilability of Darwinian doctrines of extraspecies evolution with the biblical account of creation, original sin, and the reasons for Christ's coming.

The typical press report, though, tracked Mencken's gibe that Bryan's speech "was grotesque performance and downright touching in its imbecility." McGeehan of the New York *Herald Tribune* wrote that Bryan "was given the floor and after exactly one hour and ten minutes he was lying upon it horizontally—in a figurative sense." McGeehan, regularly a sportswriter, did not often get to write about figurative self-knockouts, but he used his mind-reading talents to note that "the brethren and sisters in the rear of the courtroom looked sorrowful and disappointed," and his awareness of body language to point out that "Mr. Bryan sat in his corner in the attitude of the defeated gladiator."

Many reporters loaded their Bryan coverage with sarcastic biblical allusions: "Unleash his thunder," "Make this jury the recording angels of a great victory for revealed religion," or, "The sun seemed to stand still in the heavens, as for Joshua of old, and to burn with holy wrath against the invaders of this fair Eden of fundamentalism." Sometimes sentence after sentence mixed biblical metaphors: "Dayton began to read a new book of revelations today. The wrath of Bryan fell at last. With whips of scorn, he sought to drive science from the temples of God and failed."

New York and Chicago-based reporters were particularly insulting after the Bryan-Darrow face-off on the trial's last full day. The next day the *New York Times* observed, "It was a Black Monday for him [Bryan] when he exposed himself. . . . It has long been known to many that he was only a voice calling from a poorly-furnished brain-room." The *Herald Tribune*'s McGeehan wrote that Bryan was "losing his temper and becoming to all intents and purposes a mammal."

Overall most major newspaper reports produced so much unobservant coverage that it often seemed as if they were watching something other than the trial in front of them. One New York scribe, under the headline "Scopes Is Seen as New Galileo at Inquisition," wrote:

> The sultry courtroom in Dayton, during a pause in the argument, became hazy and there evolved from the mist of past ages a new scene. The Tennessee judge disappeared and I racked my brain to recognize the robed dignitary on the bench. Yes, it was the grand inquisitor, the head of the inquisition at Rome. Lawyers faded from view, all except the evangelical leader of the prosecution, Mr. Bryan, who was reversely incarnated as angry-eyed Pope Urban. . . . I saw the Tennessee Fundamentalist public become a medieval mob thirsty for heretical blood. . . . [It was] 1616. The great Galileo was on trial.

Many journalists in Dayton did not want to see reality. They became notorious for spending as little time with the local people as possible. H. L. Mencken, according to Pegler, had minimal contact with Dayton: "He had an airy suite on Lookout Mountain in Chattanooga, with a tub of ice and a fan blowing a cool breeze as he sat in his shorts after an hour or two a day in Dayton." McGeehan did become friendly with a local doctor who, during those days of prohibition, could offer documents more precious than rubies: prescriptions for valid liquor.

Occasionally a few journalists possessed temporarily the poetic gift Robert Burns wrote of, to see ourselves as others see us. Frank Kent, a perceptive *Baltimore Sun* correspondent, generally joined the hunt at Dayton with the other reporters, but for his July 15 article, he noted that Dayton residents were watching the reporters, and, as the headline put it, "Impressions Made by Visitors Will Not Be Altogether Favorable." Kent described how journalists were "scattering abroad a brand of profanity and a species of joke rather new to the natives." Journalists raced to an outdoor "Holy Rollers" gathering, "drove almost into the meeting, turned the glare of their headlights on the pitiful little group . . . laughed and joked until, abased and afraid, the Holy Rollers abandoned their prayers and slunk off to their homes in the hills."

Kent also wrote about rudeness at a boarding house: "On the table for breakfast were bacon and eggs, fruit, hot biscuits, coffee. Said this man in terrible tone to the little bride, who waits on the table: 'Have you no corn flakes?' Unhappily she replied: 'I am very sorry, sir, but we haven't any.' 'Hell!' said this metropolitan gentleman, and, pushing his chair over, he stalked from the room, slamming the door behind with a bang." Yet, after showing perceptiveness, the very next day Kent returned to the trial and wrote that "Bryan sits in his corner silent and watchful. . . . You can shut your eyes and imagine him leading [Daytonites] to burn the unbelievers at the stake."

"You can shut your eyes," and most journalists did at the Scopes trial.

CHAPTER 19

The Week After

BACK TO OUR NARRATIVE: Though he had been embarrassed on the witness stand, William Jennings Bryan had won his case and still had a full head of steam. In short order he was back at his rented house releasing press statements questioning Darrow's personal beliefs and motives; Darrow answered him point for point in a release of his own. Though the image of Bryan as a defeated, broken man after the trial has persisted, Bryan evidently jumped on the legal victory as the centerpiece of a proposed lecture tour to other states where antievolution laws were under consideration.

On Wednesday, the day after the trial, Bryan released an upbeat statement: "Is the Bible true is the question raised by the Tennessee law, and that question is answered in the affirmative as far as this trial can answer it." Darrow himself, in Bryan's opinion, was a cautionary example of what a godless life was like. Darrow, still savoring the image of Bryan in the witness chair gamely fielding queries about the age of the Earth and other biblical matters, replied to the press, "Of course, I cannot help having some pity for Mr. Bryan for being obligated to show his ignorance by simple and competent questions asked him on the witness stand."

In Darrow's mind he had depended on Bryan's ego to nudge him into going on the stand, and his strategy worked. Bryan was champing at the bit to do what he did so successfully: defend traditional Christian standards in the public spotlight. This was doubly true since, as eyewitnesses invariably report, his oration in court the week before had fallen flat compared with Dudley Field Malone's inspired presentation for the defense. He wanted to win back his audience. Darrow had then held Bryan's feet to the fire of scientific materialism and relied on journalists to tell the world they were scorched.

Recounting the testimony later, Darrow said defending creationism as a witness meant Bryan had "to choose between his crude beliefs and the common intelligence of modern times" or to admit ignorance. While many eyewitnesses to the testimony gave Bryan high marks for his demeanor on the stand and defending faith in the face of materialist skepticism, the *New York Times* observed, "Mr. Bryan's complete lack of interest in many of the things closely connected with such religious questions as he has been supporting for many years was strikingly shown again and again by Mr. Darrow." Creationists might argue that Bryan wasn't showing a lack of interest but rather a justifiable reluctance to speculate on God's plans and purposes.

When Mencken first encouraged Darrow to defend John Thomas Scopes, we saw that his comment was, "Nobody gives a damn about that yap schoolteacher. The thing to do is to make a fool out of Bryan." Not long after the trial ended, Darrow wrote to Mencken, "I made up my mind to show the country what an ignoramus he was, and I succeeded."

Reporting on the 1904 Democratic National Convention in Saint Louis, the twenty-three-year-old journalist had written of Bryan, "There was more eloquence in this than can ever be set down in black and white." But twenty-one summers later Mencken never failed to portray Bryan in the most unfavorable light possible. In his column for July 14, 1925, he wrote of Bryan's reaction to Darrow's speech the day before:

> During the whole time of its delivery the old mountebank, Bryan, sat tight-lipped and unmoved. There is, of

> course, no reason why it should have shaken him. He has those hill billies locked up in his pen and he knows it. His brand is on them. He is at home among them. Since his earliest days, indeed, his chief strength has been among the folk of remote hills and forlorn and lonely farms. Now with his political aspirations all gone to pot, he turns to them for religious considerations. They understand his peculiar imbecilities. His nonsense is their idea of sense. When he deluges them with his theological bilge they rejoice like pilgrims disporting in the Jordan.

Later Mencken continued, "The fellow is full of such bitter, implacable hatreds that they radiate from him like heat from a stove. He hates the learning that he cannot grasp. He hates those who sneer at him. He hates, in general, all who stand apart from his own pathetic commonness."

Describing Bryan's reaction to Malone's powerful and impressive speech on July 16, Mencken wrote the next day:

> The old boy grows more and more pathetic. He has aged greatly during the past few years and begins to look elderly and enfeebled. All that remains of his old fire is now in his black eyes. They glitter like dark gems, and in their glitter there is immense and yet futile malignancy. That is all that is left of the Peerless Leader of thirty years ago. Once he had one leg in the White House and the nation trembled under his roar. Now he is a tinpot pope in the Coca-Cola belt and a brother to the forlorn pastors who belabor half-wits in galvanized iron tabernacles behind the railroad yards.

Darrow, Mencken, and their colleagues managed to turn the national and international spotlight off of Scopes and try the simple country people of Dayton instead; they declared them guilty of close-mindedness, antiintellectualism, and plain stupidity. Next they put creationism on trial, both the belief and its most prominent believer, and condemned them as well.

Bryan, though, used to criticism, seemed to shake it off. He spent the rest of the week in Dayton, refining the closing speech that he had never gotten to deliver in court. On Friday he and his wife, Mary, drove to Chattanooga to have it typeset and printed. Saturday they drove to Tom Stewart's hometown of Winchester, Tennessee, where Bryan tried out a new Scopes speech based on his undelivered court remarks for the first time. He spoke first at a Civitan gathering, then later at a large open-air meeting. (Some sources say Stewart invited Bryan to town; others say it was Judge Raulston.) Bryan tried to use a speaker system set up on a lot in town, but an echo or some other technical problem ruined the attempt. Bryan had the amplifier turned off and spoke to the crowd directly, as he always had. The crowd could hear every word.

Stewart's eleven-year-old son remembered the huge dinner Bryan ate at his house later that afternoon and the commotion that dinner caused. Attorney General Stewart, and perhaps Judge Raulston as well, thought Bryan and his wife would eat lunch at the judge's house a few miles away. It wasn't until just before the lunch hour that Bryan declared he'd be honored to dine with the Stewarts. The whole Stewart family, and the cook besides, had been away listening to Bryan's speech so that nothing was on the stove. Frantically Mrs. Stewart canvassed the neighbors for table-ready food and collected a roasted chicken, fresh bread, vegetables, and other dishes to serve her honored guest. One neighbor donated a basket of peaches, which Bryan set on the floor beside him at the table. By the time the meal was over, he had eaten every one.

Bryan returned to Dayton Saturday night to correct the printer's proofs of his speech and make preliminary plans for his speaking tour. The outcome of the Scopes trial had concerned Bryan but almost certainly had not depressed him; rather he was newly energized and inspired to enlarge the field of battle. As he reportedly told a newspaperman in Winchester, "If I should die tomorrow, I believe that on the basis of the accomplishments of the last few weeks I could truthfully say, well done."

John Scopes had also left Dayton just after the trial but not before dealing with the thousands of letters that had poured into town over the past two weeks. The post office hired an extra mailman just to handle mail generated by the trial. When the letters filled a room at Bailey's Boarding House, Scopes started stacking them on the front porch. And still they came; the postman took to hauling mail over in washtubs.

Letters came from Germany, France, Spain, Norway, and China and with them came offers of marriage, speaking engagements, and employment; the Liberal Church appointed him "the Bishop of Tennessee with pontifical powers." One offer to the $150-a-month high school teacher was for $50,000 to lecture about evolution on the vaudeville circuit. Scopes rejected that one, he said, because "it would have put me on exhibit, which I was determined to avoid at all costs. Also there was the fact that I didn't know enough about evolution to lecture on it." He rejected every other offer as well. "I had only one life in the world," he wrote later, "and I wanted to enjoy it. I knew I could not live happily in a spotlight."

Some time late in the week, a couple of friends helped Scopes form a huge mound of letters, most of them still unopened, in the yard in front of the boarding house. From three different sides the three young men touched matches to the pile and burned them all. "Many newspaper stories reported I had been offered all kinds of fortunes and movie contracts and God knows what else," he observed. "Probably that was accurate; any kind of offer in the world would have been among the mail we burned that day, and I wouldn't have known it."

Though he had befriended several of them and had tried his own hand at their craft, Scopes was relieved to see the last wave of reporters depart on a special train bound for Washington, D.C. He helped several of them carry their bags to the station and stood on the platform to see them off. On the side of one car hung a homemade banner rechristening the train the *Protoplasma Special.*

Two of the expert witnesses, Kirtley Mather and Watson Davis, notified Scopes that they and the other witnesses had set up a scholarship fund to send him to graduate school. Before the week was out, Scopes took the train to Lexington, Kentucky, to see about entering law school in the fall. Though he had long considered a legal career, his trial experience changed him. He knew if he became a lawyer, he would be compared with Darrow and Bryan all his life. Before the summer was out he changed his mind and began a graduate degree in geology at the University of Chicago.

Returning to Dayton from Lexington on Sunday afternoon, Scopes had a layover at the train station in Knoxville where he happened to see Paul Anderson, a reporter for the St. Louis *Post-Dispatch* who had covered his trial and become his friend. They struck up a conversation. After a few minutes, Anderson said, "Are you going back to Dayton for the same reason I am?"

"I don't know, Paul," Scopes replied. "What happened?"

"Bryan died a few hours ago."

Bryan had attended the Southern Methodist church in Dayton that morning, where the preacher had called on him to lead the closing prayer at the end of the service. Then he had gone back up Market Street to his rented house for Sunday dinner and a nap. He had died in his sleep. The official cause of death was "apoplexy," the common early twentieth-century term for a stroke.

Eager to help his friend score a scoop as well as to get back to Dayton quickly himself, Scopes led Anderson on a backwoods shortcut. Instead of taking the train to Chattanooga and laying over there for the local to Dayton, they took a different train out of Knoxville and got off at Athens, Tennessee, only thirty cross-country miles from Dayton, which they covered by taxi and river ferry with the *Post-Dispatch* footing the bill.

Many commentators tied Bryan's death to the outcome of the trial. Tennessee Governor Austin Peay proclaimed the Great Commoner had died "a martyr to the faith of our fathers," and declared the day of his funeral a state holiday. In the *New York World,* Walter Lippmann wrote, "His death at this time will weight his words at Dayton with the solemnity of a parting message and strengthen their effect upon his fellow citizens."

Mencken had his own ideas about the cause of Bryan's demise. In public he joked, "God aimed at Darrow, missed, and hit Bryan instead." In private he gleefully claimed, "We killed the son of a bitch." Darrow, on vacation that weekend in the Smoky Mountains, had his own diagnosis: "Broken heart nothing; he died of a busted belly."

No formal ceremony in Dayton marked the death of this famous figure. Bryan's open casket stood at his rented house long enough for hundreds to pay their respects, a small-town version of lying in state that the Great Commoner no doubt would have appreciated. Except for Paul Anderson and the other reporters who returned to cover the latest turn in the story, the luminaries and visitors were all gone. Scopes and Anderson visited the house and found it as subdued and eerily quiet as the rest of the town. On Wednesday a special train carried the body to Washington, where Bryan received burial in Arlington National Cemetery because of his service in the Spanish-American War.

At his death Bryan was nearing the biblical allotment of threescore and ten years. He had diabetes, was a legendary overeater, and had been working long hours through some of the hottest weather in a century. Many who saw the whole trial believed Dudley Field Malone's speech on Thursday took a lot more wind out of Bryan's sails than Darrow's direct questioning the following Monday. Bryan's speech-making, interest in the publication of his trial oration, and plans for a lecture tour and voyage to the Holy Land all defined a man who was full of life and full of fight for his cause.

Here was an unlikely candidate to die of a broken heart; a stroke was surely a far more likely cause of death. Yet the myth that Darrow had destroyed him started early and grew steadily until it would eventually take on a life of its own, nurtured first by circulation-conscious newspapermen and later by agenda- and profit-driven Hollywood dream makers.

CHAPTER 20

Wrapping Up the Trial

JOHN THOMAS SCOPES and Clarence Darrow lost the battle against divine creation in the sweltering summer of 1925. But they won the war; ultimately they even won the battle. On January 15, 1927, the Tennessee Supreme Court reversed Judge John Raulston's ruling because he had assessed a $100 fine from the bench when state law required fines over $50 to be set by the jury. Attorney General Thomas Stewart may well have caught the error. The trial transcript shows him questioning the judge more than once about it; his son Thomas Jr. was convinced that his father had made his point, won the case on its legal merits, and had no interest in seeing Scopes pay a fine or go to jail. William Jennings Bryan, who had consulted with the Tennessee legislature on the original Butler Act, had lobbied the lawmakers not to put a fine in the statute since he figured a schoolteacher could ill afford it.

Darrow was disappointed to see the Dayton decision reversed on a technicality. He wrote to Scopes suggesting they have the case reassigned and appeal again. "All the lawyers are agreed that this is what we should do, so I assume you will approve. I am pretty well satisfied that the law is dead, but we want to be sure if possible." In the end the

Tennessee Supreme Court denied the motion for a new hearing, and the legal history of the Scopes trial was at an end.

John Scopes was in graduate school at the University of Chicago in 1927 on the scholarship his expert witnesses had raised for him. When a reporter called to ask him his reaction to the appeal ruling, Scopes said, "You'll have to tell me what happened. This is the first I've heard of it." He was more than glad to leave his notoriety behind though he was pleased to think the publicity of his trial kept some other states from passing their own antievolution laws.

Near the end of the school year that spring, Scopes was nominated for a prestigious graduate fellowship. His scholarship from the trial witnesses had paid for one year of his two-year doctoral program, and now this departmental honor would cover the rest of it. His plans changed, however, when he received a note a couple of weeks later from the university president who administered the fellowship: "Your name has been removed from consideration for the fellowship. As far as I am concerned, you can take your atheistic marbles and play elsewhere." Before the summer was out, Scopes was on his way to Venezuela for a job with Gulf Oil. He never got his Ph.D.

John Scopes was eager to distance himself from his celebrity and found relief in South American anonymity. Only briefly did he return to the spotlight, at his wife's insistence, for the premiere of *Inherit the Wind* in Dayton on the thirty-fifth anniversary of his trial (he had turned down invitations to see the play on Broadway and to attend the New York film premiere). At director Stanley Kramer's request, he also went on a publicity tour. "If nothing else," Scopes recalled years later, "it was time to remind the people again of the importance of preserving their basic freedoms."

In *Center of the Storm*, his autobiography published in 1967 at the height of the cold war, Darwinism's popularity, and five years after the Supreme Court first banned school prayer, Scopes also wrote:

> If a state is allowed to dictate that a teacher must teach a subject in accordance with the beliefs of one particular religion, then the state can also force schools to teach the beliefs of the person in power, which can lead to suppression of all

> personal and religious liberties. . . . The founding fathers declared in the Constitution's first amendments that there should be no interference of the church in state affairs. Yet when Congress or a court or a school is opened with a prayer based upon the Christian belief, some religion has been discriminated against no matter how small a minority it represents. The act itself is unchristian in its basic implications; it is replacing love and tolerance with discrimination. . . .
>
> I think the defense won the main battle in 1925 by exposing the literalists' unreasonable views to public scrutiny and therefore slowing down the Fundamentalist crusade, and partially because of the trial I think the day will come when we will not be bothered by Fundamentalists. . . . In larger ways, I am less optimistic. Freedom is a cause that must be defended over and over, day by day, and by many people. Liberty is always under threat and it literally takes eternal vigilance to maintain it.

John Scopes wanted to get as far away as possible from the events that made his name a household word. By contrast William Jennings Bryan lingered in town, planning to deliver a fifteen-thousand-word oration he'd been preparing for the trial since before he came to Dayton but which he didn't get to give when the trial abruptly ended. The *Chattanooga Times* was preparing to publish it.

Quoting Demosthenes and Robert Burns, Bryan imparted a highbrow tone to his remarks, though he referred to the jurors in friendly, familiar terms as "the yeomanry of the state." He insisted that the issue was not what Scopes could say or think or believe as an individual but only what he could and could not teach as an employee of the state. Evolution was nothing but "millions of guesses strung together" and was therefore insufficient grounds for challenging the Bible's teaching on creation. "Religion is not hostile to learning," he wrote. "Christianity has been the greatest patron learning has ever had. But Christians know that 'the fear of the Lord is the beginning of wisdom' now just as it has been in the past, and they therefore oppose the teaching of guesses that encourage godlessness among the students."

Near the end of his speech, Bryan summarized a position that would sound strangely familiar to creationists eighty years later:

> Science is a magnificent material force, but it is not a teacher of morals. It can perfect machinery, but it adds no moral restraints to protect society from the misuse of the machine. It can also build gigantic intellectual ships, but it constructs no moral rudders for the control of storm-tossed human vessels. It not only fails to supply the spiritual element needed but some of its unproven hypotheses rob the ship of its compass and thus endangers its cargo. . . .
>
> The world needs a Savior more than it ever did before, and there is only one Name under heaven given among men whereby we must be saved. It is this Name that evolution degrades, for, carried to its logical conclusion, it robs Christ of the glory of a virgin birth, of the majesty of His deity and mission and of the triumph of His resurrection. . . .
>
> [Evolution and the repudiation of Christ] cannot be the answer of this jury representing a Christian state and sworn to uphold the laws of Tennessee. Your answer will be heard throughout the world; it is eagerly awaited by a praying multitude. If the law is nullified, there will be rejoicing wherever God is repudiated, the Savior scoffed at and the Bible ridiculed. Every unbeliever of every kind and degree will be happy. If, on the other hand, the law is upheld and the religion of the school children protected, millions of Christians will call you blessed and, with hearts full of gratitude to God, will sing again that grand old song of triumph: ". . . Faith of our fathers—holy faith; We will be true to thee till death."

The fact that Bryan went to the trouble and expense of having his long speech published after he'd already won the case indicates that he saw a far larger issue here than a circuit court trial in Tennessee: Christianity was threatened in a broader cultural context, and Bryan was a faithful soldier jumping to the parapets.

Bryan's death the Sunday after the trial identified him with the Scopes controversy perhaps more strongly than anything he ever said in the courtroom. This is particularly true in light of the revised account of his death in *Inherit the Wind,* where it seems he died of a combination of overeating and embarrassment, ranting before an uninterested audience and dead microphone, then collapsing on the floor of the courtroom.

Not surprisingly, H. L. Mencken saw Bryan's whole life as misguided and his last days in particular as a pitiful end to a bigoted, inept, self-centered life. In his column titled "Bryan," published July 27, 1925, he revealed little respect for the dead and plenty of disdain for his ideological opponent:

> One day it dawned on me that Bryan, after all, was an evangelical Christian only by sort of afterthought—that his career in this world, and the glories thereof, had actually come to an end before he ever began whooping for Genesis. So I came to this conclusion: that what really moved him was a lust for revenge. The men of the cities had destroyed him and made a mock of him; now he would lead the yokels against them. Various facts clicked into the theory, and I hold it still. The hatred in the old man's burning eyes was not for the enemies of God; it was for the enemies of Bryan. . . .
>
> But what of his life? Did he accomplish any useful thing? Was he, in his day, of any dignity as a man, and of any value to his fellow men? I doubt it. Bryan, at his best, was simply a magnificent job-seeker. . . . He was ignorant, bigoted, self-seeking, blatant and dishonest. His career brought him into contact with the first men of his time; he preferred the company of rustic ignoramuses. . . . Imagine a gentleman, and you have imagined everything that he was not.

Judged by the (mostly pro-evolution) press accounts, crowd reaction, and Bryan's own comment, Dudley Field Malone scored the most oratorical points in the courtroom battle against Bryan. But H. L. Mencken became the *de facto* historian of the event and Clarence Darrow the figurehead leader of the Scopes camp. Darrow's public persona and his fame as a lawyer, coupled with Mencken's widely read and quoted columns that were low on accuracy and high on entertainment value, defined the case for the evolutionists.

No one was representing the creationists to the same mass audience. Bryan was gone, his treasured closing peroration unread. Attorney General Tom Stewart was concerned from the first with the letter of the law and made great pains to disassociate himself and his prosecution from the question of how life began. That wasn't the point of the statute, and he refused to be drawn into a discussion of it.

But that was the point as far as the world was concerned. Darrow and Bryan didn't square off over the "Butler Bill trial," or the "teacher/taxpayer trial," or even the "put Dayton on the map" trial. What they fought and what the world listened to as it had never listened to a single event before was the "Scopes Monkey Trial." Judge Raulston found his attempts to keep the testimony focused on the particulars of the law, which never mentioned evolution, and the charges against Scopes challenged by both sides.

Darrow had his scientific experts; although the judge wouldn't allow them to testify, their written statements in the record run to thousands of words on evidence favoring Darwinism and its compatibility with Christianity. Bryan called the trial a battle for Christianity from the beginning and positioned it that way in his remarks; the public expected nothing less, and if the Scopes case had been only a matter of taxpayer control over school curriculum, Bryan would scarcely have noticed it. As a legal proceeding it was teacher versus taxpayers. As a news event it was evolution against Christianity and science against religion or, depending on the point of view, science and learning against blind fundamentalism and ignorance. In an argument that would echo through to the end of the century and beyond, both sides claimed they were representing freedom of religion.

Despite the fact that the judge and the district attorney treated the Scopes trial as an open-and-shut case—Did John Scopes teach religion in the public school or did he not?—the world saw it differently. This was partly because of Darrow and Bryan but also because George Rappelyea, Doc Robinson, and the other Daytonians who instigated the whole business had ulterior motives of their own, as did the ACLU. Pumping up the economy of Dayton, Tennessee, was not world news, nor was the fact that the ACLU was trolling for causes to get involved in. What captured the world's imagination was the Monkey Trial: a mild-mannered teacher versus the state bureaucracy, freedom of religion versus freedom from religion, traditional morality versus individual rights, Darrow versus Bryan; creationists versus evolutionists, Christianity versus the lions of amorality and faithlessness, science versus ignorance and dogmatism.

All this and John Scopes didn't even teach biology, much less evolution.

From the day in Robinson's Drug Store that the Scopes trial was hatched, the world saw it as a religious battle. The great spokesman for one side, William Jennings Bryan, was dead a week after the verdict was read. The great spokesmen for the other side, Malone, Mencken, and Darrow, lived on to steer the historical record to suit their purposes. Their interpretations of events are more familiar today than the events themselves. The facts of the case have been obscured by half-truths and pure fiction.

Not only is the truth about the Scopes trial important today; it's more important than ever. The question of how the universe began is at the center of what our culture thinks about itself, how its laws are made and enforced, how human life is valued and set apart, how questions about moral absolutes are resolved, and how we relate to one another on every level. Though these issues were argued in the public square in 1925, American culture knew where it was headed. Eighty years on we're headed every direction at once with no way to judge which is forward and which is back.

Belief about our origins shapes our view of the world. In 1925, Darrow, Mencken, and company set the template for those beliefs by selling America their own version of events. And in their version it wasn't a country schoolteacher that was on trial; it was Christianity. In the version that many journalists and then *Inherit the Wind* sold, Christianity lost—game, set, match—and debate should cease.

But all along some creationists have refused to give up. And surprisingly, over the past fifteen years, the number of Christian rebels has increased as a new movement, Intelligent Design, led by a new strategist, Phillip Johnson, has emerged.

CHAPTER 21
Fighting the Religion of Evolution

"EVOLUTION IS A RELIGION. This was true of evolution in the beginning, and it is true of evolution still today."

Philosopher Michael Ruse made this statement to an astonished audience at the American Association for the Advancement of Science 1993 annual convention. From Darwin's time through the Scopes era and beyond, disagreement about the relationship between evolution and creationism has obscured the battle between the two. Defense counsel in the Scopes trial suggested that evolution and divine creation were not mutually exclusive. Even Darwin, as we saw in his conclusion to *The Origin of Species,* insisted that nothing in his theory of evolution should offend Christian sensibilities.

But by the time of the Darwin centennial in 1959, evolution theory had itself evolved into a religion: metaphysical, universal, and the origin of life. Ruse's admission before the AAAS was only a public acknowledgment of the obvious. Darwin based his theory on the nonscientific assumption that a good and perfect God wouldn't create and develop an evil world. Proponents who followed based their support ultimately on scientific proofs limited by materialism: if science couldn't explain it, it wasn't science.

In 1962 the U.S. Supreme Court ruled that promoting religion in the classroom was unconstitutional and ordered an immediate halt to prayer and Bible reading in public schools. But in 1980 the court effectively reintroduced religion by requiring schools to teach evolution. Historian Jacques Barzun wrote that the "so-called warfare between science and religion [could] be seen as the warfare between two philosophies and perhaps two faiths, [a] dispute between the believers in consciousness and the believers in mechanical action; the believers in purpose and the believers in pure chance."

Christianity and divine creation, the foundation of Western thought for nearly two millennia, seemed to be fading fast, in part due to the appeal of a world without God and, therefore, a world without moral absolutes or accountability. With God out of the way, the free spirits of the 1960s boldly embraced a new way of looking at the world: If it feels good, do it!

In her book *Total Truth,* Nancy Pearcey suggests that another reason Christians lost the high ground was that they spent too much time fighting among themselves over young earth versus old earth, the Genesis gap, the length of a creation day, and other points of internal disagreement, instead of defending Christianity against the secular materialism of Darwinian theory.

Pearcey is a senior fellow at the Discovery Institute and former managing editior of the science journal *Origins & Design*. Her interest in the creation question began in the 1970s at L'Abri, theologian Francis Schaeffer's famous retreat in Switzerland. There she heard Schaeffer's arguments on the state of the universe that in their simplicity foreshadowed the theory of intelligent design. She writes that "either the universe is a closed system of cause and effect, or it is an open system, the product of a Personal Agent. Everything that follows stems from that fundamental choice." One lesson in particular framed the whole issue for her as an either-or question: the world starts either with "time plus chance plus the impersonal" or with "a Personal Being who thinks, wills, and acts."

Pearcey understood that Darwinism had become the "universal acid" described in *Darwin's Dangerous Idea* by Daniel Dennett, which "eats through just about every traditional concept and leaves in its wake a revolutionized world-view." (Interviewed on the PBS series *Evolution,* Dennett said Darwin's great accomplishment was to reduce the origins of life to "purposeless, meaningless matter in motion.") Pearcey counters in *Total Truth* that such a statement has no basis in science: "It is not a scientific theory at all, but merely Dennett's personal philosophy." Generations of Darwinians have accused their opponents of pushing a personal religious agenda rather than letting the scientific facts speak for themselves. History reveals that Darwin based his theory on metaphysical assumptions. Darwinians for decades claimed the high ground of pure science and were allowed to get away with it. "By showing that a nonpersonal starting point fails to account for the world, we can eliminate a vast variety of philosophical systems within that category—materialism, determinism, behaviorism, Marxism, utilitarianism—without needing to investigate the myriad details that distinguish them."

In the 1980s the battle against Darwin badly needed a leader who could strategize and develop new ways to unify the creationists side and focus the intellectual attack. To fight the stereotype that creationists were backward, it would help for such a person to have an outstanding academic pedigree.

Enter Phillip E. Johnson. Though he might have looked like any other avuncular and slightly rumpled college professor, his unassuming appearance was deceiving. After earning degrees from Harvard and the University of Chicago, he had clerked for Earl Warren, chief justice of the U.S. Supreme Court, then gone on to a distinguished academic career with the University of California at Berkeley, where he held an endowed chair at the law school.

In the summer of 1987, Professor Johnson was in a new season of his life. Over the past few years, he had ended an unhappy marriage and begun afresh with his second wife, Kathie. Partly under her influence he had also become a Christian. With his belief came a sense that he should "do something" for his faith, though he didn't know what. He was at the top of the ladder in his profession and looking for new intellectual challenges as well.

He was teaching at University College in London that summer. One day as he walked from the bus stop to his office, the title of a book in a shop window caught his eye: *The Blind Watchmaker: Why the Evidence of Evolution Reveals a Universe without Design.* The title intrigued him on two levels. First, as a relatively new Christian, he wanted to know how evolution could square with (or prevail over) biblical teaching. Second, as a legal scholar he was curious to know what evidence allowed anyone to make so bold a claim that the universe came into existence "without design."

Johnson had a passing familiarity with the whole evolution/creation argument but was fascinated by author Richard Dawkins's pro-Darwin theory. The more he read, the more he was convinced that all of evolution theory was built on logically indefensible assumptions. The apparent deception started with Darwin and continued through more than a century and a quarter of debate.

To Johnson's keen legal mind, Darwinian evolution was fatally flawed and always had been. And religion had nothing to do with it.

The problem as he identified it was that the process of natural selection Darwin so meticulously described could not account for the variety of life on Earth or the development of new species. Assuming all of Darwin's observations and experiments were true and correct, nothing in any of it demonstrated that natural selection—or "evolution" in any of its definitions—caused a living organism to change gradually from one kind of animal or one species to another. All the actual steps were inferred or supposed or extrapolated from the physical evidence; actual evidence of permanent evolution-based change was nonexistent.

Professor Johnson explains, "The central issue that I'm always presenting is that the assumed creative power of the Darwinian mechanism, natural selection, was never proved. In fact, the scientific evidence viewed without bias not only fails to support the claim that random mutation and natural selection can create marvels of intricate, organized complexity. The evidence actually tends to show that the mechanism has no such power."

He observed that scientists universally refuse to buck the system and admit any fault in Darwinian theory, even if they suspect something wrong, because if they did they would be professional outcasts and their research funds would dry up. They argue their case on the claim of authority—"Everybody believes it so it must be true"—and *ad hominem* arguments criticizing the speaker personally rather than debating the facts—"He's crazy to be telling you that"—to which Johnson might jovially respond, "OK, if I'm crazy, prove me wrong using your own scientific method."

The secret to the success of Johnson's theory in the marketplace of ideas has been that, though he is a Christian, his argument is completely independent of the biblical Creator. "I say it doesn't matter what you think of the Bible. It isn't necessary in order to make the case that natural selection has no creative power. The only thing natural selection has ever been known to do is to produce trivial and temporary population shifts." Furthermore, he says, "new discoveries are further undoing the theory" of evolution, making it a poorer argument now than it was in Darwin's time.

As a professor of law, Phillip Johnson is the first to admit he is no scientist, but he recognized a faulty argument when he saw one, and to him the Darwinist position was full of holes. Since he had no scientific reputation or peer standing to worry about, he could pursue his investigation of the evidence in favor of Darwin without worrying about his career. His purpose going forward was "to examine the scientific evidence on its own terms, being careful to distinguish the evidence itself from any religious or philosophical bias that might distort our interpretation of that evidence. . . . The question I want to investigate is whether Darwinism is based upon a fair assessment of the scientific evidence, or whether it is another kind of fundamentalism."

Johnson christened his theory the theory of intelligent design. He believed it was impossible, without many sweeping assumptions, to prove in scientific terms that life evolved through a long process of mutation and natural selection. On the other hand, the evidence was overwhelming that life on Earth developed in an organized, purposeful way requiring an intelligent force. Humans didn't develop haphazardly from particles and primordial soup but are the product of craftsmanship by intelligent design.

Johnson didn't question the fact that natural selection occurs. Weak animals die before bearing offspring, reducing the pool of weak examples and strengthening the population. But, Johnson noted,

"Darwinism asserts a great deal more than merely that species avoid genetic deterioration due to natural attrition among the genetically unfit." The problem with Darwinian theory was that it claimed "this same force of attrition has a building effect so powerful that it can begin with a bacterial cell and gradually craft its descendants over billions of years to produce such wonders as trees, flowers, ants, birds, and humans. How do we know that all this is possible?"

According to the theory of intelligent design, we don't.

Two famous and oft-repeated examples evolutionists use to make their case are the peppered moth and the Galapagos finch. Johnson saw fatal flaws in both arguments. In the case of the peppered moth, when tree trunks in Great Britain were darkened by industrial pollution, darker colored moths were harder for birds to see, and so they ate the lighter moths. This supposedly proved that a random mutation brought about natural selection that would in time transform the moth. But years later when environmental controls reduced pollution and the tree trunks got lighter again, birds ate the lighter moths and spared their darker counterparts.

It was what Johnson called an "oscillating" result that moved first in one direction and then back toward its original position. Ultimately the moths were unchanged, and nothing implied that mutation would ever cause any permanent dramatic change, much less form a new species. A final blow to this legendary example of Darwinism was the discovery that the peppered moth does not naturally live on tree trunks; in the famous photos of the experiment the moths had been glued to the bark.

In the case of the Galapagos finches, a drought caused plants bearing small seeds to die off, leaving larger seeds for the finches to eat. Big-beaked finches could eat the seeds easier than small-beaked ones, and so eventually the average finch had a larger beak than before. But again the process reversed as soon as conditions reversed: when the drought ended and little seeds returned, small-beaked finches returned too, and there was no evidence that a new species might eventually result.

Neither these nor any other "proofs," according to Johnson, "provides any persuasive reason for believing that natural selection can produce new species, new organs, or other major changes, or even minor changes that are permanent." The change in finch beaks "has no tendency whatever to prove that similar forces caused birds to come into existence in the first place."

His thinking led Johnson to a pivotal question: "Everyone who studies the [peppered moth] experiment knows it has nothing to do with the origin of any species, or even any variety, because dark and white moths were present throughout the experiment. Only the ratios of one variety to the other changed. How could intelligent people have been so gullible as to imagine that the experiment in any way supported the ambitious claims of Darwinism?"

One of the main reasons, he deduced, was that scientific groups insisted that science consisted exclusively of "naturalistic explanations" for everything and not "supernatural means inaccessible to human understanding." If only materialism could be used to explain the origin and development of life, scientists were forced to tug and pull at the idea and make it work, whether it seemed to or not. Johnson wrote that "there is an important difference between going to the empirical evidence to test a doubtful theory against some plausible alternative, and going to the evidence to look for confirmation of the only theory that one is willing to tolerate."

Rather than use scientific inquiry and experiment to develop a theory of evolution, it seemed to Johnson that science had jumped to the assumption that Darwin was right and had been looking ever since for ways to prove it; scientific advancement since Darwin's time, however, had made evolution even more suspect.

Back in California after teaching abroad, Professor Johnson kept researching the arguments in favor of evolution. The deeper he dug, the more surprised he was that Darwinian evolution theory, one of the foundation stones of science, seemed built entirely on supposition, extrapolation, and William Jennings Bryan's "guesses strung together." In 1991 Johnson published his theory of intelligent design in *Darwin on Trial.* At just over 150 pages, it was not a big book. But his simple argument that science had never proven evolution as a fact threw volatile fuel onto the fires of Darwinian controversy.

In trying to prove God created the Earth and all the life on it, Christian creationists often veered off into arguments over how long a biblical day was, whether the "Genesis gap" existed, whether men and dinosaurs lived at the same time, and other matters that to Johnson were secondary. *Darwin on Trial* made its case primarily not by defending creationism or Christianity but by demonstrating step-by-step, using Johnson's powers of analysis and debate as a legal scholar, that nothing Darwin described could account for the results Darwin claimed, and that the scientific evidence pointed away from evolution rather than toward it.

Perhaps Johnson's most dramatic conclusion in *Darwin on Trial* was that the fossil record showed none of the intermediate steps animals would have taken if they evolved incrementally over the ages. Two examples he and others returned to time and again were the wing and the eye. These structures are complex and highly specialized. If they evolved from a single cell, a fossil record (at least with the wing) would be expected to show a primitive sort of limb that evolved over many years. The fossil record shows just the opposite: every example of a fossilized wing is fully developed and functional.

Another question Johnson posed was how a primitive wing could be preserved through natural selection if it were useless until completely evolved. The theory of natural selection held that mutations producing a benefit for the organism would be preserved because more individuals with that mutation would live to produce the next generation. A wing wasn't a benefit until completely evolved, so individuals with a proto-wing would not have any advantage over wingless examples and therefore would not be "naturally selected."

The eye was another example, one that had astounded even Darwin. Anything less than a complete eye doesn't function as an eye: if 20 percent of the biological components are in place, the individual has not 20 but 0 percent of the vision capability of a fully formed eye.

In writing about the eye, Richard Dawkins, author of *The Blind Watchmaker,* believed, "An ancient animal with 5 percent of an eye might indeed have used it for something other than sight, but it seems to me as likely that it used it for 5 percent vision." Responding in *Darwin on Trial,* Johnson wrote, "The fallacy in that argument is that '5 percent of an eye' is not the same thing as '5 percent of normal vision.' For an animal to have any useful vision at all, many complex parts must be working together. Even a complete eye is useless unless it belongs to a creature with the mental and neural capacity to make use of the information by doing something that furthers survival or reproduction."

Furthermore, today the nautilus with its primitive pinhole eye and the eagle with its incredible accuracy of sight exist side by side. The nautilus eye has never evolved into something more complex, and the eagle eye shows no signs of an earlier, simpler form. One is not a refinement of the other because they operate in completely different ways. How could so complex an organ as the eye be preserved by natural selection if it was useless until completely evolved? Why would it have evolved in the first place?

One of Johnson's key arguments was what he called "the fossil problem." If all life on earth evolved from one life form, many now-extinct plants and animals should have exhibited characteristics of the old-style parent and the new-style offspring. In other words, if somewhere in the ancient past the whale and the bat had a common mammal ancestor, the fossil record should take us back through the millennia to show how the two evolved. A fossil record of one type of animal gradually evolving from another should exist. But, popular supposition to the contrary, the fossil record shows no such progression. Types of plants and animals appear and disappear over time, tied together in a time line only by the hypotheses of scientists who start with the assumption that evolution is true and then interpret the evidence accordingly.

Johnson writes, "Today it is widely assumed that the existence of fossil remains of numerous extinct species necessarily implies evolution, and most people are unaware that Darwin's most formidable opponents were not clergymen but fossil experts. Where are the links, ancient or modern, between one type of animal and another?"

Darwin admitted that for his theory to be true, "the number of intermediate and transitional links, between all living and extinct species, must have been inconceivably great." To Johnson this meant that the rocks should be full of "fossil evidence of transitional forms." What scientists have discovered instead is that species appeared fully formed in the fossil record.

Why then did Darwinism survive, unsupported by science? Johnson answers, "Suppose that paleontologists became so committed to the new way of thinking that fossil studies were published only if they supported the theory, and were discarded as failures if they showed an absence of evolutionary change. As we shall see, that is what happened. Darwinism apparently passed the fossil test, but only because it was not allowed to fail."

Both contemporary life and fossils supply ample evidence of "microevolution," such as the change in Galapagos finch beaks or the color of the peppered moth. Johnson observed that "everyone agrees that microevolution occurs, including creationists." The point, though, "is not whether microevolution happens, but whether it tells us anything important about the processes responsible for creating birds, insects, and trees in the first place."

Then Johnson moved on to examine the molecular evidence. To prove Darwinian theory, he explained, the evidence would have to show that

> the common ancestors and transitional intermediates really existed in the living world of the past, and that natural selection in combination with random genetic changes really has the kind of creative power claimed for it. It will not be enough to find that organisms share a common biochemical basis, or that their molecules as well as their visible features can be classified in a pattern of groups within groups. The important claim of Darwinism is not that relationships exist, but that those relationships were produced by a naturalistic process in which parent species were gradually transformed into quite different descendant forms through long branches (or even thick bushes) of transitional intermediates, without intervention by any Creator or other non-naturalistic mechanism.

The facts of molecular biology tell us man and apes are 95 percent similar, or that man and a banana are 25 percent similar, in their physiological makeup. But the facts don't tell us how the similarities or dissimilarities came to exist. Scientists fill in that blank the way they do because they assume Darwinian evolution is true. Could a pool of prehistoric protoplasm have randomly evolved into a butterfly? Into a cheetah? A marathon runner? Beethoven? Johnson answers:

> The simplest organism capable of independent life, the prokaryote bacterial cell, is a masterpiece of miniaturized complexity which makes a spaceship seem rather low-tech. Even if one assumes that something much simpler than a bacterial cell might suffice to start Darwinist evolution on its way, . . . the possibility that such a complex entity could assemble itself by chance is still fantastically unlikely, even if billions of years had been available. . . . A metaphor by Fred Hoyle has become famous because it vividly conveys the magnitude of the problem: that a living organism emerged by chance from a prebiotic soup is about as likely as that "a tornado sweeping through a junkyard might assemble a Boeing 747."

Johnson's challenge to scientific orthodoxy met stiff resistance.

> The scientists have fooled themselves because this is the rule in science: first you deceive yourself; then you deceive others. So first they deceived themselves and now the leaders of evolutionary science, the persons I like to call the Mandarins of Science, are deceiving others. I don't suggest that they don't sincerely believe in this materialist, naturalistic theory of creation. Of course they do. They have convinced themselves that it's true, because it's easy to convince yourself of something that you desperately want to believe.
>
> Darwinists insist that the challenge must be fought out on grounds of their own choosing under rules that they will make. It's the very nature of my challenge that what I've done is to challenge the rules. . . . I say that we must evaluate the evidence independently of any commitment to naturalism. And this horrifies the Mandarins of Science.

The Mandarins were indeed unhappy. But Johnson's challenge was on the table to stay. And he soon attracted some articulate allies.

CHAPTER 22

Explaining Intelligent Design

JOHNSON'S ARGUMENTS did not sway evolution's stalwarts. Harvard professor Stephen Jay Gould, one of the most prolific and high-profile Darwin defenders, had spoken for many a few years earlier when he said, "Facts are the world's data. Theories are structures of ideas that explain and interpret facts. Facts do not go away while scientists debate rival theories for explaining them. Einstein's theory of gravitation replaced Newton's, but apples did not suspend themselves in mid-air pending the outcome. And human beings evolved from apelike ancestors whether they did so by Darwin's proposed mechanism or by some other, yet to be identified." In other words, regardless of the details, evolution is as real as gravity.

Johnson disagreed: "The analogy is spurious. We observe directly that apples fall when dropped, but we do not observe a common ancestor for modern apes and humans. . . . Because Gould draws the line between fact and theory in the wrong place, the distinction is virtually meaningless."

Richard Dawkins in Britain and Stephen Jay Gould in the United States remained two of Darwin's most passionate supporters. Along with Niles Eldredge and others, they dealt from a position of strength because the scientific establishment closed ranks behind them and avoided discussing the issue on neutral ground. Scientific organizations continued to insist that any force outside the materialist world—anything that smacked of a creator or guiding intelligence in forming the earth—was unscientific. The result was the hopelessly circular argument known as a tautology: because there are no forces outside the material world, there can be no forces outside the material world. The beginning assumption dictates the final result.

George E. Webb, among others, wrote in *The Evolutionist Controversy in America* (1994) that creationism was just another name for religion and the creator was a metaphor for God. From *Inherit the Wind* to the Moral Majority, Webb asserted that Darwinists believed opponents of evolution were against common sense, unassailable facts, and a secular, scientifically explainable materialistic universe. Scientist and television personality Carl Sagan popularized the romantic idea of a beautiful, magically random universe in his TV series *Cosmos.* In his 1998 book *Unweaving the Rainbow,* Richard Dawkins followed to some extent in Sagan's footsteps, saying he wanted to appeal to "the sense of wonder in science."

Dawkins continued, "The feeling of awed wonder that science can give us is one of the highest experiences of which the human psyche is capable. It is a deep aesthetic passion to rank with the finest that music and poetry can deliver." That is close to saying all creation longs for something beyond the material world. But to admit that would be to admit the material world isn't all there is and that it's wrong to repudiate the spiritual realm.

However diligently Attorney General Tom Stewart in 1925, the Supreme Court in 1962, or the ACLU in 2004 strained to separate evolutionary theory from religion, they ultimately found it impossible to do because the taproot of Darwinism has nothing to do with science and everything to do with subjective repudiation of a traditional Christian worldview. As a letter from a professor in the scientific journal *Nature* put it, "Even if all the data point to an intelligent designer, such an hypothesis is excluded from science because it is not naturalistic."

Harvard biologist Richard Lewontin provided an even more transparent statement of the evolutionist position in the *New York Review of Books* when he wrote that scientists "are forced by our *a priori* adherence to material causes to create an apparatus of investigation and a set of concepts that produce material explanations," which must be "absolute, for we cannot allow a divine foot in the door."

And so Dawkins and many evolutionists have remained firm in their commitment. Dawkins's quotation from "Oppressed by Evolution" by American anthropologist Matt Cartmill clearly defines one view of the battle: "Anybody who claims to have objective knowledge about anything is trying to control and dominate the rest of us. . . . There are no objective facts. All supposed 'facts' are contaminated with theories, and all theories are infested with moral and political doctrines. . . . Therefore, when some guy in a lab coat tells you that such and such is an objective fact . . . he must have a political agenda up his starched white sleeve."

Phillip Johnson acknowledged that there were political agendas in the creationist movement and that belief in intelligent design could lead to belief that God was the intelligent designer. But his argument was a challenge to what Darwinism said it proved, not an attempt to replace the Darwinian mechanism with something else. Evolutionists might marginalize creationists by pigeonholing them as the radical fundamentalist lowbrows of *Inherit the Wind*, but they have so far failed to answer Johnson's charges that evolution doesn't follow from the evidence unless we start by assuming it.

Michael Behe, a professor of biochemistry at Lehigh University, picked up the Intelligent Design banner in his book *Darwin's Black Box: The Biochemical Challenge to Evolution*. His point was that since Darwin's time science has discovered vast quantities of information about biochemistry showing a complexity in even the smallest living systems that Darwin and his peers could never have imagined. Writing about the complexities of blood clotting, Behe spends six and a half pages describing how the process works, trying to go as easy as possible on his nonscientific audience but nevertheless throwing around terms like *fibrinogen*, *gamma-carboxyglutamate*, and *modified calcium-prothrombin complex*.

The idea he comes back to is that, as familiar and routine as blood clotting is, it is an incredibly complicated chain of events that could not work with one step or ingredient missing. It could not have evolved incrementally over time because 99 percent of the process in place would not produce a 99 percent effective blood clot: it would produce nothing. Furthermore, if there were no intelligent design at work, all the pertinent ingredients and processes would not be developing toward the conscious goal of clotting blood. It would happen purely by accident with no indication that blood clotting was necessary or desirable.

Behe used these and other microscopic examples to make the case for what he called "irreducible complexity." This was the idea that systems could not have evolved from the simplest state of life because at some point working backwards, the system fails to work if one more component is removed.

He used a mousetrap as an example, listing its five parts: platform, holding bar, spring, hammer, and catch. If one part is missing, the trap isn't four-fifths effective, nor will it catch four-fifths of a mouse; it won't work at all. Behe was famously challenged by evolutionist Kenneth Miller during a debate when Miller brought a paper bag to his lectern; inside was a four-part mousetrap. Miller said it was proof that irreducible complexity was a flawed theory; Behe replied that Miller had used purposeful intelligent design to effect change.

Another champion of Intelligent Design is William Dembski, associate research professor at Baylor University and author of *Intelligent Design: The Bridge Between Science & Theology.* Dembski began thinking in the direction of Intelligent Design after a conference on randomness in 1988. It brought home the fact that the reason evolutionists spent so much time trying to identify randomness in nature is because nature isn't random; it is purposeful and organized.

Like Phillip Johnson and other contemporary Intelligent Design proponents, Dembski has top-flight academic credentials: a Ph.D. in philosophy and another in mathematics from the University of Chicago, an M.Div. from Princeton Theological Seminary, postdoctoral work in mathematics at MIT, and more. Though he is a Christian, he is far from the stereotyped Bible-thumping fundamentalist. Like Johnson, he saw evidence of a divine Creator but never made his argument based on it.

In 1999 Dembski accepted a position at Baylor as head of a new center to study the relationship between science and religion. The Polanyi Center was named after Hungarian chemist Michael Polanyi, who had given the idea of purposeful creation a boost by questioning whether the physical world could be explained by natural laws alone.

Before the year was out, Baylor's faculty was in an uproar. The school, founded by the Baptists in 1845 and grown to be the largest private university in Texas, had fought for a generation with the denomination as the Baptist churches generally retained their traditional conservatism while the faculty and the culture of academia grew more liberal. In 1990 the trustees had broken abruptly with the Southern Baptists and declared themselves accountable only to a self-sustaining university board. When the Polanyi Center Web site went up, academics and clergy vigorously attacked it for being "fundamentalist." It was the breakaway board's worst nightmare. They had separated from the Baptists in order to shake the conservative and fundamentalist labels; now they were lumped in with the ranting backwoods preachers of Dayton and *Inherit the Wind.*

A Baylor professor of psychology and neuroscience, Charles Weaver, spoke for many of his colleagues when he worried that Dembski's association with Intelligent Design would "discourage promising premed students and respected faculty from coming to Baylor." Provost Donald Schmeltekopf defended the school's position, explaining that it was important for Baylor to "get into the conversation and to be a participant" in the issue.

In April 2000 Dembski hosted a symposium that asked whether there was anything in the universe beyond nature, and scheduled physicist and Nobel laureate Steven Weinberg to deliver the keynote address. (Weinberg's presentation was titled "No.") For the most part Baylor faculty boycotted the event, and days later the faculty senate voted 26–2 with one abstention to dismantle the center and rebuild it from scratch with their input.

University president Robert Sloane, who had hired Dembski in the first place, refused to shut down the Polanyi Center but agreed to submit Dembski's work for peer review. Dembski was unhappy subjecting himself to what he saw as a politically motivated challenge to his academic credentials by people who didn't know anything about Intelligent Design. To his relief the outside scholars who conducted the review reported that "research on the logical structure of mathematical arguments for intelligent design have a legitimate claim to a place in the current discussions of the relations of religion and science."

Feeling vindicated and delighted, Dembski sent out a press release saying in part, "Dogmatic opponents of design who demanded the Center be shut down have met their Waterloo. Baylor University is to be commended for remaining strong in the face of intolerant assaults on freedom of thought and expression."

He had celebrated victory too soon. Faculty members were enraged at his words. The administration gave him a chance to retract or "contextualize" his statement. When he refused, he was demoted to associate research professor, and the center was left leaderless (and nameless—the Polanyi name was removed). As the *Houston Press* reported, "Dembski was not demoted because of his positions. He was demoted because his positions had become a political hot potato."

Whereas a Tennessee schoolteacher lacked the academic freedom to teach evolution in 1925, a Texas professor—even at a school that emphasized Christian profession—lacked the freedom to teach otherwise in 2000. Though the culture switched sides over seventy-five years, the debate did not fade away.

Dembski and the faculty senate could have avoided locking horns if only they had agreed that the issue was consideration of Intelligent Design, not support for a wild-eyed fundamentalist stereotype. Of all places to debate the creation question, a Christian university should be one of the fairest. Yet the argument confirmed Phillip Johnson's observation that evolutionists want to argue only according to their rules, which insist that all of science is limited to the physical, material world.

The Discovery Institute, a Seattle-based think tank founded in 1990 to promote intelligent design in schools, academia, and the culture, cosponsored the Polanyi Center symposium. Not long after Dembski's donnybrook, the *Seattle Times* described the Institute, cofounded by "onetime Reagan assistant Bruce Chapman and politico-turned-futurist George Gilder," as an institution at the center of a new movement challenging the validity of Darwinian evolution. "The movement has created a stir based on the identity of some of its proponents: They are not Bible-thumping creationists, but academics at mainstream institutions. . . .

"These folks have come up with sophisticated arguments for something they call 'intelligent design,' which, like creationism, points to some kind of creator or 'designer' of the universe but, unlike creationism, evades the subject of who that creator is."

According to cofounder Bruce Chapman, The Discovery Institute began not to bring Christianity back into the classroom but to promote design intelligence as a way to "combat the growing reliance on genetic explanations for human behavior and what he sees as an undermining of personal responsibility." Chapman saw his challenge to Darwinism as far more than tossing down the gauntlet to scientific assumptions; it was a challenge to the whole contemporary American welfare system that indiscriminately hands out money and other material things with no regard for family structure, past decisions, moral outlook, or other nonmaterial factors. If Intelligent Design is right, treating only the physical symptoms is a waste of money; if Darwin was right, all problems are material problems and so are all solutions.

Like other Intelligent Design supporters, Bruce Chapman is content to keep open the identity of the Designer since religion is such a flash point in the discussion within the halls of science, academia, schools, and the courts. Phillip Johnson also separates faith from the argument. "What I don't try to do," Johnson says, "is provide a detailed model of how supernatural creation might operate, what component of time it might take to tie it to the Genesis account. I am quite satisfied to leave it that evolutionary science has attempted to provide an alternative to the creation and has failed. . . . In fact I say it doesn't matter what you think of the Bible. I don't think any reference to the Bible is necessary to show that natural selection has no creative power."

According to Johnson, Behe, Dembski, and the Discovery Institute point of view, the source of intelligent design could be anything. "It could be space aliens or time travelers," Johnson says:

> There are atheists who believe in Intelligent Design. However, for Christians, once they've accepted the idea of an intelligent designer, it's obvious to them who the designer is. In my own development I first addressed the issue without reference to the Bible at all. I came to the conclusion that the scientific evidence just doesn't support the central claims of the Darwinian theory at all. It tends to refute them. But then I thought, "If you can't do the creating without an intelligent designer, a Creator, then there must be a Creator."
>
> Then at this point I brought the Bible into the argument. I looked for the best place to start and I found that in the prologue to the Gospel of John: "In the beginning was the Word." And I asked the question, "Does scientific evidence tend to support this conclusion or the contrary conclusion of the materialists that 'in the beginning were the particles'?" If we start with that basic explanation of the meaning of the creation in John 1, we see that is far better supported by scientific investigation than the contrary. So what's the objection to believing that that's true?
>
> At this point we haven't proved that the Bible's claims about creation are true, but we've removed a powerful obstacle in the way of such belief. And that's all I really want to do with the scientific evidence is to clear away the obstacle that it presents to a belief that the Creator is the God of the Bible.

Under some circumstances, removing that powerful obstacle might have opened up opportunities for unfettered discussion of the creation question. But in the supercharged atmosphere of a secular culture determined to defend the status quo, the possibility that a discussion of intelligent design might lead to a discussion of Christianity continued to set off alarm bells from the laboratory to the classroom to the courtroom.

For example, in 2001, in the midst of an uproar about teaching creation science, the Arkansas Science Teachers Association explained, "Science strives to explain the nature of the cosmos while religion seeks to give the cosmos and the life within it a purpose." There's no knowledge in religion, only a "purpose"; and even that isn't something universal but rather an assigned meaning religion "gives."

Nancy Pearcey reports in *Total Truth* that the Arkansas Science Teachers further contend that religion is relativistic and belongs at home or "within the context of religious institutions," while the purpose of science is "to discover and investigate universally accepted natural explanations" that public schools should teach. Pearcey calls this "the two-realm theory of truth," with the material world defining truth and all else relegated to subjective belief.

> The first hurdle for Christians to overcome is simply reintroducing the very concept that religion can be genuine knowledge. . . . We must find a way to talk about Christianity as objective knowledge, not our personal values. We must stake out a cognitive territory and be prepared to defend it. . . . Christianity does make claims about the material world—about the origin of the cosmos, the character of human nature, and events in history, preeminently the Resurrection. . . . When Christians are willing to reduce our religion to noncognitive categories, unconnected to questions of truth or evidence, then we have already lost the battle.

Intelligent Design has turned the tide by taking the spotlight off the disagreements among Christians, and even off the basic claims of Christianity, to reveal that Darwinian evolution failed to prove its case by any reasonable scientific standard. ID compares scientific proof against scientific proof and one metaphysical stance against another. ID supporters who are Christians will see their religion move, as Pearcey describes, "out of the ineffectual realm of value and [stake] out a cognitive claim in the realm of objective truth. It restores Christianity to its status as genuine knowledge." As the apostle Paul wrote in 2 Corinthians 5:7, Christians "walk by faith, not by sight."

As a value or a philosophy, Christianity posed no threat to the juggernaut of Darwinism surging forward on scientific claims. But to the extent Intelligent Design successfully reconnects faith with fact, evolutionists will fight it with all the weapons in their arsenal. Pearcey identifies several "empirical markers of design" that defeat materialist evolution on its own turf.

She revisits the idea that life, mutation, and inherited characteristics all come not from chemicals or processes but from information coded in DNA. The sequence of information in DNA makes life and reproduction possible. This sequence can come about in any of three ways: by law, by chance, or by design. Pearcey illustrates empirically that only sequencing by design can account for what DNA does.

In simplifying an argument presented by William Dembski in *The Design Inference,* Pearcey proposes thinking of DNA strands as Scrabble letters. The chance of spelling a sentence by choosing letters at random is extremely remote. There's some likelihood of spelling a few short words like "as" or "to," but "a random process will not produce Shakespeare's *Hamlet.*" "In fact," she notes, "instead of creating information, chance events tend to scramble information." For example, random typos scattered throughout a page are more likely to make the text worse than make it better. It isn't a matter of odds; the famous example of a roomful of monkeys at typewriters is irrelevant. "The point is that *in principle,* chance events do not create complex information."

Chance can't sequence DNA, and neither can nature because "*in principle,* laws of nature do not give rise to information." Laws describe predictable, repeatable events and circumstances: if you set a piece of paper on fire, it will burn; if you throw a ball into the air, it will come down. "The goal of science is to reduce those patterns to mathematical formulas. By contrast, the sequence of letters in a message is *ir*regular and *non*repeating and so it cannot be the result of any law-like process."

The same applies to DNA. In Scrabble, choosing letters by law would lead to a repeated word or word pattern over and over: one letter has to follow another according to a specific rule. If DNA formed on the basis of natural law, it would repeat the same limited information again and again. To explain it another way, you can program your computer to print "Happy Birthday" repeatedly across a sheet of homemade wrapping paper; you can't program it to write *Hamlet* because the information is too complex to be rendered by a pattern. If it's true that each human cell contains more information than the whole *Encyclopaedia Britannica*, there is no way any type of repeated pattern could convey such a volume of information. Patterns intrinsically lack high information content.

Where DNA by design succeeds and chance and law fail is in specified complexity. Pearcey explained the term using the analogy of language:

> There is no law of nature that determines the meaning of a sequence of sounds like G-I-F-T. In English the sequence means *present*; in German it means *poison*; in Norwegian it means *married*. A language takes what is an otherwise arbitrary sequence of sounds . . . and confers meaning on it through a linguistic convention. . . . Of all the possible combinations of sounds, a language selects only a few and confers meaning on them.
>
> The DNA code is precisely parallel. The sequences of chemical "letters" are chemically arbitrary. There is no natural force that determines the meaning of certain combinations. Out of all the possible combinations of chemical "letters," somehow only a few carry meaning. But where did the cell's linguistic convention come from?
>
> Clearly, linguistic conventions and rules of grammar do not arise out of chemical reactions. They come from the mental realm of information and intelligence. . . . The structure of DNA is precisely parallel to the structure of languages and computer programs. Can we infer that specified complexity in DNA is likewise the product of an intelligent agent? Unless we define science from the outset in terms of naturalistic philosophy, the answer should be yes. . . .
>
> Is it a random event? Then all we need to invoke is chance. Does it occur in a regular, repeated pattern? Then it is an instance of some natural law. Is it a complex, specified pattern? Then it exhibits design and was produced by intelligence.

CHAPTER 23
Kansas, Ohio, Georgia, Tennessee

WITH THE TURN of the twenty-first century, the Intelligent Design movement gathered steam to the point where the Mandarins of Science could no longer control it. The idea first articulated by Phillip Johnson in *Darwin on Trial* worked its way from academia through the scientific community and eventually to where all creation arguments seemed historically to end up: the classroom.

Some observers traced the reemergence of public debate all the way back to the publication of John Thomas Scopes's autobiography, *Center of the Storm,* in 1967, which revisited questions about the truth of evolution for the first time since the beginning of the space race ten years before. An important step toward reigniting the public debate came with *Darwin on Trial* in 1991, followed by Michael Behe's *Darwin's Black Box* in 1996.

On July 21, 2000, National Public Radio broadcast a program on *Science Friday* commemorating the seventy-fifth anniversary of the Scopes ruling. Host Ira Flatow welcomed Behe; Edward Larson, professor of history and law and author of the Pulitzer Prize-winning book *Summer for the Gods: The Scopes Trial and America's Continuing Debate over Science and Religion*; and Kenneth Miller, professor of biology and author of *Finding Darwin's God: A Scientist's Search for Common Ground Between Science and Religion.*

As much as ID proponents worked (and continue working) to separate themselves from religious creationism, one of the first questions Flatow asked Behe on the air was who the intelligent designer is. Behe acknowledged his religious belief but reminded Flatow that religion was beside the point:

> I'm a Roman Catholic, a Christian; I certainly would think that the designer is God, and probably most people would. But that conclusion is not forced by coming to the conclusion of intelligent design. Somebody else might think it was some New Age force or a space alien or something like that. Certainly, those things strike us as strange, but the point is that the idea of intelligent design is an idea that comes straight from the evidence, from things like the molecular machines in the cell, and it does not force a supernatural conclusion.

Kenneth Miller, a friend and professional colleague of Behe but on the other side of the argument, claimed that various scientific papers explained how biochemical systems could actually evolve in only a few months. Behe countered with the example, used often in his speeches and in *Darwin's Black Box,* of the flagellum, a tiny hairlike appendage used by microscopic organisms to propel themselves through liquid or move liquid across their surface. He proposed to Miller that the two of them remove the genetic components that produced the flagellum and see if it would evolve on its own. If it happened within two years, Behe promised to renounce intelligent design.

Miller declined the offer because, he said, anyone who took up the challenge would have to

> go into a laboratory and allow a series of events, many of which were undetermined, meaning you don't know how they're going to come out, to suddenly reoccur again. And we know from evolution if you take cultures of bacteria that start out identical and put them in different flasks under identical conditions, they will evolve in different directions in

> those different flasks. So you're asking for the outcome of an experiment that is essentially unrepeatable to be repeated and, unfortunately, that's not going to work.

Flatow later asked Behe where he thought Intelligent Design belonged in the public schools. Behe answered that while schools should teach Darwinian evolution, they should also discuss Intelligent Design because it addressed evidence evolution couldn't explain. He also admitted that teaching ID in schools had "overtones of politics and parental involvement and government." (See appendix A for the entire broadcast transcript.)

Politicians, parents, and educators of every persuasion could agree with him that the battle was far from over. In the summer of 1999, when a Gallup poll showed 69 percent of Americans favored teaching both creationism and evolution in public schools, the Kansas state board of education considered whether to revise its science curriculum standards. A committee of scientists and educators had recommended describing evolution as a basic "unifying concept or process" rather than a theory. By a narrow margin the board rejected the recommendation and voted instead to allow teachers to discuss creationism even more freely than before. What Phillip Johnson called "the potentially most significant change" was a single word: defining *science* as "the human activity of seeking logical explanations for what we observe in the world around us" rather than the previous "seeking natural explanations."

When approved, the revisions met a firestorm of opposition in the press and academia. The front page of the *Washington Post* warned that Kansas was instituting a new curriculum "that wipes out virtually all mention of evolution and related concepts." It did nothing of the sort. Yet following a season of venomous unremitting criticism from the education establishment and the media, the pro-creationist board members were voted out of office and replaced with evolutionists who quickly reversed the previous decision and returned Kansas safely to the Darwinian camp.

Creationist teachers fared no better than their state board counterparts. Roger DeHart taught high school biology in the small farming community of Burlington, Washington. For nine years he told students that they should examine the evidence in favor of evolution, which was in their textbook, but also consider the possibility of intelligent design. He never mentioned God in class. In 1999 a student complained that DeHart was bringing religion into the curriculum. The ACLU filed a complaint, and school authorities ordered DeHart to stop discussing ID and stick to the science textbook. (The same year a survey indicated that only 10 percent of American Academy of Science members believed in God, but 90 percent of Americans believed in God and that he played some part in creation.) In March 2001 the school district told DeHart he couldn't bring up anything in his two-week unit on evolution that questioned Darwinism.

Despite the nine-year history of DeHart's curriculum, his principal, Beth Vander Veen, was quoted in the *Los Angeles Times* saying, "I don't think it's about showing holes in evolutionary theory any more. I think it's about getting religion into the schools." The father of one of DeHart's students added, "He taught my kid religion for two weeks, receiving money in the public schools, and didn't ask. I was outraged."

The *Times* also noted a professor at San Francisco State lost his job for teaching creationism but later received reinstatement. The article mentioned William Dembski's professional trials as well, then went on to report, "Other scientists report receiving correspondence from colleagues who confess doubts about Darwin's theories but are afraid to go public for fear of career setbacks."

Though he obeyed the school district and stopped teaching ID, DeHart hoped he would be able to find other ways to discuss the controversy until the evidence proved intelligent design right or wrong. "Some things are worth fighting for," he said, "and this is one of them"—words eerily similar to John Scopes's statement after his conviction that he would "continue in the future, as I have in the past, to oppose this law in any way I can. Any other action would be in violation of my ideal of academic freedom—that is, to teach the truth as guaranteed in our constitution."

Writing for the *Arkansas Democrat-Gazette* a month later, Pulitzer Prize-winning columnist Paul Greenburg brought up the comparison between Scopes and DeHart, then continued:

> The repression of academic freedom in our own time—aka political correctness—is alone enough to raise questions about the evolution of man. Where the spirit of intellectual inquiry is concerned, we seem to be regressing—not evolving. . . . Why not just let teachers teach—without denouncing them as demonic and demanding that the state shut them up? What could be more educational than allowing different ideas to compete in a good teacher's classroom?
>
> Besides, there is something inherently suspect about a scientific theory no one is allowed to question. It asks us to take too much on faith.

On March 11, 2002, the Ohio state board of education debated whether to put intelligent design on an equal footing with evolution in science classrooms statewide. Dr. Jonathan Wells from the Discovery Institute argued before the board that students should learn Darwin's case was not airtight, and that an informed student was one who knew about the controversy. Philosophy professor Dr. Stephen C. Meyer, another Discovery Institute fellow, added that "the methods of science are part of the debate" and that students deserved to hear both sides of the story.

Dr. Kenneth Miller spoke for the Darwinists, agreeing that students should realize science has limitations but faulting ID because it had not been submitted for peer review in scientific journals; he did not deal with the problem of scientific journals automatically refusing to publish articles from a creationist perspective. He also argued that the "scientific controversy" ID supporters referred to was virtually nonexistent. (Lack of debate, of course, might also indicate a problem.) Intelligent design, he said, was being "propped up from outside the scientific community" to pressure legislators and school boards into accepting it.

The fourth expert to speak at the education hearing, Dr. Lawrence Krauss, chairman of the physics department at Case Western Reserve University, argued that "the real danger is trying to put God in the gaps [of Darwinist theory]. What they're really attacking here is not Darwinism but science." Krauss estimated that scientists supported evolution by a ratio of 10,000 to 1. Dr. Meyer countered with a poll that showed 71 percent of voters (an even larger percentage than 1999) favored teaching alternatives to Darwinism.

No doubt the board members also remembered the fate of their counterparts in Kansas three years before who embraced the idea of questioning Darwinism in school, then were voted out of office in the next election. Even so, a poll in May showed that 78 percent of Ohioans believed students should be taught evidence pointing to an intelligent designer as well as evolution. Lynn E. Elfner, head of the Ohio Academy of Sciences, replied that popular opinion was irrelevant: "Science is not a democratic institution. We don't make decisions on popularity, we make them on evidence. . . . I'm not aware of any evidence against evolution. . . . And, there is no scientific evidence in favor of intelligent design. It's a belief. It's beyond the natural. It's supernatural. . . . I can demonstrate evolution in a test tube."

After ten months of meetings, the Ohio board agreed to add to the tenth-grade science curriculum a single sentence that read: "Describe how scientists today continue to investigate and critically analyze aspects of evolutionary theory." Some scientists insisted it was a subtle means of sneaking creationism in through the back door, but the board provisionally approved the recommendation on October 14, 2002, after only an hour's discussion. On December 10, the board voted 18–0 to allow critical analysis of evolution but added that the new requirements did not "mandate the teaching or testing of intelligent design." Darwinism was still the only required explanation for the origin of life and the only one students would be tested on. Introducing criticism was left to the discretion of the local school boards.

That same year the Cobb County, Georgia, school board unanimously approved an amendment to their policy so that "disputed views" could be discussed in classrooms. The board acted despite the threat of a lawsuit by the ACLU and made a last-minute addition to the amendment in the hope of fending off legal challenges. The addition read in part, "It is the intent of the Cobb County Board of Education that this policy not be interpreted to restrict the teaching of evolution; to promote or require the teaching of creationism; or to discriminate for or against a particular set of religious beliefs, religion in general or non-religion." Intelligent design, the board decided, was a "necessary element of providing a balanced education."

The ACLU had already filed a lawsuit against Cobb County the previous summer in response to a sticker placed in science textbooks saying "evolution is a theory and not a fact" and encouraging students to read and discuss the concept with an open mind. The ACLU had originally planned to add the intelligent design amendment to the lawsuit, but the language categorically stating schools would not promote or require creationism prompted the organization's lawyer to suggest dropping the legal challenge. This may have been the first time creationism and intelligent design were legally delineated and separated by a legal authority.

It was a significant step for ID even though the parent who filed the suit, Jeffrey Selman, insisted there was still a loophole that allowed creationism to be taught. "To deny that this whole issue is not about religion is ludicrous. It's spin," he said, ending his remarks with, "God bless all of you because I am a religious person too."

The National Academy of Science sent a scathing open letter to the school board, calling the approval of ID an attempt to avoid the Supreme Court ban on teaching religion in schools, which specifically banned creation science. However, a professor of medicine at Emory University sent a letter praising the board's action and accompanied it with similar letters from more than 150 scientists. One of them wrote, "No doubt you have heard from a number of scientists who oppose the proposal, many of whom have accused you of openly fostering religious instruction within the public school system. I believe that it is important for the members of the school board to realize that a growing number of scientists acknowledge that neo-Darwinism models cannot explain the whole of biologic phenomena."

Another said, "The school board's resolution to allow teachers the freedom to examine both the attributes and the failings of natural selection is in keeping with the desires of many scientists to maintain academic freedom even at the secondary level. By allowing students to wrestle with conflicting data and theoretical interpretations, the board will not be guilty of fostering religion, but rather the seeds of critical thinking that will enable students in whatever career they choose."

Intelligent Design seemed at last to be making headway, establishing its independence from creationism and winning legal skirmishes that creation theory would have lost in the blink of an eye. In the fall of 2003, the Discovery Institute made its case for ID before the Texas state board of education in Austin. As in other states and other public meetings, the "evolution debate" on the agenda attracted a standing room only crowd and, in this case, 160 people registered to speak. William Dembski told the packed room of the "considerable debate in scientific circles about the mechanism of evolution." He noted that all the textbooks the board was considering "grossly exaggerate the evidence for neo-Darwinian evolution, pretending that its mechanism of natural selection acting on random genetic change is a slam dunk. Not so."

Using a familiar argument, opponents branded ID a "dressed up form of creationism," reminding the board that state law since 1991 had required teaching Darwinism and that questioning it would water it down. Three scientists from the Discovery Institute in Seattle registered to speak, but when the board learned the speakers were from out of state, members voted 10–3 not to hear them. History repeated itself, though, when in the manner of Judge Raulston during that hot summer in Tennessee, the out-of-town experts were allowed to submit written statements. In the end Texas educators voted down teaching intelligent design.

The absolute power of Darwinism has also been challenged in Oklahoma, Arkansas, Pennsylvania, California, and elsewhere as the forces arrayed against it grow both in size and academic standing. Intelligent Design has brought unprecedented freedom to legally challenge Darwinism in the classroom. Yet because it is so flexible, it has also nurtured overtly religious theories of the origins of life.

While ID proponents make progress around the country in battling the propaganda that grew out of the Scopes trial, Bryan's position provided a jumping-off point for Dr. Kurt P. Wise, an expert in invertebrate paleontology and a generation younger than Johnson. Wise was a student of celebrated Darwinist Stephen Jay Gould at Harvard, but he has taken a position radically opposed to Darwinism.

Wise affirms that the conclusions evolutionary scientists (and most scientists, for that matter) reach depend on their preconceptions, their own subjective views of religion, and their concern for peer acceptance; consideration of the facts comes further down the list. Scientists, Wise says, are supposed to reach decisions intellectually and logically. "There's supposed to be internal consistency." But scientists don't work that way.

"We don't go out there looking for data and then say, 'Oh, wow, look! This must be the way the world is!' We always go out expecting particular results. There's a human compulsion to want to make sense of things. And so people will be certain even if it's certain in the wrong things. Very few people are comfortable with uncertainty. So unbelievers are going to be certain about something, and they're not going to be certain about the right thing. My perspective is that scientists have been designed by God to seek Him in the creation in order to draw them toward God."

Wise states that creation was an event, and events have to have causes. If nothing material or natural existed before the beginning of creation, then the only entity in existence before creation was supernatural.

Wise also cncurs that scientists who express any sympathy for creationism risk their funding and livelihoods: "The embarrassment and humiliation of a creationist position drives most creationists into the closet." It didn't drive Kurt Wise into the closet but to the geographic heart of the evolution debate: Dayton, Tennessee. Since he was a boy, Wise had imagined teaching science in one of the country's most prestigious colleges. He was the first student from his high school in Rochelle, Illinois, ever to go to the University of Chicago, eighty miles away. At twenty-nine he received his Ph.D. from Harvard under Dr. Gould, after interrupting his studies from time to time to earn money as a landscape gardener.

He remained convinced that creationism was true. So instead of applying to one of the high-profile schools he'd always dreamed of, he looked for work only at Christian colleges. He accepted an offer from Bryan College in Dayton and joined the faculty as assistant professor of science. Later he also became director of the Center for Origins Research and Education at Bryan. And so almost literally within sight of the Rhea County Courthouse where the creation debate once rose to international prominence, the battle William Jennings Bryan and the Tennessee legislature began continues to develop.

Wise is a young earth creationist, arguing that the world was created by God in six twenty-four hour days. As might be expected, he's accustomed to challenges from scientists and others who point to the fossil record, radioactive dating, plate tectonics, and other widely accepted evidence that the earth is billions of years old. In his 2002 book *Faith, Form, and Time,* Wise contends that when someone "tries to infer anything about the past, he assumes the past looks like the present, so he studies the present to reconstruct the past," a method known as uniformitarianism. But Wise declares that those assumptions and conclusions are invalid because God intervenes in history by such events as the flood.

To explain the huge volume of generally accepted material proof that the Earth is ancient, Wise introduces the idea of "an apparent but non-existent history," which comes from the miracles of Jesus. When Jesus fed the five thousand after his Sermon on the Mount, he created food that had the *appearance* of wheat being sown, grown, harvested, ground, and baked into bread; of fish caught, cooked, and divided into portions, yet none of this actually happened. The wine Jesus created for a wedding feast had the *appearance* of grapes that were tended, picked, crushed, fermented, bottled, and bought, none of which took place.

"Since God is directly responsible for each of these events," Wise writes, "we must conclude that God can and does create things that appear much older than they really are." Why would God make the Earth appear old when it is not? Wise claims that God has placed in the world "intentional, inherent ambiguity," so that people will come to him by faith rather than by evidence. Other Christians, though, argue that pitting faith against evidence can lead to the same anti-intellectualism that contributed to marginalizing Christianity in the twentieth century.

Phillip Johnson and Kurt Wise do agree on the inherent angst that many scientists are feeling: they both say there are scientists who honestly question evolutionary theory but fear being skewered by their professional peers. These scientists know, Johnson asserts, that nonliving chemicals cannot combine to become a living organism. He says they've "conceded, although not when the creationists are listening, that they know that very well. And yet they're confident that they'll somehow find an experiment that will validate this power. Because after all, once they get life jump-started, once they get a single replicating molecule, they think Charles Darwin showed that it can go all the way up the line to Arnold Schwarzenegger or Einstein."

The creative power of Darwinism, say ID advocates, has never been proven. As Johnson observes:

> Take that away, and there's nothing left except a story, a rather discredited theory. And that's why the cultural consequences will be so enormous when this comes out that the materialists are rightly frightened about that.
>
> Imagine what would happen if the president of the National Academy of Sciences, this battery of microphones in front of him, were to say to the public, "We've been telling you for 150 years this Darwinian theory was well established, but actually it isn't. The mechanism can't do any creating. The whole thing's a mistake. We're sorry."

What, Johnson muses, would become of the Mandarins of Science and culture, all those Ivy League professors and people who write editorials for the *New York Times* and the *Washington Post,* if they were to have their evolutional rug pulled out from under them?

CHAPTER 24

The Wedge

LESS THAN A DECADE after launching the Intelligent Design Movement with his book *Darwin on Trial*, Phillip Johnson ushered the creation debate to a new level as leader of an informal group of scholars, scientists, and thinkers he called the Wedge. In his book *The Wedge of Truth: Splitting the Foundations of Naturalism*, Johnson established the metaphor for materialist Darwinian theory as a big log dropped on the road to understanding the origins of life. The log appears to be huge, strong, monolithic, and impossible to move. But on closer examination, there's a crack going deep into the heartwood. On each side of the crack is a modernist definition of science:

> On one hand, modernists say that science is impartial fact-finding, the objective and unprejudiced weighing of evidence. Science in that sense relies on careful observation, calculations, and above all, repeatable experiments. That kind of objective science is what makes technology possible, and where it can be employed it is indeed the most reliable way of determining the facts. On the other hand, modernists also identify science with naturalistic philosophy. In that case science is committed to finding and endorsing naturalistic

> explanations for every phenomenon—*regardless of the facts.* That kind of science is not free of prejudice. On the contrary it is *defined* by a prejudice. The prejudice is that all phenomena can ultimately be explained in terms of purely natural causes, which is to say unintelligent causes.

Johnson saw Intelligent Design as the narrow end of an ideological wedge that would ultimately split the log of science dependent on the materialist assumption that "in the beginning were the fundamental particles that compose matter, energy and the impersonal laws of physics." As the point of the wedge, Intelligent Design would open a path for others to follow, gradually thickening the wedge of scientific creationism with new thoughts, theories, and proofs to the point where the seemingly invincible theory of purposeless random evolution fell apart under the weight of its own inner inconsistency.

In contrast to the Mandarins of Science, who loudly dismissed any hint of opposing views, Johnson and the Wedge movement welcomed skeptics. "The naysayers are not our enemy," he explained in *The Wedge of Truth.* "On the contrary, they are an essential part of the dialogue, to help us make sure we are testing our own ideas as we should." The enemy was instead the "obfuscators" who "resist any clear definition of terms or issues, who insist that the ruling scientific organizations be obeyed without question and who are content to paper over logical contradictions with superficial compromises."

One important way the Wedge was different from the original Intelligent Design Movement was that having fully made his case against evolution without mentioning God, Johnson could now move beyond the flaws in reasoning that derailed Darwinism. He could connect the story of creation with the story of Christ: "It is time to set out more fully how the Wedge program fits into the specific Christian gospel (as distinguished from a generic theism), and how and where questions of biblical authority enter the picture."

Johnson suggested that the most important issue for the moment was how to tell reason from rationalization. He saw rationalization among Darwinists as an indication that deep down they knew how weak their case was. He quoted Amherst biology professor Paul Ewald insisting about Darwinism, "It has to be true—it's like arithmetic." Yet time after time Darwinists failed to come up with specific examples of the results they claimed evolution could produce.

Johnson told the story of an interview Richard Dawkins gave to an Australian documentary film producer in 1998, when Dawkins was arguably the most famous Darwinist in the world. The interviewer asked if Dawkins could cite a single example of a mutation or other evolutionary step that was information enhancing. (This would confirm the key assumption of Darwinism that small micromutations occur, some of which are advantageous and thus preserved by natural selection; over many generations these many small changes form a new species or an entirely new type of organism. To do this, evolved genetic material has to carry information that its ancestor did not have. The interviewer was asking for any specific example of this added information.)

Dawkins was struck speechless on camera and finally gave an irrelevant answer that seemed to indicate he didn't have an example. In a later interview Dawkins declared, "It is a question that nobody except a creationist would ask. A real biologist finds it an easy question to answer." To Johnson this was only one high-profile example of countless instances where under direct questioning evolutionists could offer "no explanation of how random mutations . . . can be causing massive increases in genetic information." How then did primeval ooze eventually evolve into Mozart?

Johnson refined his explanation as to why so many men and women of science take such a seemingly irrational position and exclude any evidence outside the material realm, even when material explanations are insufficient. Any theory of special creation of individual species, writes Johnson, "is considered unscientific and hence ineligible for consideration because it necessarily involves a supernatural intervention in nature that is inaccessible to scientific investigation. . . . With supernatural creation disqualified as 'religious,' Darwinian evolution is just about the only remotely tenable theory to account for the changes required to make a world of diverse complex organisms. . . . The theory's logical appeal to the materialist mind is so powerful that a few confirming illustrations are sufficient" even though those illustrations, including the inevitable finch beak and peppered moth examples, were misleading at best.

Using physicist Paul Davies as one example, Johnson showed how scientists' logic brought them to the brink of accepting the fact that evolution could not account for life on earth, but many scientists then retreated under close questioning because of their personal theological preferences and fear of peer reaction. Quoting from Davies's book *The Fifth Miracle*, Johnson underscored the fact that evolution cannot explain where new genetic information comes from; whereas evolutionists emphasized the mechanism of evolving life, creationists emphasized the hereditary information that defines life. Here even Davies seemed to admit evolution couldn't supply all the answers:

"A law of nature of the sort we know and love will not create biological information, or indeed any information at all. . . . The secret of life lies, not in its chemical bases, but in the logical and informational rules it exploits. . . . Real progress with the mystery of biogenesis will be made, I believe, not through exotic chemistry, but from something conceptually new." On the surface, this statement by a renowned physicist sounded like a ringing endorsement of Intelligent Design. Davies acknowledged that "the idea that the laws of nature may be slanted towards life, while not contradicting the letter of Darwinism, certainly offends its spirit."

After *The Fifth Miracle* was published, Johnson attended a conference where Davies was buttonholed by Nobel laureate Christian de Duve, author of *Vital Dust: Life as a Cosmic Imperative*, who believed that life was the product of "law-driven chemical steps, each one of which must have been highly probable in the right circumstances." Under intense one-on-one questioning from de Duve after his presentation, Davies reversed his evident position and assured de Duve that he still believed chemical reactions created all the information necessary for life and the development of various kinds of plants and animals.

> Put to the test, Davies retreated headlong from the revolutionary implications of his own logic. . . . When I asked Davies why he refused to go further, he told me frankly that

> he was attracted to the idea that there is some rational principle behind the cosmos that steers matter in the direction of evolving into life and intelligence. However, he was very much against any idea of a personal God who might interfere with the operation of natural law. . . . So theological preference was one reason for not bringing a freely acting intelligence into the history of life. Another reason, as evidenced by the dialogue with de Duve, was that Davies was unwilling to risk being labeled as a creationist or a vitalist.

During his own lecture at the conference, Johnson "drew out the implications of Davies's thinking and asked frankly whether the first commitment of science was to impartial investigation of the evidence, or to upholding materialist preferences regardless of the evidence." Afterward de Duve "sternly reproved" Johnson for "attacking science," and, reports Johnson, "lectured me over lunch on the theme that 'evolution has occurred.'"

The most important message in *The Wedge of Truth* is that in the end the evolution debate isn't a scientific argument but a titanic clash of worldviews. From the Scopes trial of 1925 to the educational and legal wrangling of 2005, the evolution battle is a battle of the heart. If "in the beginning were the particles," the world is ruled by random, purposeless chemical reactions, and the physical realm is the whole of existence. But if "in the beginning was the Word," which became the Creator God in human form, then the world is ruled by a divine order reflecting an absolute standard of good and evil, and the material world and its goals are subservient to the realm of the soul and spirit.

> In the final analysis it is not any specific evidence that convinces me that Darwinism is a pseudoscience that will collapse once it becomes possible for critics to get a fair hearing. It is the way the Darwinists argue their case that makes it apparent that they are afraid to encounter the best arguments against their theory. A real science does not employ propaganda and legal barriers to prevent relevant questions from being asked, nor does it rely on enforcing rules of reasoning that allow no alternative to the official story.

Out of the void of collapsed Darwinism, Johnson sees the eventual triumph not only of theism but Christianity in particular. While there's no substitute for the elegant and masterful argument of *The Wedge of Truth* in full, the following sentences scattered across the last two chapters outline the essence of it:

> Only persons have purposes and make choices. If a personal entity is at the foundation of reality, then we have a secure basis for discussing what the world is *for* rather than merely the material means by which it works. Only the Word creates, although the living things the Word creates have a capacity to vary in response to different environments. This is why no natural mechanism has been discovered for the creation of new complex genetic information. No such mechanism exists.
>
> Pseudoscience has its origin in the sin of pride, which refuses to respect the limitations inherent in our status as both created and fallen beings. Motivated by the sinful wish to control everything, pseudoscience distorts reality to conform it to our desires. Materialism is the characteristic concept by which twentieth century pseudoscience has accomplished this.
>
> What do we exist *for*, and why should we not live for pleasure, or in order to kill as many other people as possible before committing suicide? We are not capable of resolving that predicament on our own, least of all by the unassisted power of reason, because our reasoning powers are the very means we employ to construct whatever idol we are currently worshiping. To what or to whom can we turn for a new starting point?

Johnson says it is pointless to turn to God if God is a product of human imagination, thus controlled by human philosophy. "What we need is for God himself to speak, to give us a secure foundation on which we can build. If God has not spoken, then we have no alternative to despair. If God has spoken, then we need to build on that framework rather than try to fit what God has done into some framework that comes from human philosophy."

But Johnson points out that God has spoken: in the Bible and in the person of Jesus Christ. Naturalism leaves him out; creationism places him in the center of all existence. Naturalism makes it logical to banish Jesus from the classroom and science and public debate. The only viable alternative to naturalism—and from the standpoint of scientific proof, the only answer at all—is acknowledgment of God as the Creator and Christ as his human form. That, says Johnson, is why "our educational planners consider it enormously important that school children learn about evolution but entirely unimportant whether they learn enough about Jesus to evaluate his claims." The one thing that can explain the origin of the universe is the one thing public school students in America are forbidden to discuss.

Johnson concludes: "After seeing that trying to build everything on a foundation of matter has led us into a blind alley, we will have to look for something better. Once the question is put that way, Christians have an answer. Scientists as such do not, although many scientists as citizens may have a lot to contribute. If other faiths have different answers, let them be heard so we can give them serious consideration."

What will the future hold? In 2004 *World* magazine asked Phillip Johnson, William Dembski, and two other leaders of the Intelligent Design Movement to have some fun: Imagine writing in 2025, on the one hundredth anniversary of the famous Scopes monkey trial, and explain how Darwinism had bit the dust, unable to rebut the evidence that what we see around us could not have arisen merely by time plus chance.

The two other fanciful historians: Jonathan Wells, a senior fellow at the Discovery Institute and author of *Icons of Evolution* (2000), who received a Ph.D. in biology from the University of California at Berkeley and a Ph.D. in theology from Yale University; and Jeffrey M. Schwartz, research professor of psychiatry at the UCLA School of Medicine, and the author of more than one hundred scientific publications in the fields of neuroscience and psychiatry.

Here's an abridged version of Johnson's contribution, titled "The Demise of Naturalism" (see appendix B for the complete text of the *World* magazine feature):

Methodological naturalism used to be a regulative principle for science and for all serious academic thought. Not any longer. It is now (in 2025) an outdated dogma, and the Scopes trial stereotype, as depicted in the movie *Inherit the Wind,* is now effectively dead.

In 1980, astronomer Carl Sagan commenced the influential National Public Television series *Cosmos,* by announcing its theme. "The cosmos is all there is, ever was, or ever will be." In those years, celebrity scientists like Sagan freely promoted a dogmatic naturalistic philosophy as if it were a fact that had been discovered by scientific investigation, just as previous generations of celebrities had promoted racism, class warfare, and Freudian fantasy in the name of science. The celebrities felt themselves free to ignore both evidence and logic, because the approval of the rulers of science, who had a vested interest in persuading the public to adopt a philosophy that maximized their own influence, was all that was needed to induce the media to report an ideological dogma as a scientific conclusion.

Millions of schoolchildren and credulous adults were led to accept the voice of Sagan as the voice of science and thus to believe that scientists had proved that God does not exist, or at least is irrelevant to our lives. In brief, the message of this government-promoted television series was that philosophical naturalism and science are one and the same. Throughout the second half of the twentieth century, the popular media relentlessly pursued the theme that liberation and fulfillment are to be found through technology, with the attendant implication that the supernatural creator revealed in the Bible is a superfluous and obsolete entity doomed to expire from terminal irrelevance.

Social scientists further affirmed this myth with their secularization thesis, which predicted that supernatural religion would steadily lose adherents throughout the world as public education enlightened the multitudes, and as people came to see scientific technology as the only route to health, happiness, and longevity. Problems such as pollution and warfare were acknowledged, but these too could be mastered if we insisted that our politicians heed the advice of the ruling scientists.

The cultural path that led to this apotheosis of scientific naturalism began just after the middle of the twentieth century, with the triumphalist Darwin Centennial Celebration in 1959 and the 1960 film *Inherit the Wind,* a stunning but thoroughly fictionalized dramatization of the Scopes trial. As the twentieth century came to an end, science and history teachers were still showing *Inherit the Wind* to their classes as if it were a fair portrayal of what had happened in Dayton, Tennessee, in 1925.

Superficially, it seemed that scientific naturalism was everywhere triumphant at the start of the twenty-first century. Scientific rationalists were nonetheless uneasy, for two reasons. First, literary intellectuals had pushed naturalism to the limits of its logic and drawn the conclusion that, since an uncreated nature is indifferent to good and evil, all values are merely subjective, including even the value of science. It seemed to follow that nothing is forbidden, and pleasure can be pursued without limit. Both highbrow literature and popular entertainment became strongly nihilistic, scorning all universal standards of truth, morality, or reason.

Second, public opinion polls showed that a clear majority of the American public still believed that God is our creator despite the heavy-handed indoctrination in evolutionary naturalism to which they had been subjected for several decades in textbooks, television documentaries, and museum exhibits. The seemingly solid wall of Darwinian orthodoxy was crumbling.

Naturalism was losing its essential scientific backing, and then it also suddenly lost its hold on the popular and literary imagination, as the American public tired of nihilism and began to count the cost of all that had been destroyed during the century of scientism. New historical scholarship reflected in a stunning PBS television documentary exposed the *Inherit the Wind* portrayal of the Scopes trial as a hoax, kicking off an era of historical revisionism in which book after scholarly book exposed how propaganda techniques had been employed to create a mythology of inevitable progress towards naturalism, similar to the governing mythology of the Soviet Union, which had proclaimed the inevitable replacement of capitalism by communism.

The collapse of the Soviet Union put an end to the Soviet myth, just as the scientific collapse of Darwinism, preceded as it was by the discrediting of Marxism and Freudianism, prepared the way for the culture to turn aside from the mythology of naturalism to rediscover the buried treasure that the mythology had been concealing. A hilarious Broadway comedy titled *Inherit the Baloney* enacted a sort of Scopes Trial in reverse, with the hero a courageous Christian college professor badgered incessantly by dim-witted colleagues and deans who keep telling him that the only way to preserve his faith in a postmodern world is to jettison all the exclusivist truth-claims: they wanted him to admit that Jesus was sorely in need of sensitivity training from some wise counselor like Pontius Pilate, because "nobody can surf the web every day and still believe that there is such a thing as 'truth' or goodness." Overnight, the tendency of naturalistic rationalism to decay into postmodern irrationalism became a national joke.

Then the rise of Islamic extremism at the start of the new century came just as scholars and journalists were finally taking notice of the rapid spread of active, vibrant Christian faith in Africa, South America, and Asia, especially China. The secularization thesis was consistent with the facts only in a few parts of the world where long established Christian Churches had succumbed to complacency and the slow poison of naturalism. Where life was hardest and persecution frequent, the flame of faith burned brighter than ever. For those with a global outlook, the question was not whether God was still important in our lives, but rather, "What does God want us to do?" Once Darwinism had joined Marxism and Freudianism in the dustbin of history, the entire world seemed new and full of exciting possibilities.

The crucial turning point in America came in the year 2004. In that year the "same sex marriage" explosion, abetted by public officials, brought to public attention the extent to which long-settled understandings of law and morality had been undermined as judges, mayors, and citizens internalized the nihilistic moral implications of naturalistic philosophy. That same year, with the spectacular success of two great movies, *The Return of the King* and *The Passion of the Christ*, it became clear that the public was hungering for art and entertainment which affirmed traditional values rather than flouting them. Surprise: the Bible still provided, as it had for many centuries, the indispensable starting point for the artistic imagination.

Artists and humanities scholars recognized that the human imagination had been stunted by blind adherence to a philosophy that denied the artist or poet any sense of the divine power that gives meaning to the realm of nature. As sanity reasserted itself, even the secular intellectuals saw that the fact of creation provides the essential foundation not only for the artistic imagination, but even for the scientific imagination, because science itself makes no sense if the scientific mind is itself no more than the product of irrational material forces.

As that insight spread, naturalism became yesteryear's fashion in thought, and the world moved forward to the more realistic understanding of the human condition that we in 2025 now take for granted. Only the fool says that there is no God, or that God has forgotten us. Folly like that is as dead today as the discredited *Inherit the Wind* stereotype, which fit the facts of history no better than the secularization thesis. We no longer expect to meet intelligent beings on other planets, for we have learned how uniquely fitted to shelter life our own planet has been created to be. Now we have a much more exciting adventure. We can dedicate our minds and our courage to sharing the truth that makes us free.

CHAPTER 25
Consequences

DARROW, THE ACLU, and their media allies succeeded in labeling the Christianity of William Jennings Bryan and his followers reactionary, exclusive, overbearing, and out of touch. They asserted that biblical faith took a suspension of disbelief in the facts of modern science that only an idiot could make.

Their greatest strategic victory was in laying claim to the definition of what a Christian is. Once the Darwinians defined the terms of the argument, the Christians were stuck on the defensive. They lost focus and momentum, lost public support, and in time lost the battle to maintain America's historically Christian popular culture. Today that loss profoundly affects the most essential aspects of our national identity.

Darrow succeeded in defining a Christian as a closed-minded, uneducated fundamentalist who feared and hated anything he didn't understand and called down hellfire on anyone who didn't agree with him. An agnostic himself, Darrow masterfully portrayed Tennessee lawmakers and their celebrity cocounsel as impediments to progress, learning, academic and political freedom, and bereft of common sense.

At the end of Bryan's appearance as a witness, Darrow condemned Bryan's brand of Christianity as "fool ideas that no intelligent Christian on earth believes." Darrow insisted that Bryan's theology wasn't real Christianity although Darrow was scarcely qualified to tell the world what an intelligent Christian would or would not believe. Many newspaper readers were willing to overlook that detail as they eagerly devoured the news of Bryan's dramatic grilling. Even Bryan's most faithful supporters must have felt the sting as newspapers around the country picked up on Darrow's characterization of his opponent as an obstructionist blind to the advances and realities of the modern scientific world.

What the public never understood, because Bryan never explained it and the press didn't report it, was that Bryan based his definition of Christianity on biblical principles. Fundamentalism has a bad connotation today as it did in Scopes's time but literally means only a belief in the fundamentals of Christianity: the virgin birth, the Trinity, the miracles of Jesus, Jesus' death and resurrection, his sacrifice to atone for the sins of mankind. Fundamentalism also holds that the Bible is literally true, though some of it is unexplainable in material terms and must be accepted on faith.

The scientific experts who taught Sunday school had no problem teaching the miracles of Jesus on Sunday and the miracles of chemical compounds on Monday. But Bryan and millions of other Americans did not want Christianity to become merely a Sunday faith, ignored on the other six days. If science, and the popular newspaper-reading audience, refused to consider metaphysical causes under the umbrella of science, then science and Christianity were no longer allies but opponents.

In the defense motion to quash the indictment against Scopes and have the charge against him dismissed, Darrow claimed the Butler Act violated the state constitution's guarantee of a citizen's "natural and indefeasible right to worship God according to the dictates of their own conscience." Judge Raulston denied the motion, stating, "I fail to see how this act in any way interferes or in the least restrains any person from worshiping God in the manner that best pleaseth him. It gives no preference to any particular religion or mode of worship. Our public schools are not maintained as places of worship, but, on the contrary, were designed, instituted, and maintained for the purpose of mental and moral development and discipline."

With this ruling, Judge Raulston pointed to a split between Christianity and the trends of American culture. To achieve "mental and moral development and discipline" requires a standard of development and discipline. A standard derived from man's law or man's rationality is unavoidably relative and changeable; only a standard from outside man's control can give constant and absolute guidance. From the landing of the Pilgrims to the motion to quash the Scopes indictment, that standard in America had been based on the Bible. That was not to say citizens were compelled or even encouraged to worship Jesus or anybody or anything else, simply that the assumed and accepted standards at the base of all laws, rules, and expectations were derived directly from biblical teaching.

One result of the Scopes trial was that biblical belief came to be viewed by many thought leaders not as a faith that (among other things) encouraged mental and moral development but one that infantilized its adherents. Christianity was defined as the small-minded insular ignorance of a man who believed Jonah could live three days in the belly of a big fish and that the latest scientific advances shouldn't be taught in school because they conflicted with the Bible. Three decades later the film *Inherit the Wind* turned Bryan's brand of Christianity into a joke for the masses.

Movie scriptwriters and directors, like newspaper writers, badly misrepresented Bryan's fundamentalism. Some of it was his own doing: his oratorical flourishes and playing to the crowd made him an easy target for Darrow's cold scientific materialism and expert sarcasm. What Bryan resolutely defended was the fundamentalist position that the Bible was the literal truth and that Darwinism was at odds with the Bible. Time and again, when pressed for specific explanations of miraculous events, he said one way or another that he couldn't explain them but took them on faith.

One famous question on the topic, which made it into the film script, was whether Bryan had discovered where Cain, Adam's son, got his wife if Eve was the only woman God had created so far.

"I leave the agnostics to hunt for her," he answered.

Bryan's explanations of Bible events were consistent with Christian teaching, but his inability or unwillingness to explain what skeptics saw as inconsistency made it easy for adversarial reporters. They saw Bryan as not all that different from semiliterate hillbillies accused of holding back progress in the name of Jesus. Darrow and the ACLU defined Christianity on their terms, charged it with crimes they selected, and found it guilty as charged. Popular culture condemned Christianity on these trumped-up terms for generations and continues to do so.

The Scopes trial was a high-profile event on the road to a cataclysmic change in American culture. Between 1925 and today, the historic position of Christianity in the United States has been completely upended. Judge Raulston and Attorney General Stewart used the Constitution to defend teaching creation science in schools; a generation later the courts used the same Constitution to order any acknowledgment of God banned from the classroom.

From the schoolroom the conflict over religion in public life expanded in the 1960s and afterward as courts found their interpretation of the Constitution different from historical precedent and changed the enforcement of the law to conform with their new vision. By 1980 creation science was banned from the classroom by reinterpreting the same statutes Judge Raulston had cited in protecting it. In 2002 the Ninth Circuit Court of Appeals ruled that the official Pledge of Allegiance was unconstitutional because it contained the words, "under God," added in 1954. Eventually the U.S. Supreme Court overturned the ruling on a technicality.

Children stopped learning, and people stopped discussing, the Christian origins of the Thanksgiving holiday; Christmas became "winter vacation"; public Christmas displays, some in place year after year for decades, were suddenly ruled unconstitutional. It was only as Christianity disappeared from the public square that some Americans began to see the Darrow-Mencken definition of Christianity as self-serving, shortsighted, and wrong. They saw that biblical values had made the United States the freest and most prosperous country in the history of the world.

Ironically, one freedom that had all but disappeared by the turn of the twenty-first century was the freedom to acknowledge God in the course of public discourse. Under the pressures of legal redress and political correctness, religion has gone underground. Richard John Neuhaus has called the result "the naked public square": naked in its lack of religious discussion. Politicians and public figures now make a point of leaving religion at home or in the church and keeping this private matter private.

The justification for this was that it would produce a neutral state where everyone's views had an equal chance to be heard. It has brought us to the point, very unusual in world history, where many intellectual leaders boast of their detachment from religion personally or professionally (or both). Harvard, Yale, Columbia, and other great universities were founded to teach Christianity. Many American presidents based their policies on biblical principles. Yet today's leaders, with few exceptions, carefully disassociate their public personas with religious belief.

The result is not neutrality but the fog of relativism. Without an absolute authority to declare right and wrong, the decision falls into the hands of judges, politicians, and individual citizens, the most noble of whom are, in the theology of the founders, self-serving sinners incapable of making their own law. To the founders law was a gift from God, and government's responsibility was to safeguard that gift. With God retired from the public square, a government of fallible human beings took control. It's as if with the locomotive barreling down the line, somebody pulled up the tracks.

With no rails to guide them, "each man did what was right in his own eyes." And so the warning of the Bible came true. Right was no longer established by God but by man. One God had established one right; now each man had as much right to his idea of right as the next.

That led to an explosion in pornography, illegitimacy, divorce, and a revolution in entertainment standards. The Supreme Court declared pornography protected speech and divined a previously undetected constitutional right for women to have abortions. The words of the laws hadn't changed, but the biblical moral foundation the authors of those laws depended on was suddenly knocked away. Even definitions of the most basic words came under fire in the murky world of relativism. "Marriage" no longer meant what it had meant for millennia because some homosexual citizens and sympathetic judges decided on their own that it should mean something else.

Removing religion from schools and the public arena didn't make a level playing field but an agnostic culture at best and atheistic at worst. Many Americans now espouse the religion of individual relativism: If it feels good, do it. If it smacks of sacrifice or responsibility, ignore it. America wasn't founded on those principles and, as current trends reveal, will not be long sustained by them. Now at last, in the first decade of the twenty-first century, there are signs people have had enough.

In state after state, parents and school boards are reintroducing material that acknowledges shortcomings and unanswered questions about Darwinism. Not many are implemented but some are, and the very fact the discussion is taking place points to a new interest in examining the faith-based story.

Promise Keepers and True Love Waits have attracted millions of people looking for the assurance and hope of absolute standards in personal behavior and family responsibility. According to a 2004 study by the Heritage Foundation, girls who take a pledge of virginity are 40 percent less likely to have a child out of wedlock than other girls.

Speaking at Howard University in Washington to mark the fiftieth anniversary of school desegregation, comedian Bill Cosby openly challenged black parents to take responsibility for children who get in trouble: "Where were you when he was two? Where were you when he was twelve? Where were you when he was eighteen? And how come you didn't know that he had a pistol? And where is the father?" Political correctness bars white politicians from such honest remarks; even Cosby took heat in some quarters, but people knew he was right.

President George W. Bush was the first president in years to declare his Christianity openly. When asked at a news conference whether he asked his father, former president George H. W. Bush, for advice. "You know, he is the wrong father to appeal to in terms of strength," the president reportedly said. "There is a higher Father that I appeal to."

Other trends: In recent years Christians have stood fast with the Boy Scouts in their refusal to accept homosexual members and leaders and formed organizations to battle for Christianity in the very courts that once made it their business to protect Christian values. After years of minimal activity, more Christians are learning how to serve and witness overseas. Between 1996 and 2001 the number of volunteer laymen making short-term trips to foreign countries rose tenfold to 350,000.

Mainline denominations such as Episcopal, Methodist, and Lutheran that have abandoned historic biblical positions on homosexuality and marriage are rapidly losing members, while evangelical denominations such as the Southern Baptists and the Presbyterian Church in America (PCA) that strongly endorse traditional views are strong and growing. In April 2004 five Episcopal congregations in Ohio called in retired conservative bishops to conduct confirmation services rather than invite the current serving bishop, who endorsed ordination of a practicing homosexual as bishop of New Hampshire.

In response to the churches' actions, the Episcopal House of Bishops released an official statement saying the act was one of "defiance" and "a willful violation of our Constitution and Canons." The retired bishops answered, "The action of the 2003 General Convention [ordaining a homosexual], in repudiating 4,000 years of biblical teaching regarding sexuality and the action of the House of Bishops in repudiating their consecration vows regarding Holy Scripture, were acts of defiance." Conservative Episcopalians are gaining support from fast-growing Anglican churches in Africa.

Across the spectrum of public life many Christians (as well as non-Christians) are beginning to see the folly of abandoning the culture's foundational values, of standing "naked in the public square." Christians with faith, patience, and tenacity may well see the tide continue to turn. The culture is hungry for assurance and safe harbor, and it is God who can bestow them.

To make any real headway, Christians must address and dispel a list of stereotypes that began with Bryan and Darrow and have hounded them ever since.

CHAPTER 26
Surmounting Stereotypes

THANKS TO THE MODERN PRESS, the fundamental stereotypes developed in 1925 are as strong as ever. If ever they were to be abandoned, the brief period of national unity that arose after the September 11, 2001, terrorist attacks was a likely time. But five days after 9/11, *New York Times* correspondent Serge Schmemann wrote that terrorists opposed "values cherished in the West as freedom, tolerance, prosperity, religious pluralism and universal suffrage, but abhorred by religious fundamentalists (and not only Muslim fundamentalists) as licentiousness, corruption, greed and apostasy." His implication was clear: conservative Christians in America associate liberty with licentiousness and prosperity with greed.

Another example: The October 7, 2001, *New York Times Magazine* ran an essay by Andrew Sullivan that labeled the war on terrorism "a religious war—but not of Islam versus Christianity and Judaism. Rather it is a war of fundamentalism against faiths of all kinds that are at peace with freedom and modernity." His definition of fundamentalism: "the blind recourse to texts embraced as literal truth, the injunction to follow the commandments of God before anything else, the subjugation of reason and judgment and even conscience to the dictates of dogma." Among the blind subjugators of reason: fundamentalist Christians.

Times columnist Thomas L. Friedman on November 27, 2001, wrote that Islam, Judaism, and Christianity all have to choose between "an ideology that accepts religious diversity" and the belief of "Christian and Jewish fundamentalists" that there is "just one religious path." The *Times* did print a letter by David Zwiebel of the Orthodox Jewish group Agudath Israel that took issue with Mr. Friedman's either-or stipulation. Mr. Zwiebel wrote that the "vision of America as a country where religious belief is welcome only if it abandons claims to exclusive truth is truly chilling—and truly intolerant."

Fifty-year *Times* man Anthony Lewis, in his farewell column on December 15, wrote that "the phenomenon of religious fundamentalism is not to be found in Islam alone. Fundamentalist Christians in America, believing that the Bible's story of creation is the literal truth, question not only Darwin but the scientific method that has made contemporary civilization possible." In an interview the following day, Mr. Lewis equated Osama bin Laden and John Ashcroft: both men sure of what they believe and thus supportive of indecent and inhumane policies, for "certainty the enemy of decency and humanity is people who are sure they are right."

Other leading publications display similar biases. A *Washington Post* article on December 30, 2001, postulated Christian-Muslim equivalence: "Today, there are Christian fundamentalists who attack abortion clinics in the United States and kill doctors; Muslim fundamentalists who wage their sectarian wars against each other." Editors evidently saw no need to point out that the rare abortionist killings have been condemned widely within Christendom, while the rampant rage within Islam has received broad encouragement.

The *Washington Post* on January 17, 2002, noted that American "religious conservatives" opposed cloning while "at the same time, the United States was fighting a war to free a faraway nation from the grip of religious conservatives who were denounced for imposing their moral code on others." The *Post* reporter complained that support for protecting embryos "could legitimize an effort to codify fundamentalist views into law."

The *Atlantic Monthly*'s February 2002 cover story, "Oh, Gods!" ended with analysis of how fast Christianity is growing in Africa and South America and suggested that concern about Islam is overblown, for "the big 'problem cult' of the twenty-first century will be Christianity."

Time's Margaret Carlson complained on February 20, 2002, that John Ashcroft "has a history of using his bully pulpit, as Attorney General, as a pulpit. He has prayer sessions every morning in his office. He doesn't agree, apparently, with pluralism—he believes that there is one form of religion—and it should be practiced as an official matter of state." Mr. Ashcroft, of course, has often said exactly the opposite, but Ms. Carlson apparently contends that a government official who prays in his office cannot be pluralistic.

Those comments and many more are legacies of the Scopes trial and its media portrayal. The stereotypes the Scopes trial pinned on Christians eighty years ago show no signs of fading. Christians won that early legal battle but lost the public relations war. When American culture transformed itself in the 1960s, those stereotypes made an easy target. They still do.

Twenty-first-century conservative Christians give critics plenty of ammunition. But it's also possible to stop playing to stereotype, to emerge from the shadow of a great but mischaracterized nineteenth-century orator and reclaim the high ground in public discourse. It's time to shake off the crippling legacy of the Scopes trial and show the true face of evangelical Christianity to a world more desperate than ever for truth, assurance, and answers. To do that Christians have to respond to a tenacious series of stereotypes and either prove them false or render them false. The time to begin is now.

Continuing Stereotype 1: Christians try to impose biblical views and morals on the entire population.

Ever since Clarence Darrow lured William Jennings Bryan onto the witness stand, the cultural left has set traps for conservative Christians. A typical contemporary ploy is to display some "work of art" calculated to outrage evangelicals and traditional Catholics, who respond on cue by demanding that the outrage be removed. The result is more publicity and popularity for the offensive display. One of countless examples was the opening of an exhibit at the Brooklyn Museum of Art on October 2, 1999, featuring a dung- and pornography-bedecked painting of "The Holy Virgin Mary." While two hundred demonstrators protested the exhibit, ninety-two hundred attended the opening.

As ready to criticize Christians in 1999 as in 1925, the *New York Times* ran a page-one story juxtaposing the record number of attendees with a protestor who prayed outside the museum "for hours, so much so that some people leaving the exhibition mockingly parroted the prayer as they headed for their cars." Articles in other major newspapers suggested that one religious group, and a dumb one at that, was trying to impose its morals on the general populace.

Ephesians 4:15 teaches Christians that a believer's role in spreading the gospel is "speaking the truth in love." It's then up to the Holy Spirit to move in the hearts of others to bring them to the saving grace of Christ. It isn't up to Christians to compel others to share their beliefs; it's up to Christ. Taking the bait and giving the liberal media an easy target is counterproductive. Christians must have faith in God to work his perfect will, in individuals and in cultures, as he sees best.

Continuing Stereotype 2: Christians blindly follow leaders like Bryan.

Since the Moral Majority movement of the 1970s and 1980s, evangelist and educator Jerry Falwell, evangelist and presidential candidate Pat Robertson, and others have been put forth in the press as the "new Bryan." A decade ago the *Washington Post* famously stereotyped Christians as poor, dumb, and easily led. Christians responded by faxing in their bank balances and academic degrees.

Bryan and some of his theological heirs have attracted huge crowds. There's nothing wrong with that, media spin to the contrary, unless the crowds transfer their fealty from the message to the messenger. At least in theory, Christians should be less likely than others to bow down to any human authority. Christians obey a higher authority and are taught by the Bible not to put their trust in princes.

Christians should be political skeptics in relation to Washington orthodoxy and strict constructionists concerning both the Bible and the Constitution. Most important, Christians must read for themselves what the Bible says about Christianity, letting Scripture—and not those with axes to grind—interpret Scripture. Christians must also read the Constitution to see what the nation agreed to in 1787 and 1788, and how the nation has changed since through the amendment process, not take what today's judges say it is.

The founders of the United States admired Sir Henry Blackstone and his *Commentaries on the Law of England*. The admiration produced a strong connection between the American Constitution and the Declaration of Independence and Blackstone's commentaries on law. Foremost among them was the conviction that the law came from God.

Blackstone wrote:

> Man, considered as a creature, must necessarily be subject to the laws of his creator, for he is entirely a dependent being. . . . And consequently as man depends absolutely on his maker for everything, it is necessary that he should in all points conform to his maker's will. This will of his maker is called the law of nature. For God, when he created matter, and endued it with a principle of mobility, established certain rules for the perpetual direction of that motion; so, when he created man, and endued him with freewill to conduct himself in all parts of life, he laid down certain immutable laws of human nature, whereby that freewill is in some degree regulated and restrained, and gave him also the faculty of reason to discover the purpose of these laws.

John Adams and other colonial leaders bought copies of Blackstone's work in an edition privately printed in Philadelphia in 1771. More than fifteen years before the Constitution was written, its authors recognized the link between the laws of a free people and the laws of God. Referring directly to the law and not some intermediate interpretation reveals how far Washington orthodoxy has strayed from the truth.

Continuing Stereotype 3: Christians want to legislate morality from the top down.

The failure of Prohibition shows how impossible it is to dictate the morality of millions of people. Sometimes it sounds like evangelical Christians do want to legislate morality, but Christians should actually be less likely than others to fixate on particular schemes to reform society because we know triumph will come only when Christ returns.

Christians know, or should know, that laws can't wipe out sin because sin is in everyone. The goal instead should be to keep sin from gaining government backing. Logically, Christians should not be trying to gain power to force change upon "the masses" from the top down because, among other reasons, that approach doesn't work. Thinking Christians do not believe that we can retain childhood innocence by avoiding such topics in school: the doctrine of original sin teaches that such innocence does not exist. Christians should realize that no societal restructuring will liberate the natural goodness of man because Christianity tells us natural goodness doesn't exist.

Continuing Stereotype 4: Christians are opposed to educational choice.

Everyone with any interest in the Scopes trial should realize (in retrospect) that the Butler Act was poorly drafted. The real issue was parental and taxpayer control of tax-funded schools, an issue that should have been addressed in other ways. Today it is the traditional Christian point of view that's likely to be left out of public discussion, so Christians generally welcome educational choice; secular liberals want to limit teaching to their side of the evolution issue alone. The same goes for various other issues.

Christians for the most part support educational choice: theories of intelligent design should be taught alongside theories of evolution. Christians should not be against high school or college students reading parts of the Quran; we should also be pushing for them to be reading parts of the Bible.

More broadly we should fight for educational choice in general so that private schools will be an option for everyone, not just the rich. The large-scale failure of public schools is making this need apparent to more people. More liberals, particularly in inner cities, are finally demanding and getting educational choice because they see the results of decades without choice. Carrying the trend onward, Christians seek—and the culture may yet embrace—choice for unborn babies, who should not be killed before they have a chance to make any choices in life. We should push for choice in social services so addicts, alcoholics, and others among the poor can be offered faith-based programs along with conventional liberal ones.

Many non-Christians are seeing that Christian solutions offer a dimension other solutions cannot. Many school districts have asked for a secularized version of True Love Waits, the Christian program that has been so successful in reducing premarital sex among teenagers. To their credit, its founders regretfully refused, explaining that the Christian element was essential for recognizing the moral absolutes the program was based on.

One example where Christian programs have been accepted despite their religious connections is Chuck Colson's Prison Fellowship. Now at work in more than one hundred countries around the world, Prison Fellowship prepares prisoners for life outside the walls with overtly Christian programs of Bible study, prayer, peer support, and mentoring. On average, more than two-thirds of exconvicts are rearrested within three years of their release. With Prison Fellowship, 80 percent get out of prison and stay out. The results are simply too good to ignore. And they come from Christian principles inseparable from the program.

Continuing Stereotype 5: Christians oppose the First Amendment's guarantee of religious freedom.

Christians need to make clear that the problem is not the First Amendment's guarantee of religious freedom but the movement of high courts over the past fifty years to turn this amendment on its head and use it to deny Christians the very freedom it was written to preserve. James Madison, the amendment's lead author, assured members of Congress that its purpose was to keep federal officials from placing one sect or denomination on a pedestal to the disadvantage of all the others and "to which they would compel others to conform."

In "Federalist Number 43," published January 23, 1788, Madison recalled both Blackstone and the Declaration of Independence when he wrote of "the transcendent law of nature and of nature's God, which declares that the safety and happiness of society are the objects at which all political institutions aim, and to which all such institutions must be sacrificed."

A little history clarifies the point. Nine of the original thirteen colonies had tax-supported churches, all of which discriminated against Baptists. John Leland, the leading Baptist evangelist in the colonies, opposed ratification of the U.S. Constitution because he was afraid it would lead to a tax-supported national church. Madison promised him that if he would support ratification, Madison would introduce an amendment assuring no national church would be established.

Years later on New Year's Day, 1802, after Leland made a courtesy call on President Thomas Jefferson, Jefferson wrote to the Danbury Baptist Association in Connecticut: "Believing with you that religion is a matter which lies solely between man and his God, that he owes account to none other for his faith or his worship, that the legislative powers of government reach actions only, and not opinions, I contemplate with sovereign reverence that act of the whole American people which declared that their legislature should 'make no law respecting an establishment of religion, or prohibiting the free exercise thereof,' thus building a wall of separation between Church and State."

His point clearly is that Congress should stay out of religious matters of conscience. But he said nothing about separating God from government. Two days after Leland's visit, Jefferson attended a worship service in the House of Representatives with Leland preaching. Jefferson's point that government ought to stay out of religion was upheld into the middle of the twentieth century by Supreme Court

Justice Potter Stewart, who said, "What our Constitution indispensably protects is the freedom of each of us, be he Jew or Agnostic, Christian or Atheist, Buddhist or free thinker, to believe or disbelieve, to worship or not to worship, to pray or keep silent, according to his own conscience, uncoerced and unrestrained by government."

As Richard Land notes in *For Faith and Family*, "The First Amendment was never intended to keep religion out of public policy, but to keep government out of religion."

Continuing Stereotype 6: Christians demand conformity.

There's some truth to this one. Christianity establishes absolutes and Christians are called to defend them. Christians also know, however, that sinful man can never reach the perfect standard to which the Creator calls us; we should strive for that standard while acknowledging its unreachability this side of heaven.

Today in practical terms, opponents of Christianity demand conformity in public schools and elsewhere. Today Christians want to see more diversity of ideas in media and academic circles; more fair treatment of a diversity of views, not just a stultifying extension of politically correct secular liberalism; less discrimination against Christians at colleges and universities.

Continuing Stereotype 7: Christians don't prize liberty.

Sometimes this has been a true charge. It depends on what type of liberty we're talking about. In essence many Christians haven't distinguished sufficiently between ancient Israel and modern America.

Ancient Israel, to use today's parlance, was a holiness theme park. The laws laid down by Moses set up Israel to be a holy people separated from others and dedicated to God. The land itself was a theme park, with everything stressing holiness: geography, economics, laws, customs. In the end, of course, the insufficiency of all those aids to reverence showed man's desperate need for Christ.

The United States is a liberty theme park. We are the envy of much of the world because of the freedom we have to speak, write, worship, and work. We are free to build businesses and to travel. We are also free to consume pornography, practice adultery and homosexuality, and act in other ways that threaten life and the pursuit of long-term happiness.

Anyone who does not understand the American commitment to liberty will go the way of Bryan. Americans will not be compelled or coerced into conformity to Christian principles. Showing by example the peace and fulfillment the faith bestows and praying for God's guidance are among the steps Christians can take to appeal to a free yet semi-godless people.

Free yet godless—is that the future of America, and if so, how long will freedom last? Some who claim the name of Christ have tried to make their peace with godlessness: editors of the *Christian Century,* a liberal theological weekly, wrote on February 20, 1909, that "the religion that is typical of modern times is getting on friendly terms with other human interests. It is abdicating its absolutism and bending down to the life men really live."

Bending down or bowing down? G. Stanley Hall, a founder of American psychology, wrote in 1924 about his delight when he discovered evolution as a student and learned that "all worlds and all in them had developed very gradually . . . all religions, gods, heavens, immortalities, were made by mansoul." Hall put Man the Creator at the center of things and rejoiced at the Scopes trial verdict the following year, but the last three-fourths of the twentieth century—with its tens of millions of deaths at the hands of Hitler, Stalin, Mao, Pol Pot, and others with faith in materialism—suggested that godless freedom quickly turns into slavery.

And if that conclusion is seen as blaming a doctrine for the faults of its followers, or as tying innocent American tendencies to evil abroad, let's review the framing of the Scopes trial story by the ACLU and the leading liberal magazine of the era, the *Nation*. The ACLU's Arthur Garfield Hays saw the trial as "a battle between two types of minds—the rigid, orthodox, accepting, unyielding, narrow, conventional mind and the broad, critical, cynical, skeptical and tolerant mind." According to Joseph Wood Krutch in the *Nation,* the Scopes trial showed "that the danger, often referred to by liberals, of the laws that will reduce the United States to a bondage more complete than that of the darkest Puritan village of colonial New England, is not fanatic danger but one real and present."

Schematized in that way, the mission for those who prize liberty over conformity was clear: fight biblical Christianity. With that as the goal and Christians as the enemy, the door is wide open to the absolutism of atheists, and liberal adoption of a "no enemy to the left" strategy. One result is that the tables are now turned from eighty years ago: Darwinians demand total control of the classroom and refuse to allow other theories to be taught or even hard questions to be asked. The absolution we should fear is not that of weakened church groups but triumphalistic progressives.

Americans, whether Christian or non-Christian, should learn from the Dayton debacle and avoid both the stereotypes and the reality. No group should try to impose its will on a diverse population and demand that its view and no others should be taught in public schools. In both public schools and media presentations, we should teach the debate and not demand conformity to either biblical or atheistic understandings. Many Christians learned from the Scopes trial and its aftermath that students should become aware of views other than those presented in church. But some Darwinists learned that they should seize the opportunity to exclude religious viewpoints, and both students and the cause of free inquiry have suffered.

Only truth, unburdened at last of politics and preconceptions, will ultimately resolve the conflict. It could have done so eighty years ago and can do so tomorrow morning. The challenge for all of us is to summon the diligence to seek that truth, the patience to find it, the wisdom to see it, and the courage to accept it.

APPENDIX A

"Scopes 75th Anniversary Broadcast" *Science Friday* with host Ira Flatow, July 21, 2000, WNYC and National Public Radio

Scopes Trial and the Theory of Evolution v. Creation

Ira Flatow, host: This is *Talk of the Nation/Science Friday.* I'm Ira Flatow.

Today is the seventy-fifth anniversary of the day a Tennessee jury, after deliberating for nine minutes, handed John Scopes a guilty verdict. The crime: violating Tennessee's law that banned the teaching of evolution in public schools. That trial was by no means the end of the story, as we know, but the trial and a movie, *Inherit the Wind,* did help shape public opinion about teaching evolution in public schools.

First up this hour we're going to talk about the scientific climate in the days leading up to the trial and the trial itself. And you're going to be surprised at how different it actually was from the movie. And then we'll spend the rest of the hour talking about the evolution versus creation debate, and intelligent design, a concept that has eclipsed scientific creationism in the creation/evolution debate. So if you'd like to talk about it, we'd love to hear from you. Our number is

1 (800) 989-8255; 1 (800) 989-TALK. And as always you can surf over to our Web site at sciencefriday.com to find links to our topic this hour.

I want to introduce my first guest. Edward J. Larson is the author of the Pulitzer Prize-winning *Summer for the Gods: The Scopes Trial and America's Continuing Debate over Science and Religion,* published by Harvard University Press. Dr. Larson is professor of history and law, University of Georgia in Athens. He joins by phone today.

Welcome to the program, Dr. Larson.

Dr. Edward J. Larson (professor, Georgia University; author, *Summer for the Gods*): Thank you very much. Glad to be here.

Flatow: Thank you. Do you think people have gotten the wrong impression about that trial from the movie?

Larson: Well, they get a different impression from the movie. I had the good fortune to be able to meet and work with both Jerome Lawrence and Bob Lee, the writers of the play, in preparing my book. And as they were always candid from the very beginning, they weren't writing a play about the Scopes trial; they were writing a play about McCarthyism. It was written during the period of the blacklisting of authors and playwrights; indeed, actually, some blacklisted playwrights helped in writing it. And they were just projecting back, much as was done with *The Crucible* by Arthur Miller, projecting back to another event, and then making a play about, trying to expose, really, how awful McCarthyism was. And so it's a wonderful play, but it tells you about the '50s not the '20s.

Flatow: So what was the trial really like, in terms of flavor and atmosphere and what was being done there versus what we saw in the movie?

Larson: Well, the movie tries to create the image. In fact, they say right in the movie that the crowd has to be always looming there; this ominous crowd being manipulated by a, you know, demagogue. And that's the sinister image it creates. Actually, Dayton was like a circus. It was a publicity stunt. It wasn't a mob-motivated event. Scopes was not a victim; he was a willing volunteer.

What had happened is that Tennessee had outlawed the teaching of human evolution. I mean, that was the real story. It wasn't the indictment of John Scopes. The real story was that Tennessee had passed a law outlawing the teaching of evolution. Out in East Tennessee, in the rising hill country of East Tennessee, Dayton was a small town with no ties to the Democratic administration that ran Tennessee at that time. And so they thought, almost on a lark, to test the law because the ACLU had issued an announcement that they would give a high-profile defense, talking about people like Charles Evans Hughes coming in to defend any schoolteacher in the state willing to challenge the constitutionality of the law. And Dayton thought that was a wonderful time to get some attention for their town.

Actually, the idea was concocted by an opponent of the law, a person who thought the law was just dang stupid. The lead prosecutor, Tom Stewart, thought it was a dumb law as well, but he thought it was the law and it was his duty to enforce. And so what you had was sort of a festival atmosphere where it wasn't the town that was looming there; it was the press that was looming everywhere. Hundreds of reporters came in. It was the first broadcast trial, broadcast live over the radio. It was also . . .

Flatow: So it was a hyped-up media event.

Larson: It was like the Simpson trial of the '20s. The '20s . . .

Flatow: Yeah.

Larson: . . . was a sensation-loving decade, and this was billed as the trial of the century before it even began. And wonderful reporters, like H. L. Mencken and Joseph Wood Crutch, went down to cover it. It was all filmed, and films were flown out of Dayton, and it was shown in movie houses around the country.

And John Scopes was never threatened; he was never jailed. He was never ostracized. He wasn't even threatened to lose his job. The law called for a small monetary fine, which many people, including the prosecutor, William Jennings Bryan, offered to pay on his behalf if he was convicted.

Flatow: So it was basically a cooperative effort on everybody's part just to test the law out.

Larson: To test the law. Originally, the town had PR in mind and sort of summer fun. Scopes truly opposed the law, but he wasn't a biology teacher. He hadn't ever violated the law.

Flatow: He was not a biology teacher.

Larson: No, he was a football coach.

Flatow: He was . . .

Larson: But you don't need a real biology teacher to do a test case.

Flatow: Yeah. Yeah.

Larson: And he did think the law was dang stupid, no question about that. He probably even thought it was evil—might be a little strong for his views.

Flatow: Yeah.

Larson: The ACLU brought down crack lawyers. And then it really even expanded beyond what was envisioned when William Jennings Bryan, the three-time Democratic Party nominee for president, the legendary speaker, when he volunteered to assist the prosecution. And basically his intent in doing so was make sure they really defended the law and didn't just sort of roll over dead for the ACLU.

Flatow: You write in your book *Summer for the Gods,* you have a quote about William Jennings Bryan, why he objected so much to the Darwinian theory. And it wasn't so much the exact idea of evolution itself, but you quote him as saying, "Because I fear we shall lose the consciousness of God's presence in our daily lives if they accept that."

Larson: That was certainly one of his prime motivations. He was not truly a biblical literalist as he testified on the stand. He said he thought the days of creation and the Genesis story symbolized long periods of time, but he was certainly an orthodox Christian on the conservative side. And he deeply believed that God created humans. He wasn't too sure about the animals and everything else, and he didn't really care about them. His point was that humans were created, so he did believe that on a religious basis. He'd read some scientific opponents of the theory, like Louie Agassis from Harvard back he was then, you know, long dead, but he'd opposed Darwinism in the previous century, as had some others. So he didn't accept it scientifically or religiously.

But really, what got him fighting, and what he said got him fighting, was social Darwinism—the fact that some militarists, some capitalists, some imperialists, were justifying their activities publicly on a survival-of-the-fittest-type thinking as applied to humans. That is human society, that the fittest should prevail. And there was a whole variety of what we'd call conservative activities, but most prominent then was World War I and the robber barons, who were saying, "Well, science justifies what we're doing." And William Jennings Bryan had long opposed the capitalists, the imperialists, the militarists. He had resigned as secretary of state in protest of World War I. And so that really got him going.

Now, granted, he had his religious presuppositions, but he plugged those into seeing the dangers of social Darwinism, and that got him fighting. He didn't think that schools should teach as true the Darwinian theory of human evolution. Now he didn't really oppose other theories very much, but the Darwinian theory; that shouldn't be taught as true in public schools because it would encourage acceptance in social Darwinism. At least, that's what he figured, and that's what he said publicly.

Flatow: Right.

Larson: And that's how he rallied people to his side on this cause.

Flatow: Because survival of the fittest encourages war, it encourages people to just, you know, not care about their neighbor. It just violates all the tenets of any way that we should be living, right?

Larson: Well, that's the way he interpreted it.

Flatow: Yeah.

Larson: And there are people who use it that way. And there are still politicians who use it that way. Now, of course, other politicians don't, and many leading Darwinists, like Ed Wilson, totally repudiate those ideas. But there was enough that Bryan could bring plenty of anecdotal evidence to his speeches.

Flatow: What got us to that point? Why did they decide at that time in history to test the case? What were the events leading up to that?

Larson: Well, there were developments on a variety of fronts. And I suppose they all sort of coalesce together into the brew that was the Scopes trial. Certainly one was an increased appreciation of, and following for, human evolution. Scientists had accepted evolution for decades, but it was hitting the people's attention a lot more because of discoveries of humanoid fossils, such as in Africa. And they seemed to be filling in the so-called "missing link" in the fossil record between animals and humans.

Now the opponents of evolution had long used those missing links to say, "Well, you can't really believe this stuff." And when they began to find what looked like missing links, and when the press started making front-page announcements of discoveries of the missing link, especially the missing link connecting primates to humans, that made the issue seem more pressing. But then there were a variety of mundane coincidental causes, such as the simple fact that, really, much before 1920 most kids didn't go to high school. There really wasn't effective compulsory attendance, especially in the South, but there weren't many high schools before 1900.

And so what you have in the 1920s is a spread of compulsory education where children of a broad range of Americans are now being forced to go to high school. And if their parents had objected to evolution all along, it never really mattered what was happening in high school. Their kids only went to elementary school. And, of course, you don't cover evolution there; you don't get that far. So it was impacting more people. You have this rise in fossil evidence, or what appeared to be fossil evidence for human evolution, putting the issue right at home. And then you have a revival of conservative Christianity in America as a reaction to modernism.

And then in the middle of it, you get William Jennings Bryan, the great orator, the powerful speaker, and not known as a conservative, suddenly championing, along with a whole variety of liberal causes like women's suffrage, starts championing antievolutionism. That made a lot of people rethink the issue. And somehow it concocted into an explosion that was the antievolution crusade.

Flatow: And I guess that when people were realizing that their kids were going to be taught something in high school now, they wanted to make sure that evolution didn't get the sole voice there.

Larson: Well, yeah. What they wanted, what Bryan called for was just not covering the topic of origins. He believed that it would violate establishment of religious freedom to teach biblical creationism in the public schools. It was not being taught. The people were not teaching biblical creationism. So he wanted to basically not teach the other side.

Now that's a fairly repressive viewpoint. It wants to keep everything out. I don't know. I mean, you know, there may or may not be a lot of following for that today, but that was the viewpoint back then. "Let's just leave this controversial issue out of the public schools."

And that made it a good target for people like the ACLU, people concerned with academic freedom and free speech. That made it, really, an electric target for them to aim at—that here was somebody, here was a movement, trying to repress a knowledge to basically wipe out an area of knowledge, that is the subject of origins, from the public schools, and, therefore, they could draw a whole new world of followers to their side. It was a tremendous case for the American Civil Liberties Union. It really put them on the map as rather than a radical organization, as a mainstream organization. It got followers in the scientific community . . .

Flatow: All right.

Larson: . . . and among the middle of the American cultural elite to back them . . .

Flatow: Right.

Larson: . . . really for the first time.

Flatow: All right. I'm talking with Edward Larson, author of *Summer for the Gods*. We're going to come back after this short break and talk lots more about the creation/evolution debate, so don't go away. We'll be right back.

I'm Ira Flatow, and this is *Talk of the Nation/Science Friday* from National Public Radio.

(*Soundbite of music*)

Flatow: Welcome back to *Talk of the Nation/Science Friday.* I'm Ira Flatow.

We're talking this hour about the Scopes trial, it's the seventy-fifth anniversary of that decision, and the history of teaching evolution in this country with my guest Ed Larson, author of *Summer for the Gods,* published by Harvard University Press.

Ed, is it really true they took just nine minutes to . . . did they even leave the room when they debated this?

Larson: Well, the only reason it took nine minutes was they had to weave their way out of the crowd—the five hundred people—four hundred, five hundred people crowded into the courtroom. It wouldn't have taken them even that long. They never made it to the jury room. They finally just stopped in the hallway. Actually, it could be so quick because Clarence Darrow, the lead attorney for Scopes, asked them to convict Scopes; the reason was because they had tried during the trial to get the trial court to declare the law unconstitutional. When they failed at that, they wanted a conviction for Scopes. The last thing they wanted was jury nullification because they wanted to test the law.

Flatow: Right.

Larson: And the only way they could appeal the law on up to get it tested in the Tennessee Supreme Court and then maybe the United States Supreme Court was to get a conviction. So he asked them to convict Scopes. They never challenged whether or not Scopes had ever taught evolution. He actually hadn't. That's why he could never take the stand, because he hadn't taught it. But they sort of conceded that. They tried to concede it. And they had a couple of schoolchildren who went on the stand, and the only reason they could testify honestly that Scopes had taught them evolution was that they took the kids out in a car during the preparation for the trial, and had Scopes tell them about evolution in the car, so they could say, "Yeah, he taught us about evolution."

Flatow: This whole thing was just a show trial. I mean . . .

Larson: Yes, it was a show.

Flatow: Your defense lawyer asks the jury to convict your client.

Larson: And the prosecutor, William Jennings Bryan, had offered to pay the fine.

Flatow: You make up some way that the teacher in a car could make believe he's teaching so he could be then convicted of something you want him to be convicted of.

Larson: They wanted to test the law. What the ACLU wanted to try, wanted to put on trial, was not John Scopes. They wanted to put the law on trial. And that's what they did.

Flatow: Yeah. All right. So the law's on trial. Did it have any practical effect, if they weren't teaching it, if the football coach wasn't even teaching it in school?

Larson: Well, it might have had practical effect. What actually happened in the history of the law was then it's appealed up to the Tennessee Supreme Court, which is a politically elected body. And William Jennings Bryan had died during this time in the intervening period. And so they made a deft political move. They upheld the statute, but they overturned Scopes's conviction on a technicality in sentencing, which wasn't even raised by either the defense, of course, because they didn't want it overturned on a technicality, so it was an issue that had not even been raised. They overturned it on their own motion on a technicality. And then went ahead on in their decision to direct the prosecutor not to reindict Scopes. And then they went on to direct all the prosecutors of the state, to quote, "save the peace and dignity of the state by never bringing an indictment under the statute ever again," and none ever was.

Flatow: So the whole debate sort of fell out of vogue after a while.

Larson: Yeah, it certainly fell out of law.

Flatow: Yeah.

Larson: It wasn't a legal issue. The antievolution laws did not get back to the courts until the 1960s. What would that be—thirty years later? And . . .

Flatow: Mm-hmm.

Larson: Probably adding that wrong. It's probably forty years later. And it didn't get back in until the interpretation of the Constitution had changed, and then those laws were struck down as unconstitutional under sort of a new reinterpretation of the application of the law. But it wasn't challenged as if it was enforced. The ACLU brought a declaratory judgment action against a similar law in Arkansas, so the antievolution laws are now unconstitutional, but it wasn't directly because of Scopes.

Flatow: And was it the movie that brought it back, *Inherit the Wind,* in the . . . ?

Larson: Actually, what brought it back was Scopes's autobiography. In 1965, I believe it was, Scopes wrote his autobiography. That would be five years after the movie, ten years after the play. And the autobiography raised the whole issue again. And one of the newspapers in Tennessee, in Memphis, sort of picked up the issue, as sort of in honor of Scopes, let's get this statute repealed, and that got the whole thing churning again. And Tennessee repealed its statute, and Arkansas took its statute to court, and that was the end of them. Otherwise people had pretty well forgotten about the law even existed.

Flatow: Yeah. Will you stay with us? Because I want to bring on a couple more guests.

Larson: I'd be happy to.

Scopes Trial 75th Anniversary, Part 2

Correction: This published transcript incorrectly attributes some remarks to Ed Larson that were actually made by Ken Miller.

Flatow: Now joining me to talk some more about the theory of evolution and maybe how it should be taught in schools are my next guests. Kenneth Miller is a cell biologist and professor of biology at Brown. He's author of *Finding Darwin's God: A Scientist's Search for Common Ground between God and Evolution,* published by HarperCollins. He joins us by phone from Providence.

Thank you for being with us, Dr. Miller.

Dr. Kenneth Miller (biologist; professor, Brown University; author, *Finding Darwin's God*): You're welcome. Happy to be here.

Flatow: You're welcome. You're welcome.

Michael Behe is a professor of biochemistry at Lehigh University in Bethlehem, Pennsylvania. He's also a fellow at the Center for the Renewal of Science and Culture at the Discovery Institute. He's author of *Darwin's Black Box: The Biochemical Challenge to Evolution,* published by Free Press. And he joins us by phone from his office.

Thank you for joining us, Dr. Behe.

Dr. Michael Behe (professor, Lehigh University; Discovery Institute; author, *Darwin's Black Box*): Yeah, glad to be with you.

Flatow: You state, Dr. Behe, you have written many articles in which you started out believing in the theory of evolution as being able to explain everything, but now you're not a believer in it anymore.

Behe: That's right. I was always taught evolution in the schools, and I accepted it because, you know, why not? My teachers knew more than I did. But when I started to investigate it, because I was prompted, I read a book that was skeptical of evolution by a scientist named Michael Denton. When I looked, I noticed a large number of problems. And let me just kind of give you a gist of it.

In the twentieth century, science has discovered that in the cell, which was thought to be kind of a glob of protoplasm by scientists in the nineteenth century, that the cell is run by extremely complicated molecular machines. And many of them are what I call "irreducibly complex." And a good example from our everyday world of irreducible complexity is a mousetrap. You've got a mousetrap you buy at the store has a number of parts. It's got a wooden base and a spring and hammer, and so on. And if you take any of those parts away, then the thing doesn't work. And it's hard to envision how that would be put together in a gradual manner as Darwinian evolution would require.

And a good example of that in biochemistry is something called the bacterial flagellum. And a flagellum is quite literally an outboard motor that bacteria use to swim, and it's got many different parts, like the propeller and the drive shaft and the hook region. And kind of like the mousetrap, if you take any of the parts away, the flagellum just doesn't work. And so because of its irreducibility, I've argued that the flagellum is better explained not as the result of natural selection, but it and other molecular machines are better explained as the result of purposeful intelligent design.

Flatow: And who would that purposeful, intelligent design belong to?

Behe: Who's the designer?

Flatow: Yeah.

Behe: Well, certainly, I'm a Roman Catholic, a Christian; I certainly would think that the designer is God, and probably most people would. But that conclusion is not forced by coming to the conclusion of intelligent design. You know, somebody else might think it was some New Age force or a space alien or something like that. Certainly, those things strike us as strange, but the point is that the idea of intelligent design is an idea that comes straight from the evidence, from things like the molecular machines in the cell, and it does not force a supernatural conclusion.

Flatow: Dr. Miller, you spend a lot of time in your book *Finding Darwin's God* in refuting a lot of Dr. Behe's theories, especially this cell theory.

Miller: Yeah. No, that's exactly right. And I have to say, you know, for want of affiliation, Michael and I are both Roman Catholics, and, you know, I would be as delighted as anybody else to look at the inside of a cell, and I don't know how else to describe it, to find God's fingerprints there in something that you could win souls for. But I find Dr. Behe's ideas interesting, and I think they're provocative, and I think he has really done a great service to the scientific community in terms of jostling people around and saying, "Come on, you folks. If you want to argue for evolution, you ought to come up with explanations for some of these things." And I think that's a valuable service.

But I also think, fundamentally, he's mistaken. And the way in which I've tried to show that is really pretty straightforward. The first thing is that Mike is absolutely right that the cell is filled with complex biochemical machines, and boy, is it ever. And we discover more all the time. But it turns out he's actually not right when he says that you cannot explain the evolution of these things by Darwinian mechanisms, and there are actually quite a few papers that have appeared in the literature in the last couple of years that have done exactly that. The other thing that I think is significant is Dr. Behe says the reason that Darwinian evolutionary biology cannot explain the evolution of complex systems is that every one of these systems, these little machines, is irreducibly complex. And what is meant by that, of course, as you just heard, is if you take a part away, it doesn't work anymore. And since natural selection can only work on the whole machine, therefore, it can't explain its evolution.

But the interesting thing about that is, if you actually look at a couple of those machines and he, for example, uses the eukaryotic cilium, which is also sort of like a little propulsion device, as an example of irreducible complexity. When you look around in nature, you actually find cilia and flagella that are missing one part or two parts or three parts and are still fully functional. And the interesting thing about the mousetrap, the mousetrap requires five parts, and if you take a part away, it doesn't work. There actually are ways to make a mousetrap work with four or three or even fewer parts, but what's really relevant and what really matters in terms of the analogy is there are parts of the mousetrap, such as the spring and the base plate and so forth, which can be useful for other functions; in other words, useful as a paper clip, as a joke once. The last time Dr. Behe and I shared a platform, I used three of the five parts of a mousetrap as a tie clip.

And actually, that's pretty much how cells evolve complex biochemical systems, is their parts, and partial assemblies of their parts are useful for other functions, and that's how evolution produces them.

Larson: If I could hop in there.

Flatow: Sure.

Behe: Ken Miller's discussion of the mousetrap is interesting because he takes it from a Web page by Professor John MacDonald at the University of Delaware. And on his Web page, Professor MacDonald says specifically that these mousetraps are not intended as analogies of how evolution works. What happens is that one can make mousetraps with different numbers of parts, but one has to intelligently manipulate the parts, bend them, put them in the right position and so on. They're examples of intelligent design rather than examples of how Darwinian evolution would work.

Miller: Yes, but . . .

Behe: Now, Ken, I'm sorry. I'll just . . .

Flatow: Go ahead.

Behe: . . . take a short time. Ken and I can go around and around on this, but I'd like to issue a friendly challenge. Now in his book, Ken says, on page 108, after discussing micro evolution, he says that no principle of biochemistry or molecular biology would prevent natural selection from, quote, "redesigning dozens or hundreds of genes over a few weeks or months," close quote. Now that bacterial flagellum I talked about has only about thirty or forty genes, not dozens or not hundreds. So here's the challenge: Let Ken go into the lab, using molecular biology techniques, knock out the genes for the flagellum, and instead of just two months, let's give him two years. See if in two years the bacterium can reevolve a flagellum. And if it can do that, I promise publicly to renounce my view. And if it doesn't, I would ask Ken to say publicly just that he thinks intelligent design is an idea worth investigating. How's that sound, Ken?

Miller: Well, it's an interesting challenge because for the very simple reason that it flies in the face of what we actually understand about evolution, and that is that the evolution of the bacterial flagellum was a process that took place probably about three billion years ago. And what you're asking anyone who takes up the challenge to do is to go into a laboratory and allow a series of events, many of which were undetermined, meaning you don't know how they're going to come out, to suddenly reoccur again. And we know from evolution if you take cultures of bacteria that start out identical and put them in different flasks under identical conditions, they will evolve in different directions in those different flasks. So you're asking for the outcome of an experiment that is essentially unrepeatable to be repeated, and, unfortunately, that's not going to work.

Behe: Well, I understand why you're reluctant, but to somebody like me, who's skeptical of evolution, let me try to explain why, you know, I find such explanations unconvincing. Recently, a couple months ago, a man named Jerry Coyne, who's a prominent evolutionary biologist at the University of Chicago, wrote in the *New Republic* magazine. He said, quote, "In science's pecking order, evolutionary biology lurks somewhere near the bottom, far closer to phrenology than to physics."

And the reason why he was so hard on his own discipline is that he was reviewing a book called *A Natural History of Rape,* in which it was asserted that human rape is, quote, "a natural biological phenomenon that is a product of the human evolutionary heritage." And in the book, a couple of evolutionary biologists by the name of Randy Thornhill and Craig Palmer used evolutionary reasoning to try to show why they think that rape is, in fact, selected by evolution. And

Coyne was livid because he thought they were ignoring data, that their ideas were not testable and so on.

Well, to many of us, such as myself, the excuses that evolutionary biologists give for avoiding testing their theory are essentially the same flaws that Coyne sees in Thornhill and Palmer's book, that "just so" stories are easy to make up. You can make them up for why rape is adaptive, why bacterial flagellum could be put together, and so on. But nobody seems to test them.

Miller: Yes, but that's right, and I have to tell you . . .

Flatow: Wait, wait. Let me. . . . I have to interrupt. Wait, hang on, and remind everybody that I'm Ira Flatow and this is *Talk of the Nation/Science Friday* from National Public Radio, talking with Dr. Kenneth Miller and Dr. Michael Behe, and also with Ed Larson. We're talking about the seventy-fifth anniversary of the Scopes trial and kept the debate continuing here. Who was interrupting whom at that point? I want to . . .

Miller: I think we both were, but I have to say . . .

Flatow: OK.

Miller: . . . that I completely concur with Coyne's criticism of the book that you brought up. I think the people who wrote that book took a few areas of behavioral ecology, and they simply extrapolated them beyond any reason. And, in fact, very often people in the scientific field will go off on a tangent, and an unjustified tangent, and that's really exactly what these people did. But the real key thing—and Professor Behe, for example, asked for experimental evidence—is that the very premise of what he argues has not been persuasive within the scientific community. And the reason that very premise has not been persuasive is for the very simple reason that there are examples in the scientific literature of the thing he says does not exist. And I'll give you an example, and I think many of your listeners will resonate with this.

For anybody who took high school biology or Bio 101 in college, I dare say one of the least favorite parts of the course very often is the Krebs cycle. When I teach freshman biology at Brown, my students dread a couple of lectures on the Krebs cycle, even though I try to make them as exciting and invigorating as possible. And the reason for that is the Krebs cycle, which is the heart of metabolism, is a very complex biochemical system. It has nine enzymes, four cofactors; every part has to be put together for it to work properly. It's exactly the sort of thing that Professor Behe says evolution cannot explain, but interestingly, in the very same year that his book appeared, a very good explanation of the step-by-step Darwinian evolution of the Krebs cycle appeared, and it's been followed up with a couple other papers that have appeared, one last year, exploring the same area.

Mike's book has been noticed within the scientific community. It was reviewed in *American Scientist*; it was reviewed in *Nature*. I would encourage Dr. Behe to come to scientific meetings and sort of . . .

Flatow: OK.

Miller: . . . slug it out with informed audience.

Flatow: Dr. Miller, I have to interrupt one more time and take a quick break, and we'll come and slug it out a little bit more among ourselves here. So don't go away. We'll be right back after this short break.

I'm Ira Flatow and this is *Talk of the Nation/Science Friday* from National Public Radio.

(*Announcements*)

Flatow: Welcome back to *Talk of the Nation/Science Friday*. I'm Ira Flatow.

A brief program note: Join Juan Williams and his guests on Monday in this hour for a look at why the romance novel still persists. Who reads romance novels? The answer might surprise you.

We're talking this hour on *Science Friday* about the Scopes trial and the teaching of evolution in this country with my guests. Michael Behe is professor of biochemistry at Lehigh and author of *Darwin's Black Box: The Biochemical Challenge to Evolution*, published by the Free Press. Kenneth Miller, professor of biology at Brown and author of *Finding Darwin's God: A Scientist's Search for Common Ground Between God and Evolution*, published by HarperCollins. Ed Larson, professor of history and law and author of *Summer for the Gods* published by Harvard University Press.

Ed Larson, have we heard this debate before? This isn't the first time intelligent design theory has been suggested as an alternative to Darwinism, is it?

Larson: No, it's not. From the very beginning, the issue of what you could call intelligent design, the issue of irreducible complexity, was raised against Darwinism. Louie Agassiz raised it in arguments about complex ecological relationships; how could ecologically dependent beings evolve separately? He, of course, was the great zoologist at Harvard. And you had Richard Owen, the great anatomist in England, probably the greatest in the world, doing it about organs like, in fact, Darwin was so struck by these arguments that he once called the eye, which is a complex organism, the antidote to atheism, he referred to it in one of his letters.

Despite these arguments that have been raised, the vast majority of scientists came to accept Darwinism, not necessarily on these issues but because how it explained other phenomenons in science, such as the fossil record or the geographical distribution of animals. But the issue's always been there, and what Professor Behe has done, as has been said even by his opponent—on this show he has raised it again—bringing in a new variety of so-called designed organisms. So it's an old argument, but appearing in new ways and raising new issues. And it has sharpened the debate quite a bit.

Flatow: OK. Let me go to the phones, to Garrett in St. Louis. Hi, Garrett.

Garrett (caller): Ira, thank you so much for taking my call. This is a topic that has haunted me for about fifteen years, and I can get very verbose on this topic, so if I wear out my welcome, just shut me up.

Flatow: We've only got about fifteen minutes left, so . . .

Garrett: Real quickly, I'll boil it down to two points. Most importantly, I want to express my appreciation to Dr. Miller and his book *Finding Darwin's God*. I am a physiologist, and I've been a Christian for about two years, despite the fact that I accept evolution as valid. And it's nice to know that someone besides myself is a Christian who accepts evolution and is trying to resolve this apparent conflict.

And secondly, I'd like to point out that the creationists, with their ludicrous arguments, are the reason that I stayed away from God for so very long. I'm not sure that the creationists realize how much damage they're doing to Christianity. For years I felt like I would have to commit intellectual suicide if I became a Christian, and I wonder how many other scientists are being kept away from God because of creationists' arguments?

Behe: Can I just pop in? I know he's admiring Ken's book.

Garrett: And yours, too, Dr. Behe. I've read that one, too.

Behe: Oh, well, thanks very much. I'd just like to say that I agree with you. I agree with Ken. Ken and I, I think, are as one on this. I don't think I believe that, you know, one can certainly believe in God and believe that evolution is true, even evolution by natural selection. The question is, is it a true scientific theory? And my contention is solely based on the scientific evidence. I just don't think that when you look at these irreducibly complex molecular machines that natural selection is a sufficient mechanism to explain them. But I certainly agree, and I would urge listeners to clear up in their own minds that this debate, at least between Ken and myself, is not over religion, not over whether one can believe in God or not, but rather, it's over a scientific point of whether natural selection is true.

Flatow: Well, if it is a scientific point, then why not publish your theories and your ideas in scientific journals, in *Science* and *Nature,* wherever there's, you know, accepted scientific journals, and how to test it in the world of science?

Behe: Well, it has been tested in the world of science. I published a book by the Free Press, but . . .

Flatow: Well, but, you know, these are not books, not peer-review journals.

Behe: That's right, but they are reviewed by scientists. The Free Press sent my book out to a half-dozen scientists, more scientists than generally review a paper, for their comments and criticism. All of the work that I have in my book is taken from the peer-review literature. I didn't introduce any new scientific fact.

Flatow: So then why not publish it with, you know, the body of other scientific literature, in a peer review journal?

Behe: Well, because when you're bringing up a new and controversial idea, you need a lot of space to develop that idea.

Miller: Well, as long as I have Mike on the air, let me ask him something, and I think Ira would be interested in this. And I very much appreciate Garrett's comments. Thank you, Garrett. Mike is,

I believe, a member of the American Society for Biochemistry and Molecular Biology. Is that right, Mike?

Behe: I sure am. Yeah.

Miller: Absolutely. And I'm a member of the American Society for Cell Biology. So here's the deal I'll make you. I propose that the two of us write a joint letter to the presidents of those two societies, asking either of them to host or both of them to host, at their respective annual meetings, in front of a scientific audience, a one-on-one debate either between you and me or between you, Mike, and another opponent, another evolutionist favored by the president of either society. Because that's really, I think, where this debate should be thrashed out. Would you agree to that?

Behe: Oh, I accept it. Sure. That, I'd say, I would be delighted. Yeah.

Miller: It's a deal. Great.

Behe: I debated this topic over at the Royal Society of Medicine in London just a couple months ago, and I gave a lecture to the Biochemistry Department at the Mayo Clinic, oh, six months or so ago. I am delighted to bring my ideas in front of scientists.

Flatow: Let me . . .

Miller: I think we'll have an easier time getting together than Gore and Bush will.

Flatow: Let me take it one step further, Dr. Behe. Where do you believe it belongs in public schools?

Behe: In public schools?

Flatow: Yeah. Where does this debate belong in public schools?

Behe: Well, that's a whole other question. It has overtones of politics and parental involvement and government and things like that, but I think, first of all, that, certainly, Darwinian evolution should be taught. It explains a number of things quite well.

Flatow: In biology class with evolution?

Behe: I'm sorry?

Flatow: With biology class?

Behe: Sure. Sure.

Flatow: In the same class.

Behe: Yeah, sure. Darwinian evolution should be taught in biology class. And I also think that . . .

Flatow: No, no, your idea of intelligent design . . .

Behe: Oh, my idea.

Flatow: . . . should that be taught with Darwinian evolution in biology class?

Behe: I think it should. I think it should at least be introduced because there are a number of problems that Darwinian biology has, which I think that intelligent design is a good answer for, and if you look at public sentiment, now we talk about peer review. When we go into public schools, the jury of our peers is the public. And if you look at the public, the public clearly wants alternatives to Darwinian evolution taught in schools, and I think . . .

Larson: Ira, if I may . . .

Flatow: Yes.

Larson: One of the things that's interesting about this is, first of all, I would agree, as a matter of academic freedom, that teachers should be free to teach anything, bring in any evidence that they want with respect to any scientific or historical or cultural or social theory. I think that's a good idea. But the interesting thing, and I'm not talking about Professor Behe personally, but the interesting thing about other people who are opponents of evolution is that they generally haven't settled for that route. What they've usually done is to try to do an end run around the scientific community and appeal to agencies of government to insert their ideas in the curriculum. And examples of that are the creation science laws that were passed in Louisiana and Arkansas before they were invalidated by the courts, and most recently going around the scientific community to try to get boards of education in various states, notably Kansas, to sort of remove evolution, and also the age of the Earth from Earth science curriculum, and the big bang from cosmology and so forth.

Behe: Well, I think it's also true that Darwinists do the same thing. For example . . .

Larson: I don't think so, and I'd be happy to say why.

Behe: OK. Well, you can say it right after I'm done. That the Darwinists have control of many of the governmental institutions which set science standards, and they are using them, in my opinion, to push science textbooks to say things in favor of Darwinism which the scientific literature does not support. For example, in the recent Science Standards sent out by the National Academy of Sciences, they clearly want the discussion of the origin of life, which everybody admits is a wide-open question, to be discussed solely in terms of the undirected chemical reactions of elements that might have been present on the early Earth. And even many scientists, such as Paul Davies, who wrote a book on this recently, think that entirely new ideas have to be introduced here. But nonetheless, Darwinists want discussion to be confined just to their preferred answers. But if a question is open, then it's not legitimate to try to limit the discussion to any one point of view.

Flatow: But is the answer "God did it" you know, the simple answer "God did it" as opposition to scientific method, does that belong in a biology class? You know?

Behe: No. Well, of course not. And I didn't say that one should insert something that says, "God did it." You point out the fact that life is information rich, that every organism we know of has coded information; that information has to be translated by a genetic code, and that from what we currently know, there is no physical process that could produce that code.

Flatow: All right. Let me remind everybody that this is *Talk of the Nation/Science Friday* from National Public Radio. Ken Miller . . .

Miller: Ira, I certainly don't subscribe to the view that the reason that evolution is taught in classrooms is because of a conspiracy of Darwinists at high levels. I think the reason for that is actually pretty simple, and that is when you teach science, when you look to put together a science curriculum, what do you teach? You teach the scientific consensus. You teach what is general, and I'm not talking bureaucrats; I'm talking about the mass of people in the wide-open, freewheeling scientific community.

And just to give you one very quick example, and you've talked about this a lot on your program, there is an alternative theory for what causes AIDS. It's advanced by Peter Duesberg and several other scientists. What do we teach in the classroom? Well, all science should be taught skeptically, but in general, we tell students the consensus view, which is that AIDS is an infectious disease that is caused by a virus that we call HIV that is transmitted from person to person. Now Duesberg might say the establishment is in control, but Duesberg, in my opinion, has done the right thing, which is he's behaved like a scientist. He's tried to win the scientific battle. With very few exceptions, intelligent-design people have done a step around the scientific community, and they've gone directly to agencies of government without trying to win the battle of ideas. And I think that's the way they should be.

Behe: Well, that's clearly not true. If you . . .

Miller: And that's the reason I'd like to debate Mike.

Behe: That's clearly not true. We have published a number of books outlining our ideas.

Miller: That's not the same thing.

Behe: And I agree with you that, in general, a consensus view could be taught, but in this particular instance, the public smells a rat. They think that the arguments are being stacked in favor of a theory that does not have the evidential support that the Darwinists claim it has, and they want to see something different.

Flatow: Ed Larson, can you teach it, is it legal to teach it in classrooms now?

Larson: Well, we have clear decisions, as Dr. Miller has pointed out, we have clear decisions saying that creation science, because the court has ruled that that is a form of religious instruction or religious belief, religious dogma cannot be taught in public schools. We also have rulings that would raise severe questions of whether a board of education could direct that creation science or something other than evolution be taught. Where the interesting question would arise, and this is where I think the issue sort of joined, is making this a scientific debate. If an individual science teacher chose to teach objections to Darwinism in a pedagogically sound method, not as a way to promote religion but reflecting his own views of science.

Flatow: All right.

Larson: Then we have court rulings that suggest that that would be appropriate.

Flatow: All right. We've run out of time. We're going to pick this up, you can be sure, later on and talk more about this. And I have to thank my guests this hour: Ed Larson, professor of history and law and author of *Summer for the Gods,* published by Harvard University Press; Dr. Michael Behe, professor of biochemistry at Lehigh and author of *Darwin's Black Box: The Biochemical Challenge to Evolution,* published by the Free Press; Dr. Kenneth Miller, professor of biology at Brown and author of *Finding Darwin's God: A Scientist's Search for Common Ground between God and Evolution,* published by HarperCollins and due out in paperback in October.

Thank you, gentlemen, for joining us this hour.

Larson: Thank you, Ira.

Miller: My pleasure.

Flatow: You're welcome.

(Credits)

Flatow: If you have comments or questions, write to us: *Talk of the Nation/Science Friday,* WNYC Radio, One Center Street, New York, New York 10007. If you missed any of the links, you can surf over to our Web site at sciencefriday.com.

I'm Ira Flatow. Have a great weekend. I'm in New York.

Science Friday is a science and technology news-talk radio program produced by Samanna Productions, in association with NPR member station WNYC New York.

APPENDIX B

"The View from 2025: How Design Beat Darwin," Reprinted from *World* magazine, April 3, 2004

WORLD ASKED FOUR LEADERS of the intelligent design movement to have some fun: Imagine writing in 2025, on the one hundredth anniversary of the famous Scopes monkey trial, and explain how Darwinism has bit the dust, unable to rebut the evidence that what we see around us could not have arisen merely by time plus change. Our fanciful historians are:

- Phillip Johnson, *World*'s Daniel of the Year for 2003, is a law professor at the University of California at Berkeley and the author of *Darwin on Trial* (1991) and many other books, including *Defeating Darwinism by Opening Minds, Reason in the Balance, The Wedge of Truth,* and *The Right Questions.*
- Jonathan Wells, a senior fellow at the Discovery Institute and the author of *Icons of Evolution* (2000). Mr. Wells received both a Ph.D. in biology from the University of California at Berkeley and a Ph.D. in theology from Yale University.
- William Dembski, associate research professor at Baylor and a senior fellow of the Discovery Institute. Mr. Dembski received a Ph.D. in mathematics and a Ph.D. in philosophy from the

University of Chicago and is the author of, among other books, *The Design Inference* (1998) and *The Design Revolution* (2004).
- Dr. Jeffrey M. Schwartz, research professor of psychiatry at the UCLA School of Medicine, is the author of more than one hundred scientific publications in the fields of neuroscience and psychiatry. His latest book is *The Mind and the Brain* (released in paperback last year).

The Demise of Naturalism

By Phillip Johnson

In 1980, astronomer Carl Sagan commenced the influential National Public Television series *Cosmos,* by announcing its theme. "The cosmos is all there is, ever was, or ever will be." Sagan's mantra was spoken more than twenty years before the landmark Santorum Amendment to the Federal Education Act of 2001 encouraged science educators to teach students to distinguish between testable scientific theories and philosophical claims that are made in the name of science.

In those unsophisticated pre-Santorum years, celebrity scientists like Sagan freely promoted a dogmatic naturalistic philosophy as if it were a fact that had been discovered by scientific investigation, just as previous generations of celebrities had promoted racism, class warfare, and Freudian fantasy in the name of science. The celebrities felt themselves free to ignore both evidence and logic because the approval of the rulers of science, who had a vested interest in persuading the public to adopt a philosophy that maximized their own influence, was all that was needed to induce the media to report an ideological dogma as a scientific conclusion.

Millions of schoolchildren and credulous adults were led to accept the voice of Sagan as the voice of science and thus to believe that scientists had proved that God does not exist, or at least is irrelevant to our lives. In brief, the message of this government-promoted television series was that philosophical naturalism and science are one and the same. The series did contain scientific information, much of it inaccurate or misleading, but primarily it was an appeal to the imagination, promoting the worship of science and the adventurous vision of exploring the universe.

The perennially popular *Star Trek* television series further conditioned the youth of America to dream of a technological utopia in which disease and distance were conquered and the great adventure of mankind was to explore the many inhabited planets supposedly existing throughout the universe. Throughout the second half of the twentieth century, which we now know as the "century of scientism," the popular media relentlessly pursued the theme that liberation and fulfillment are to be found through technology, with the attendant implication that the supernatural Creator revealed in the Bible is a superfluous and obsolete entity doomed to expire from terminal irrelevance.

Social scientists further affirmed this myth with their secularization thesis, which predicted that supernatural religion would steadily lose adherents throughout the world as public education enlightened the multitudes, and as people came to see scientific technology as the only route to health, happiness, and longevity. Problems such as pollution and warfare were acknowledged, but these too could be mastered if we insisted that our politicians heed the advice of the ruling scientists.

The cultural path that led to this apotheosis of scientific naturalism began just after the middle of the twentieth century, with the triumphalist Darwin Centennial Celebration in 1959 and the 1960 film *Inherit the Wind*, a stunning but thoroughly fictionalized dramatization of the Scopes trial of 1925. The real Scopes trial was a publicity stunt staged by the ACLU, but Broadway and Hollywood converted it to a morality play about religious persecution in which the crafty criminal defense lawyer Clarence Darrow made a monkey of the creationist politician William Jennings Bryan and in the process taught the movie-going public to see Christian ministers as ignorant oppressors and Darwinist science teachers as heroic truth-seekers. As the twentieth century came to an end, science and history teachers were still showing *Inherit the Wind* to their classes as if it were a fair portrayal of what had happened in Dayton, Tennessee, in 1925.

Superficially, it seemed that scientific naturalism was everywhere triumphant at the start of the twenty-first century. Scientific rationalists were nonetheless uneasy, for two reasons. First, literary intellectuals had pushed naturalism to the limits of its logic and drawn the conclusion that, since an uncreated nature is indifferent to good and evil, all values are merely subjective, including even the value of science. It seemed to follow that nothing is forbidden, and pleasure can be pursued without limit. Both highbrow literature and popular entertainment became strongly nihilistic, scorning all universal standards of truth, morality, or reason.

Second, public opinion polls showed that a clear majority of the American public still believed that God is our Creator despite the heavy-handed indoctrination in evolutionary naturalism to which they had been subjected for several decades in textbooks, television documentaries, and museum exhibits. The seemingly solid wall of Darwinian orthodoxy was crumbling under the pressures described in the accompanying article by Jonathan Wells.

Naturalism was losing its essential scientific backing, and then it also suddenly lost its hold on the popular and literary imagination, as the American public tired of nihilism and began to count the cost of all that had been destroyed during the century of scientism. New historical scholarship reflected in a stunning PBS television documentary exposed the *Inherit the Wind* portrayal of the Scopes trial as a hoax, kicking off an era of historical revisionism in which book after scholarly book exposed how propaganda techniques had been employed to create a mythology of inevitable progress toward naturalism, similar to the governing mythology of the Soviet Union, which had proclaimed the inevitable replacement of capitalism by communism.

The collapse of the Soviet Union put an end to the Soviet myth, just as the scientific collapse of Darwinism, preceded as it was by the discrediting of Marxism and Freudianism, prepared the way for the culture to turn aside from the mythology of naturalism to rediscover the buried treasure that the mythology had been concealing. A hilarious Broadway comedy, titled *Inherit the Baloney,* enacted a sort of Scopes Trial in reverse, with the hero a courageous Christian college professor badgered incessantly by dim-witted colleagues and deans who keep telling him that the only way to preserve his faith in a postmodern world is to jettison all the exclusivist truth claims: they wanted him to admit that Jesus was sorely in need of sensitivity training from some wise counselor like Pontius Pilate because "nobody can surf the Web every day and still believe that there is such a thing as truth or goodness." Overnight the tendency of naturalistic rationalism to decay into postmodern irrationalism became a national joke.

Then the rise of Islamic extremism at the start of the new century came just as scholars and journalists were finally taking notice of the rapid spread of active, vibrant Christian faith in Africa, South America, and Asia, especially China. The secularization thesis was consistent with the facts only in a few parts of the world where long-established Christian churches had succumbed to complacency and the slow poison of naturalism. Where life was hardest and persecution frequent, the flame of faith burned brighter than ever. For those with a global outlook, the question was not whether God was still important in our lives but rather, What does God want us to do? Once Darwinism had joined Marxism and Freudianism in the dust bin of history, the entire world seemed new and full of exciting possibilities.

The crucial turning point in America came in the year 2004. In that year the "same sex marriage" explosion, abetted by public officials, brought to public attention the extent to which long-settled understandings of law and morality had been undermined as judges, mayors, and citizens internalized the nihilistic moral implications of naturalistic philosophy. That same year, with the spectacular success of two great movies, *The Return of the King* and *The Passion of the Christ,* it became clear that the public was hungering for art and entertainment that affirmed traditional values rather than flouting them. Surprise: the Bible still provided, as it had for many centuries, the indispensable starting point for the artistic imagination.

Artists and humanities scholars recognized that the human imagination had been stunted by blind adherence to a philosophy that denied the artist or poet any sense of the divine power that gives meaning to the realm of nature. As sanity reasserted itself, even the secular intellectuals saw that the fact of creation provides the essential foundation not only for the artistic imagination, but even for the scientific imagination, because science itself makes no sense if the scientific mind is itself no more than the product of irrational material forces.

As that insight spread, naturalism became yesteryear's fashion in thought, and the world moved forward to the more realistic understanding of the human condition that we in 2025 now take for granted. Only the fool says that there is no God or that God has forgotten us. Folly like that is as dead today as the discredited *Inherit the Wind* stereotype, which fit the facts of history no better than the secularization thesis. We no longer expect to meet intelligent beings on other planets, for we have learned how uniquely fitted to shelter life our own planet has been created to be. Now we have a much more exciting adventure. We can dedicate our minds and our courage to sharing the truth that makes us free.

Whatever Happened to Evolutionary Theory?

By Jonathan Wells

In 1973, geneticist Theodosius Dobzhansky wrote: "Nothing in biology makes sense except in the light of evolution." By *evolution*, he meant the synthesis of Charles Darwin's nineteenth-century theory that all living things have descended from a common ancestor through natural selection and random variations, and the twentieth-century theory that new variations are produced by mutations in DNA. By 2000, the biological sciences had become almost totally dominated by this view. Millions of students were taught that Darwinian evolution was a simple fact, like gravity. Oxford professor Richard Dawkins even proclaimed that anyone who doubted it must be ignorant, stupid, insane, or wicked.

Now, a mere quarter of a century later, Darwinian evolution is little more than a historical footnote in biology textbooks. Just as students learn that scientists used to believe that the sun moves around the Earth and maggots are spontaneously generated in rotting meat, so students also learn that scientists used to believe that human beings evolved through random mutations and natural selection. How could a belief that was so influential in 2000 become so obsolete by 2025? Whatever happened to evolutionary theory?

Surprising though it may seem, Darwinism did not collapse because it was disproved by new evidence. (As we shall see, the evidence never really fit it anyway.) Instead, evolutionary theory was knocked off its pedestal by three developments in the first decade of this century—developments centered in the United States but worldwide in scope. Those developments were: (1) the widespread adoption of a "teach the controversy" approach in education, (2) a growing public awareness of the scientific weaknesses of evolutionary theory, and (3) the rise of the more fruitful "theory of intelligent design."

The first development was a reaction to late twentieth-century efforts by dogmatic Darwinists to make evolutionary theory the exclusive framework for biology curricula in American public schools. Biology classrooms became platforms for indoctrinating students in Darwinism and its underlying philosophy of naturalism—the antireligious view that nature is all there is and God is an illusion. In the ensuing public backlash, some people demanded that evolution be removed from the curriculum entirely. A larger number of people, however, favored a "teach the controversy" approach that presented students with the evidence against evolutionary theory as well as the evidence for it.

The U.S. Congress implicitly endorsed this approach in its No Child Left Behind Act of 2001. A report accompanying the legislation stated that students should learn "to distinguish the data and testable theories of science from religious or philosophical claims that are made in the name of science," and that students should "understand the full range of scientific views that exist" with regard to biological evolution. Despite loud protests and threats of lawsuits from the Darwinists, hundreds of state and local school boards across America had adopted a "teach the controversy" approach by 2005.

In the second major development, students who were free to examine the evidence for and against evolution quickly realized that the former was surprisingly thin. Although Darwinists had long boasted about having "overwhelming evidence" for their view, it turned out that they had no good evidence for the theory's principal claim: that species originate through random mutation and natural selection. Bacteria were the best place to look for such evidence because they reproduce quickly, their DNA can be easily mutated, and they can be subjected to strong selection in the laboratory. Yet bacteria had been intensively studied throughout the twentieth century, and bacteriologists had never observed the formation of a new species.

If there was no good evidence that a Darwinian mechanism could produce new species, still less was there any evidence that a Darwinian mechanism could produce complex organs or new anatomical features. Darwinists discounted the problem by arguing that evolution was too slow to observe, but this didn't change the fact that they lacked empirical confirmation for their theory.

Of course, there was plenty of evidence for minor changes in existing species, but nobody had ever doubted that existing species can change over time. Domestic breeders had been observing such changes—and even producing them—for centuries. Unfortunately, this was not the sort of evidence that evolution needed. After all, the main point of evolutionary theory was not how selection and mutation could change existing species but how that mechanism could produce *new* species—indeed, *all* species after the first—as well as new organs and new body plans. That's why Darwin titled his magnum opus *The Origin of Species,* not *How Existing Species Change over Time.*

A growing number of people realized that the "overwhelming evidence" for evolutionary theory was a myth. It didn't help the Darwinists when it became public knowledge that they had faked some of their most widely advertised evidence. For example, they had distorted drawings of early embryos to make them look more similar than they really are (in order to convince students that they had descended from a common ancestor), and they had staged photos showing peppered moths on tree trunks where they don't normally rest (in order to persuade students of the power of natural selection).

In the first few years of this century, the cultural dominance of Darwinism was so strong, especially in academia, that critics were slow to speak up. By 2009, however, when Darwin's followers had hoped to stage a triumphal celebration of their leader's two hundredth birthday, millions of people were laughing at the emperor with no clothes.

The third and perhaps most decisive development was a series of breakthroughs in biology and medicine inspired by the new theory of intelligent design. Everyone, even the Darwinists, agreed that living things look as though they were designed. Darwinists insisted that this was merely an illusion, produced by the combined action of random mutation and natural selection; but design theorists argued that the design was real. For years the controversy remained largely philosophical; then, in the first decade of this century, a few researchers began applying intelligent design theory to solving specific biological problems.

One of these was the function of so-called "junk DNA." From a Darwinian perspective, "genes" were thought to determine all the important characteristics of an organism, and gene mutations were thought to provide the raw materials for evolution. When molecular biologists in the third quarter of the twentieth century discovered that certain regions of DNA encode proteins that determine some of the characteristics of living cells and equated these with genes, Darwinists assumed that their theory was complete. They even proclaimed DNA to be "the secret of life."

Yet molecular biologists learned in the 1970s that less than 5 percent of human DNA encodes proteins. Darwinists immediately declared the other 95 percent "junk," molecular accidents that had accumulated in the course of evolution. Since few researchers were motivated (or funded) to investigate garbage, most human DNA was neglected for decades. Although biologists occasionally stumbled on functions for isolated pieces of "junk," they began to make real progress only after realizing that the DNA in an intelligently designed organism is unlikely to be 95 percent useless. The intensive research on noncoding regions of human DNA that followed soon led to several medically important discoveries.

Another insight from intelligent design theory advanced our understanding of embryo development. From a Darwinian perspective, all the information needed for new features acquired in the course of evolution came from genetic mutations. This implied that all essential biological information was encoded in DNA. In contrast, intelligent design theory implied that organisms are irreducibly complex systems in which DNA contains only part of the essential information. Although a few biologists had been arguing against DNA reductionism for decades, biologists guided by intelligent design theory in 2010 discovered the true nature of the information that guides embryo development.

All three of these developments—teaching the controversy, educating people about the lack of evidence for evolutionary theory, and using intelligent design theory to make progress in biomedical research—were bitterly resisted by Darwinists in the first decade of this century. Defenders of the Darwinian faith engaged in a vicious campaign of character assassination against their critics in the scientific community. Meanwhile, their allies in the news media conducted a massive disinformation campaign, aimed primarily at convincing the public that all critics of Darwinism were religious zealots.

More and more people saw through the lies, however, and within a few short years Darwinism had lost its scientific credibility and public funding. By 2015 it was well on its way to joining its intellectual cousins, Marxism and Freudianism, in the dust bin of discarded ideologies. By 2020, Darwinism was effectively dead.

The New Age of Information

By William Dembski

At the time of the Scopes trial, and for the remainder of the twentieth century, science was wedded to a materialistic conception of nature. The architects of modern science, from René Descartes to Isaac Newton, had proposed a world of unthinking material objects ruled by natural laws. Because these scientists were theists, the rule of natural law was for them not inviolable—God could, and from time to time did, invade the natural order, rearrange material objects, and even produce miracles of religious significance. But such divine acts were gratuitous insertions into a material world that was capable of carrying on quite nicely by itself.

In the end the world bequeathed to us by modern science became a world of unthinking material objects ruled by unbroken natural laws. With such a world, God did not, and indeed could not, interact coherently, much less intervene. Darwinian evolution, with its rejection of design and its unwavering commitment to purely material forces (such as natural selection), came to epitomize this materialist conception of science. If God played any role in the natural world, human inquiry could reveal nothing about it.

This materialist conception of the world came under pressure in the 1990s. Scientists started asking whether information might not be the fundamental entity underlying physical reality. For instance, mathematician Keith Devlin mused whether information could perhaps be regarded as "a basic property of the universe, alongside matter and energy (and being ultimately interconvertible with them)." Origin-of-life researchers like Manfred Eigen increasingly saw the problem of the origin of life as the problem of generating biologically significant information. And physicist Paul Davies speculated about information replacing matter as the "primary stuff," therewith envisioning the resolution of age-old problems, such as the mind-body problem. Thus he remarked, "If matter turns out to be a form of organized information, then consciousness may not be so mysterious after all."

Such speculations became serious scientific proposals in the first decade of this century as proponents of intelligent design increasingly clashed with Darwinian evolutionists. The irony here is that the very sorts of arguments that Darwinists had been using to try to discredit intelligent design and relegate it to the sphere of religion rather than science ended up discrediting Darwinian evolution itself and exposing its unscientific presuppositions.

To see how this happened, recall how exchanges between Darwinists and the early design theorists used to go. The design theorists would go to great lengths to analyze a given biological structure, show why it constituted an obstacle to Darwinian and other materialistic forms of evolution, and lay out how the structure in question exhibited clear marks of intelligence. To such carefully drawn lines of scientific argument and evidence, the Darwinist invariably offered stock responses, such as,

There you go with your religion again.
You're just substituting supernatural causes for natural causes.
You just haven't figured how evolution did it.
You're arguing from ignorance.
You're lazy; get back in the lab and figure out how evolution did it.

These responses were effective at cowing critics of Darwinism so long as the scientific community agreed with the Darwinists that science was about understanding the natural world solely in terms of unguided material processes or mechanisms. But in the first decade of this century, it became clear that this definition of science no longer worked. Science is, to be sure, about understanding the natural world. But science is not about understanding the natural world solely in terms of material processes.

The problem is that material processes, as understood by the Darwinists and most of the scientific community at the time, could not adequately explain the origin of biologically significant information. Darwinist Michael Ruse saw the problem clearly, though without appreciating its significance. Describing the state of origin-of-life research at the turn of the century, he remarked: "At the moment, the hand of human design and intention hangs heavily over everything, but work is going forward rapidly to create conditions in which molecules can make the right and needed steps without constant outside help. When that happens, . . . the dreaming stops and the fun begins."

Unfortunately for the Darwinists, the dreaming never stopped, and the fun never began. Instead, the work of theoretical and applied intelligent-design theorists went forward and showed why scientific explanations of biologically significant information could never remove the hand of design and intentionality. The watchword for science became *information requires intelligence*. This came to be known as the No Free Lunch Principle, which states that apart from intelligent guidance, material processes cannot bring about the information required for biological complexity.

The No Free Lunch Principle led to a massive change in scientific perspective. One notable consequence for biology was a thoroughgoing reevaluation of experimental work on prebiotic and biotic evolution. Invariably, where evolutionary biologists reported interesting experimental results, it was because "intelligent investigators" had "intervened" and performed "experimental manipulations" that nature, left to its own devices, was utterly incapable of reproducing.

This led to an interesting twist. Whereas Darwinists had been relentless in disparaging intelligent design as a pseudoscience, Darwinism itself now came to be viewed as a pseudoscience. Intelligent design had been viewed as a pseudoscience because it refused to limit nature to the operation of blind material processes. Once it became clear, however, that material processes were inherently inadequate for producing biologically significant information, the Darwinian reliance, and indeed insistence, on such processes came to be viewed as itself pseudoscientific.

What would you think of a chemist who thought that all explosives were like TNT in that their explosive properties had to be explained in terms of electrostatic chemical reactions? How would such a chemist explain the explosion of a nuclear bomb? Would this chemist be acting as a scientist in requiring that nuclear explosions be explained in terms of electrostatic chemical reactions rather than in terms of fission and fusion of atomic nuclei? Obviously not.

Scientific explanations need to invoke causal powers that are adequate to account for the effects in question. By refusing to employ intelligence in understanding biologically significant information, the Darwinian biologists were essentially like this chemist, limiting themselves to causal powers that were inherently inadequate for explaining the things they were trying to explain. No wonder Darwinism is nowadays considered a pseudoscience; it does not possess, and indeed self-consciously rejects, the conceptual resources needed to explain the origin of biological information. Some historians of science are now even going so far as to call Darwinism the greatest swindle in the history of ideas. But this is perhaps too extreme.

The information-theoretic perspective did not just come to govern biology but took hold throughout the natural sciences. Physics from the time of Newton had sought to understand the physical world by positing certain fundamental entities (particles, fields, strings), specifying the general form of the equations to characterize those entities, prescribing initial and boundary conditions for those equations, and then solving them. Often these were equations of motion that, on the basis of past states, predicted future states. Within this classical conception of physics, the holy grail was to formulate a "theory of everything," a set of equations that could characterize the constitution and dynamics of the universe at all levels of analysis.

But with information as the fundamental entity of science, this conception of physics gave way. No longer was the physical world to be understood by identifying an underlying structure that has to obey certain equations no matter what. Instead, the world came to be seen as a nested hierarchy of systems that convey information, and the job of physical theory was to extract as much information from these systems as possible. Thus, rather than see the scientist as Procrustes, forcing nature to conform to preconceived theories, this informational approach turned the scientist into an inquirer who asks nature questions, obtains answers, but must always remain open to the possibility that nature has deeper levels of information to divulge.

Nothing of substance from the previous "mechanistic science" was lost with this informational approach. As Roy Frieden had shown, the full range of physics could be recovered within this informational approach (*Physics from Fisher Information: A Unification*, Cambridge University Press, 1998). The one thing that did give way, however, was the idea that physics is a bottom-up affair in which knowledge of a system's parts determines knowledge of the system as a whole. Within the informational approach, the whole was always truly greater than the sum of its parts, for the whole could communicate information that none of the parts could individually.

The primacy of information throughout the sciences has had profound consequences for religion and faith. A world in which information is not primary is a world seriously limited in what it can reveal about God. This became evident with the rise of modern science; the world it gave us revealed nothing about God except that God, if God exists at all, is a lawgiver. But with information as the primary stuff, there are no limits on what the world can in principle reveal about God. Theists of all stripes have therefore found this newfound focus of science on information refreshing.

Mind Transcending Matter

By Jeffrey Schwartz

Looking back, it seems inevitable that advances in brain science during the twentieth century led almost all people esteemed as scientifically literate to believe that eventually all aspects of the human mind would be explained in material terms. After all, in an era when the unquestioned cultural assumption was "for science all causes are material causes," how could one be expected to think differently? What's more, tremendous advances in brain-imaging technologies during the last two decades of that most materialist of centuries enabled scientists to investigate the inner workings of the living human brain. This certainly seemed to further buttress the generally unexamined and often smugly held belief that the deep mysteries of the brain and the "laws" through which it created and ruled all aspects of the human mind would someday be revealed.

Thus arose the then virtually hegemonic belief that human beings and everything they do are, like all other aspects of the world of nature, the results of material causes by which the elites of the time simply meant results of material forces interacting with one another. While primitive, uneducated, and painfully unsophisticated people might be beguiled into believing that they had minds and wills capable of exerting effort and rising above the realm of the merely material, this was just, as Daniel Dennett, a widely respected philosopher of the day, delighted in putting it, an example of a "user illusion"—the quaint fantasy of those who failed to realize, due to educational deficiencies or plain thickheadedness, that "a brain was always going to do what it was caused to do by local mechanical disturbances." Were you one of the rubes who believed that people are capable of making free and genuinely moral decisions? Then of course haughty contempt, or at best pity, was the only appropriate demeanor a member of the intellectual elite could possibly direct your way.

On a societal and cultural level, the damage such spurious and unwarranted elite opinions wreaked on the world at large was immense. For if everything people do results solely from their brains, and everything the brain does results solely from material causes, then people are no different from any other complicated machine, and the brain is no different in principle from any very complex computer. If matter determines all, everything is passive, and no one ever *really* does anything; or to be more precise, no one is really *responsible for* anything they think, say, or do. What's more, if anything they think, say, or do causes problems for them or society at large, then, believed the sophisticates of that thankfully bygone era, the ultimate way to solve the problem would be to make the required changes in the brain that would make it work the way a properly functioning machine is supposed to. This naturally led to the widespread use of drugs as a primary means of treating what generally came to be called "behavioral problems." After all, if the brain is the final cause of everything a person thinks, says, and does, why bother with old-fashioned and outdated notions like self-control or even "making your best effort" to solve a problem? If the brain is the ultimate cause underlying all the problems, then the sophisticated thing to do to rectify things is to give a chemical (or even place an electrode!) that gets right in there and fixes things. "God helps those who help themselves"? Not in the real world, where science knows all the answers, sneered the elites of the time.

Fortunately for the future of humanity, in the early years of the twenty-first century, this all started to change. The reasons, on a scientific level, grew out of the coming together of some changes in perspective that had occurred in physics and neuroscience during the last decades of the previous century. Specifically, the theory of physics called quantum mechanics was seen to be closely related, especially in humans, to the discovery in brain science called neuroplasticity: the fact that throughout the life span the brain is capable of being rewired, and that in humans at least, this rewiring could be caused directly by the action of the mind.

Work using new brain imaging technologies of that era to study people with a condition called obsessive-compulsive disorder (OCD) played a key role in this development. OCD is a medical condition in which people suffer from very bothersome and intrusive thoughts and feelings that give them the sense that "something is wrong" in their immediate surrounds, usually the thought or feeling that something is dirty or contaminated or needs to be checked because it isn't quite right. This is what is called an obsession. The problem the medical condition causes is that although the sufferers generally know this feeling that "something is wrong" is false and doesn't really make sense, the feeling keeps bothering them and doesn't go away, due to a brain glitch that was discovered using brain imaging. Sufferers often respond to these gut-wrenching thoughts and feelings by washing, checking, straightening things, etc. over and over again, in a desperate but futile attempt to make things seem right. These futile repetitive acts are called compulsions.

In the 1990s it was discovered that OCD sufferers were capable of learning how to resist capitulating to these brain-related symptoms by using a mental action called "mindful awareness" when confronting them. In a nutshell, mindful awareness means using your mind's eye to view your own inner life and experiences the way you would if you were standing, as it were, outside yourself. Most simply put it means learning to use a rational perspective when viewing your own inner experience. When OCD patients did this, and as a result came to view the bothersome intrusive thoughts and feelings just as medical symptoms that they had the mental power to resist, they found they were empowered to direct their attention in much more useful and wholesome ways by focusing on healthy and/or work-related activities. Over several weeks, and with much mental effort and faith in their ability to overcome the suffering, many OCD patients were found to be capable of regularly resisting the symptoms. This greatly strengthened their mental capacity to focus attention on useful, wholesome activities and overcome compulsive urges. The major scientific finding that was discovered using brain imaging was that when OCD sufferers used the power of their minds to redirect regularly their focus of attention in wholesome ways, they literally *rewired their own brains* in precisely the brain circuit that had been discovered to cause the problem.

In the early years of the current century, brain imaging was used to reveal many similar and related findings. For instance, people with spider phobia, or people viewing stressful or sexually arousing films, were found to be entirely capable of using mental effort to apply mindful awareness and reframe their perspective on their experience. By so doing it was clearly demonstrated that they could systematically change the response of the brain to these situations and so cease being frightened, stressed, or sexually aroused, whatever the case may be. This latter finding was realized by some at the time to be potentially relevant to teaching sexual abstinence strategies to adolescents; for if you have the power to control your brain's response to sexual urges, then practicing sexual abstinence in arousing situations will not only strengthen your moral character; it will also increase your mental and physical capacity to control the workings of your own brain, an extremely wholesome and empowering act!

All this work came together when physicist Henry Stapp realized that a basic principle of quantum mechanics, which because of the nature of the brain at the atomic level must be used for proper understanding of the brain's inner workings, explains how the action of the mind changes how the brain works. A well-established mechanism called the Quantum Zeno Effect (QZE) readily explains how mindfully directed attention can alter brain circuitry adaptively. Briefly, we can understand the Quantum Zeno Effect (QZE) like this: the mental act of focusing attention tends to hold in place brain circuits associated with whatever is focused on. In other words, focusing attention on your mental experience maintains the brain state arising in association with that experience. If, using mindful awareness, a brain state arises associated with a wholesome perspective, the sustained application of that mindful perspective will literally, because of the QZE mechanism, hold in place the brain circuitry associated with the wholesome process. Of course, the QZE mechanism would be expected to work the same way to hold in place the brain's response to meditation or prayer, and brain-imaging research in the early years of this century demonstrated that to be the case.

The rest, as they say, is history. Once a solid scientific theory was in place to explain how the mind's power to focus attention could systematically rewire the brain and that the language of our mental and spiritual life is necessary to empower the mind to do so, the materialist dogma was toppled. We may not have all lived happily ever after in any simplistic sense, but at least science is no longer on the side of those who claim human beings are no different in principle from a machine.

APPENDIX C

Malone Replies to Bryan

Complete official transcript of Dudley Field Malonoe's response to William Jennings Bryan, Thursday, July 16, 1925.

DUDLEY FIELD MALONE—If it the court please, it does seem to me that we have gone far afield in this discussion. However, probably this is the time to discuss everything that bears on the issues that have been raised in this case, because after all, whether Mr. Bryan knows it or not, he is a mammal, he is an animal, and he is a man. But, your honor, I would like to advert to the law and to remind the court that the heart of the matter is the question of whether there is liability under this law.

I have been puzzled and interested at one and the same time at the psychology of the prosecution, and I find it difficult to distinguish between Mr. Bryan, the lawyer in this case; Mr. Bryan, the propagandist outside of this case; and the Mr. Bryan who made a speech against science and for religion just now—Mr. Bryan my old chief and friend. I know Mr. Bryan. I don't know Mr. Bryan as well as Mr. Bryan knows Mr. Bryan, but I know this, that he does believe—and Mr. Bryan, your honor, is not the only one who believes in the Bible. As a matter of fact, there has been much criticism, by indirection and implication, of this text, or synopsis, if you please, that does not agree with their ideas. If we depended on the agreement of the theologians, we would all be infidels. I think it is in poor taste for the leader of the prosecution to cast reflection or aspirations upon the men and women of the teaching profession in this country. God knows, the poorest paid profession in America is the teaching profession, who devote themselves to science, forego the gifts of God, consecrate their brains to study, and eke out their lives as pioneers in the fields of duty, finally hoping that mankind will profit by his efforts, and to open the doors of truth.

Mr. Bryan quoted Mr. Darwin. That theory was evolved and explained by Mr. Darwin seventy-five years ago. Have we learned nothing in seventy-five years? Here we have learned the truth of biology, we have learned the truth of anthropology, and we have learned more of archeology? Not very long since the archeological museum in London established that a city existed, showing a high degree of civilization in Egypt fourteen thousand years old, showing that on the banks of the Nile River there was a civilization much older than ours. Are we to hold mankind to a literal understanding of the claim that the world is six thousand years old because of the limited vision of men who believed the world was flat, and that the Earth was the center of the universe, and that man is the center of the Earth.

It is a dignified position for man to be the center of the universe, that the earth is the center of the universe, and that the heavens revolve about us. And the theory of ignorance and superstition for which they stood are identical, a psychology and ignorance which made it possible for theologians to take old and learned Galileo, who proposed to prove the theory of Copernicus, that the Earth was round and did not stand still, and to bring old Galileo to trial—for what purpose? For the purpose of proving a literal construction of the Bible against truth, which is revealed.

Haven't we learned anything in seventy-five years? Are we to have our children know nothing about science except what the church says they shall know? I have never seen harm in learning and understanding, in humility and open-mindedness, and I have never seen clearer the need of that learning than when I see the attitude of the prosecution, who attack and refuse to accept the information and intelligence, which expert witnesses will give them. Mr. Bryan may be satisfactory to thousands of people. It is in so many ways that he is satisfactory to me; his enthusiasm, his vigor, his courage, his fighting ability these long years for the things he thought were right. And many a time I have fought with him, and for him; and when I did not think he was right, I fought just as hard against him. This is not a conflict of personages; it is a conflict of ideas, and I think this case has been developed by men of two frames of mind. Your honor, there is a difference between theological and scientific men.

Theological and Scientific Minds Differ

Theology deals with something that is established and revealed; it seeks to gather material, which they claim should not be changed. It is the Word of God, and that cannot be changed; it is literal, it is not to be interpreted. That is the theological mind. It deals with theology. The scientific is a modern thing, your honor. I am not sure that Galileo was the one who brought relief to the scientific mind because, theretofore, Aristotle and Plato had reached their conclusion and processes by metaphysical reasoning because they had no telescope and no microscope. These were things that were invented by Galileo. The difference between the theological mind and the scientific mind is that the theological mind is closed because that is what is revealed and is settled. But the scientist says no, the Bible is the book of revealed religion, with rules of conduct, and with aspirations—that is the Bible. The scientist says, take the Bible as a guide, as an inspiration, as a set of philosophies and preachments in the world of theology.

And what does this law do? We have been told here that this was not a religious question. I defy anybody, after Mr. Bryan's speech, to believe that this was not a religious question. Mr. Bryan brought all of the foreigners into this case. Mr. Bryan had offered his services from Miami, Florida; he does not belong in Tennessee. If it be wrong for American citizens from other parts of this country to come to Tennessee to discuss issues which we believe, then Mr. Bryan has no right here, either. But it was only when Mr. Darrow and I had heard that Mr. Bryan had offered his name and his reputation to the prosecution of his young teacher, that we said, "Well, we will offer our services to the defense." And, as I said in the beginning, we feel at home in Tennessee; we have been received with hospitality, personally.

Our ideas have not taken effect yet; we have corrupted no morals so far as I know, and I would like to ask the court if there was any evidence in the witnesses produced by the prosecution, of moral deterioration due to the course of biology which Prof. Scopes taught these children, the little boy who said he had not been hurt by it and who slipped out of the chair possibly and went to the swimming pool, and the other who said that the theory he was taught had not taken him out of the church. This theory of evolution, in one form or another, has been up in Tennessee since 1832, and I think it is incumbent on the prosecution to introduce at least one person in the state of Tennessee whose morals have been affected by the teaching of this theory.

After all, we of the defense contend, and it has been my experience, your honor, in my twenty years, as Mr. Bryan said, as a criminal lawyer, that the prosecution had to prove its case, that the defense did not have to prove it for them. We have a defendant here charged with a crime. The prosecution is trying to get your honor to take the theory of the prosecution as the theory of our defense. We maintain our right to present our own defense, and present our own theory of our defense, and to present our own theory of this law because we maintain, your honor, that if everything that the state has said in its testimony be true—and we admit it is true—that under this law the defendant Scopes has not violated that statute. Haven't we the right to prove it by our witnesses if that is our theory, if that is so?

Moreover, let us take the law—"Be it enacted by the state of Tennessee that it shall be unlawful for any teacher in any universities, normals, or any other schools in the state, which are supported in whole or in part by public funds of the state, to teach any theory that denies the story of divine creation of man as taught in the Bible, and to teach him that man is descended from a lower order of animals." If that word had been *or* instead of *and*, then the prosecution would only have to prove half of its case. But it must prove, according to our contention, that Scopes not only taught a theory that man had descended from a lower order of animal life, but at the same time, instead of that theory, he must teach the theory which denies the story of divine creation set forth in the Bible. And we maintain that we have a right to introduce evidence by these witnesses that the theory of the defendant is not in conflict with the theory of creation in the Bible. And, moreover, your honor, we maintain we have the right to call witnesses to show that there is more than one theory of the creation in the Bible. Mr. Bryan is not the only one who has spoken for the Bible; Judge McKenzie is not the only defender of the Word of God. There are other people in this country who have given their whole lives to God. Mr. Bryan, to my knowledge, with a very passionate spirit and enthusiasm, has given most of his life to politics, we believe.

Bible Not Book of Science

I would like to say, your honor, as personal information, that probably no man in the United States has done more to establish certain standards of conduct in the mechanics and world of politic than Mr. Bryan. But is that any reason that I should fall down when Bryan speaks on theology? Is he the last word on the subject of theology?

Well do I remember in my history of the story of the burning of the great library at Alexandria, and just before it was burned to the ground that the heathen, the Mohammedans, and the Egyptians, went to the hostile general and said, "Your honor, do not destroy this great library because it contains all the truth that has been gathered," and the Mohammedan general said, "But the Koran contains all the truth. If the library contains the truth that the Koran contains, we do not need the library; and if the library does not contain the truth that the Koran contains, then we must destroy the library anyway."

But these gentlemen say the Bible contains the truth. If the world of science can produce any truth or facts not in the Bible as we understand it, then destroy science, but keep our Bible. And we say, "Keep your Bible." Keep it as your consolation, keep it as your guide, but keep it where it belongs, in the world of your own conscience, in the world of your individual judgment, in the world of the Protestant conscience that I heard so much about when I was a boy. Keep your Bible in the world of theology where it belongs, and do not try to tell an intelligent world and the intelligence of this country that these books written by men who knew none of the accepted fundamental facts of science can be put into a course of science, because what are they doing here? This law says what? It says that no theory of creation can be taught in a course of science, except one which conforms with the theory of divine creation as set forth in the Bible. In other words, it says that only the Bible shall be taken as an authority on the subject of evolution in a course on biology.

The Court—Let me ask you a question, colonel? It is not within the province of this court to determine which is true, is it?

Mr. Malone—No, but it is within the province of the court to listen to the evidence we wish to submit to make up its own mind, because here is the issue.

The Court—I was going to follow that with another question. Is it your theory—is it your opinion that the theory of evolution is reconcilable with the story of the divine creation as taught in the Bible?

Mr. Malone—Yes.

Scientists Are God-Fearing Men

The Court—In other words, you believe—when it says—when the Bible says that God created man, you believe that God created the life cells and that then out of that one single life cell the God created man by a process of growth or development—is that your theory?

Mr. Malone—Yes.

The Court—And in that you think that it doesn't mean that he just completed him, complete all at once?

Mr. Malone—Yes, I might think that and I might think he created him serially—I might think he created him anyway. Our opinion is this—we have the right it seems to us, to submit evidence to the court of men without question who are God-fearing and believe in the Bible and who are students of the Bible and authorities on the Bible and authorities on the scientific world—they have a right to be allowed to testify in support of our view that the Bible is not to be taken literally as an authority in a court of science.

The Court—That is what I was trying to get, your position on. Here was my idea. I wanted to get your theory as to whether you thought it was in the province of the court to determine which was true, or whether it was your theory that there was no conflict and that you had a right to introduce proof to show what the Bible—what the true construction of interpretation of the Bible story was.

Mr. Malone—Yes.

The Court—That is your opinion.

Mr. Malone—Yes. And also from scientists who believe in the Bible and belong to churches and who are God-fearing men—what they think about this subject, of the reconcilement of science and religion—of all science and the Bible, your honor, because yesterday I made a remark, your honor, which might have been interpreted as personal to Mr. Bryan. I said that the defense believed we must keep a clear distinction between the Bible, the church, religion, and Mr. Bryan. Mr. Bryan, like all of us, is just an individual, but like himself he is a great leader. The danger from the viewpoint of the defense is this, that when any great leader goes out of his field and speaks as an authority on other subjects, his doctrines are quite likely to be far more dangerous than the doctrines of experts in their field who are ready and willing to follow, but what I don't understand is this, your honor, the prosecution inside and outside of the court has been ready to try the case, and this is the case.

What is the issue that has gained the attention not only of the American people but people everywhere? Is it a mere technical question as to whether the defendant Scopes taught the paragraph in the book of science? You think, your honor, that the News Association in London, which sent you that very complimentary telegram you were good enough to show me in this case, because the issue is whether John Scopes taught a couple of paragraphs out of his book? Oh, no, the issue is as broad as Mr. Bryan himself has made it. The issue is as broad as Mr. Bryan has published it, and why the fear? If the issue is as broad as they make it, why the fear of meeting the issue? Why, where issues are drawn by evidence, where the truth and nothing but the truth are scrutinized, and where statements can be answered by expert witnesses on the other side, what is this psychology of fear?

I don't understand it. My old chief—I never saw him back away from a great issue before. I feel that the prosecution here is filled with a needless fear. I believe that if they withdraw their objection and hear the evidence of our experts, their minds would not only be improved but their souls would be purified. I believe and we believe that men who are God fearing, who are giving their lives to study and observation, to the teaching of the young—are the teachers and scientists of this country in a combination to destroy the morals of the children to whom they have dedicated their lives? Are preachers the only ones in America who care about our youth? Is the church the only source of morality in this country? And I would like to say something for the children of the country. We have no fears about the young people of America. They are a pretty smart generation. Any teacher who teaches the boys and girls today, an incredible theory.

No Need to Worry about Children

We need not worry about those children of this generation paying much attention to it. The children of this generation are pretty wise. People, as a matter of fact, I feel that the children of this generation are probably much wiser than many of their elders. The least that this generation can do, your honor, is to give the next generation all the facts, all the available data, all the theories, all the information that learning, that study, that observation has produced—give it to the children in the hope of heaven that they will make a better world of this than we have been able to make it.

We have just had a war with twenty million dead. Civilization is not so proud of the work of the adults. Civilization need not be so proud of what the grown-ups have done. For God's sake let the children have their minds kept open—close no doors to their knowledge; shut no door from them. Make the distinction between theology and science. Let them have both. Let them both be taught. Let them both live. Let them be reverent, but we come here to say that the defendant is not guilty of violating this law.

We have a defendant whom we contend could not violate this law. We have a defendant whom we can prove by witnesses whom we have brought here and are proud to have brought here, to prove, we say, that there is no conflict between the Bible and whatever he taught. Your honor, in a criminal case we think the defendant has a right to put in his own case, on his own theory, in his own way. Why! Because your honor, after you hear the evidence, if it is inadmissible, if it is not informing to the court and informing to the jury, what can you do? You can exclude it—you can strike it out.

What is the jury system that Mr. Bryan talked so correctly about just about a week ago, when he spoke of this jury system, when he said it was a seal of freedom for free men, in a free state? Who has been excluding the jury for fear it would learn something? Have we? Who has been making the motions to take the jury out of the courtroom? Have we? We want everything we have to say on religion and on science told, and we are ready to submit our theories to the direct cross-examination of the prosecution. We have come in here ready for a battle. We have come in here for this duel. I don't know anything about dueling, your honor. It is against the law of God. It is against the church. It is against the law of Tennessee, but does the opposition mean by a duel that our defendant shall be strapped to a board and that they alone shall carry the sword, is our only weapon the witnesses who shall testify to the accuracy of our theory—is our weapon to be taken from us, so that the duel will be entirely one-sided? That isn't my idea of a duel. Moreover it isn't going to be a duel.

Truth Is Imperishable and Eternal

There is never a duel with the truth. The truth always wins, and we are not afraid of it. The truth is no coward. The truth does not need the law. The truth does not need the forces of government. The truth does not need Mr. Bryan. The truth is imperishable, eternal, and immortal and needs no human agency to support it. We are ready to tell the truth as we understand it, and we do not fear all the truth that they can present as facts. We are ready. We are ready. We feel we stand with progress. We feel we stand with science. We feel we stand with intelligence. We feel we stand with fundamental freedom in America. We are not afraid. Where is the fear? We meet it, where is the fear? We defy it, we ask your honor to admit the evidence as a matter of correct law, as a matter of sound procedure and a matter of justice to the defense in this case. (Profound and continued applause.)

APPENDIX D

Text of Bryan's Proposed Address in Scopes Case

AS A MEMBER of the counsel of prosecution in the Scopes evolution case in Dayton, William Jennings Bryan had prepared an address in defense of Tennessee's law against the teaching of evolution in the public schools. This address was not delivered during the trial because arguments to the jury by counsel on both sides were dispensed with by agreement. Arrangements for publications of it were made by Mr. Bryan only a few hours before his death. The text of the address follows:

May It Please the Court, and Gentlemen of the Jury:

Demosthenes, the greatest of ancient orators, in his "Oration on the Crown," the most famous of his speeches, began by supplicating the favor of all the gods and goddesses of Greece. If, in a case which involved only his own fame and fate, he felt justified in petitioning the heathen gods of his country, surely we, who deal with the momentous issues involved in the case, may well pray to the Ruler of the universe for wisdom to guide us in the performance of our several parts in this historic trial.

Let me, in the first place, congratulate our cause that circumstances have committed the trial to a community like this and entrusted the decision to a jury made up largely of the yeomanry of the state. The book in issue in this trial contains on its first page two pictures contrasting the disturbing noises of a great city with the calm serenity of the country. It is a tribute that rural life has fully earned. I appreciate the sturdy honesty and independence of those who come into daily contact with the earth, who, living near to nature, worship nature's God, and who, dealing with the myriad mysteries of earth and air, seek to learn from revelation about the Bible's wonder-working God. I admire the stern virtues, the vigilance, and the patriotism of the class from which the jury is drawn and am reminded of the lines of Scotland's immortal bard, which, when changed but slightly, describe your country's confidence in you:

> O Scotia, my dear, my native soil!
> For whom my warmest wish to Heaven is sent,
> Long may thy hardy sons of rustic toil
> Be blest with health, and peace, and sweet content!
> And oh, may Heav'n their simple lives prevent
> From luxury's contagion, weak and vile!
> Then, howe'er crowns and coronets be rent,
> A virtuous populace may rise the while,
> And stand, a wall of fire, around their much-loved isle.

Let us now separate the issues from the misrepresentations, intentional or unintentional, that have obscured both the letter and the purpose of the law. This is not an interference with freedom of conscience. A teacher can think as he pleases and worship God as he likes, or refuse to worship at all. He can believe in the Bible or discard it; he can accept Christ or reject him. This law places no obligations or restraints upon him. And so with freedom of speech, he can, so long as he acts as an individual, say anything he likes on any subject. This law does not violate any right guaranteed by any constitution to any individual. It deals with the defendant, not as an individual, but as an employee, an official or public servant, paid by the state, and therefore under instructions from the state.

Right of the State to Control Public Schools

The right of the state to control public schools is affirmed in the recent decision in the Oregon case, which declares that the state can direct what shall be taught and also forbid the teaching of anything "manifestly inimical to the public welfare." The above decision goes even farther and declares that the parent not only has the right to guard the religious welfare of the child but is in duty bound to guard it. That decision fits this case exactly. The state had a right to pass this law, and the law represents the determination of the parents to guard the religious welfare of their children.

It need hardly be added that this law did not have its origin in bigotry. It is not trying to force any form of religion on anybody. The majority is not trying to establish a religion or to teach it—it is trying to protect itself from the effort of an insolent minority to force irreligion upon the children under the guise of teaching science. What right has a little irresponsible oligarchy of self-styled "intellectuals" to demand control of the schools of the United States, in which 25,000,000 children are being educated at an annual expense of nearly $2,000,000,000?

Christians must, in every state of the Union, build their own colleges in which to teach Christianity; it is only simple justice that atheists, agnostics, and unbelievers should build their own colleges if they want to teach their own religious views or attack the religious views of others.

The statute is brief and free from ambiguity. It prohibits the teaching, in the public schools, of "any theory that denies the story of divine creation as taught in the Bible," and teaches, "instead, that man descended from a lower order of animals." The first sentence sets forth the purpose of those who passed the law. They forbid the teaching of any evolutionary theory that disputes the Bible record of man's creation and, to make sure that there shall be no misunderstanding, they place their own interpretations on their language and specifically forbid the teaching of any theory that makes man a descendant of any lower form of life.

The evidence shows that the defendant taught, in his own language as well as from a book outlining the theory, that man descended from lower forms of life. Howard Morgan's testimony gives us a definition of *evolution* that will become known throughout the world as this case is discussed. Howard, a fourteen-year-old boy, has translated the words of the teacher and the textbook into language that even a child can understand. As he recollects it, the defendant said, "A little germ or one-cell organism was formed in the sea; this kept evolving until it got to be a pretty good-sized animal, then came on to be a land animal, and it kept evolving, and from this was man." There is no room for difference of opinion here, and there is no need of expert testimony. Here are the facts, corroborated by another student, Harry Shelton, and admitted to be true by counsel for defense. Mr. White, superintendent of schools, testified to the use of Hunter's *Civic Biology,* and to the fact that the defendant not only admitted teaching evolution but declared that he could not teach it without violating the law. Mr. Robinson, the chairman of the school board, corroborated the testimony of Superintendent White in regard to the defendant's admissions and declaration. These are the facts; they are sufficient and undisputed. A verdict of guilty must follow.

But the importance of this case requires more. The facts and arguments presented to you must not only convince you of the justice of conviction in this case but, while not necessary to a verdict of guilty, they should convince you of the righteousness of the purpose of the people of the state in the enactment of this law. The state must speak through you to the outside world and repel the aspersions cast by the counsel for the defense upon the intelligence and enlightenment of the citizens of Tennessee. The people of this state have a high appreciation of the value of education. The state constitution testifies to that in its demand that education shall be fostered and that science and literature shall be cherished. The continuing and increasing appropriations for public instruction furnish abundant proof that Tennessee places a just estimate upon the learning that is secured in its schools.

Declares Religion Not Hostile to Learning

Religion is not hostile to learning. Christianity has been the greatest patron learning has ever had. But Christians know that "the fear of the Lord is the beginning of wisdom" now just as it has been in the past, and they therefore oppose the teaching of guesses that encourage godlessness among the students.

Neither does Tennessee undervalue the service rendered by science. The Christian men and women of Tennessee know how deeply mankind is indebted to science for benefits conferred by the discovery of the laws of nature and by the designing of machinery for the utilization of these laws. Give science a fact and it is not only invincible, but it is of incalculable service to man. If one is entitled to draw from society in proportion to the service that he renders to society, who is able to estimate the reward earned by those who have given to us the use of steam, the use of electricity, and enabled us to utilize the weight of water that flows down the mountainside? Who will estimate the value of the service rendered by those who invented the phonograph, the telephone, and the radio? Or, to come more closely to our home life, how shall we recompense those who gave us the sewing machine, the harvester, the threshing machine, the tractor, the automobile, and the method now employed in making artificial ice? The department of medicine also opens an unlimited field for invaluable service. Typhoid and yellow fever are not feared as they once were. Diphtheria and pneumonia have been robbed of some of their terrors, and a high place on the scroll of fame still awaits the discoverer of remedies for arthritis, cancer, tuberculosis, and other dread diseases to which mankind is heir.

Christianity welcomes truth from whatever source it comes and is not afraid that any real truth from any source can interfere with the divine truth that comes by inspiration from God himself. It is not scientific truth to which Christians object, for true science is classified knowledge, and nothing therefore can be scientific unless it is true.

Evolution Not Truth; Merely a Hypothesis

Evolution is not truth; it is merely a hypothesis—it is millions of guesses strung together. It had not been proven in the days of Darwin; he expressed astonishment that with two or three million species it had been impossible to trace any species to any other species. It had not been proven in the days of Huxley, and it has not been proven up to today. It is less than four years ago that Professor Bateson came all the way from London to Canada to tell the American scientists that every effort to trace one species to another had failed—every one. He said he still had faith in evolution but had doubts about the origin of species. But of what value is evolution if it cannot explain the origin of species? While many scientists accept evolution as if it were a fact, they all admit, when questioned, that no explanation has been found as to how one species developed into another.

Darwin suggested two laws, sexual selection and natural selection. Sexual selection has been laughed out of the classroom, and natural selection is being abandoned, and no new explanation is satisfactory even to scientists. Some of the more rash advocates of evolution are wont to say that evolution is as firmly established as the law of gravitation or the Copernican theory. The absurdity of such a claim is apparent when we remember that anyone can prove the law of gravitation by throwing a weight into the air, and that anyone can prove the roundness of the earth by going around it, while no one can prove evolution to be true in any way whatever.

Chemistry is an insurmountable obstacle in the path of evolution. It is one of the greatest of the sciences; it separates the atoms—isolates them and walks about them, so to speak. If there were in nature a progressive force, an eternal urge, chemistry would find it. But it is not there. All of the ninety-two original elements are separate and distinct; they combine in fixed and permanent proportions. Water is H_2O, as it has been from the beginning. It was here before life appeared and has never changed; neither can it be shown that anything else has materially changed.

There is no more reason to believe that man descended from some inferior animal than there is to believe that a stately mansion has descended from a small cottage. Resemblances are not proof—they simply put us on inquiry. As one fact, such as the absence of the accused from the scene of the murder, outweighs all the resemblances that a thousand witnesses could swear to, so the inability of science to trace any one of the millions of species to another species, outweighs all the resemblances upon which evolutionists rely to establish man's blood relationship with the brutes.

Man's Urge Comes Not from Within but from Above

But while the wisest scientists cannot prove a pushing power, such as evolution is supposed to be, there is a lifting power that any child can understand. The plant lifts the mineral up into a higher world, and the animal lifts the plant up into a world still higher. So, it has been reasoned by analogy, man rises, not by a power within him, but only when drawn upward by a higher power. There is a spiritual gravitation that draws all souls toward heaven, just as surely as there is a physical force that draws all matter on the surface of the Earth toward the Earth's center. Christ is our drawing power; he said, "I, if I will be lifted up from the earth, will draw all men unto me," and his promise is being fulfilled daily all over the world.

It must be remembered that the law under consideration in this case does not prohibit the teaching of evolution up to the line that separates man from the lower forms of animal life. The law might well have gone farther than it does and prohibit the teaching of evolution in lower forms of life; the law is a very conservative statement of the people's opposition to an anti-biblical hypothesis. The defendant was not content to teach what the law permitted; he, for reasons of his own, persisted in teaching that which was forbidden for reasons entirely satisfactory to the lawmakers.

Most of the people who believe in evolution do not know what evolution means. One of the science books taught in the Dayton high school has a chapter on "The Evolution of Machinery." This is a very common misuse of the term. People speak of the evolution of the telephone, the automobile, and the musical instrument. But these are merely illustrations of man's power to deal intelligently with inanimate matter; there is no growth from within in the development of machinery.

Equally improper is the use of the word *evolution* to describe the growth of a plant from a seed, the growth of a chicken from an egg, or the development of any form of animal life from a single cell. All these give us a circle, not a change from one species to another.

Evolution Wrong Word Even in Plant Life

Evolution—the evolution involved in this case, and the only evolution that is a matter of controversy anywhere—is the evolution taught by the defendant, set forth in Hunter's *Civic Biology*. The author of the books now prohibited by the new state law, and illustrated in the diagram printed on page 194 of Hunter's *Civic Biology*, estimates the number of species in the animal kingdom at 518,900. These are divided into eighteen classes, and each class is indicated on a diagram by a circle, proportionate in size to the number of species in each class and attached by a stem to the trunk of the tree. It begins with protozoa and ends with the mammals. Passing over the classes with which the average is unfamiliar, let me call your attention to a few of the larger and better known groups. The insects are numbered at 360,000, over two-thirds of the total number of species in the animal world. The fishes are numbered at 13,000, the amphibians at 1,400, the reptiles at 3,500, and the birds are 13,000, while 3,500 mammals are crowded together in a little circle that is barely higher than the bird circle. No circle is reserved for man alone. He is, according to the diagram, shut up in the little circle entitled "Mammals," with 3,499 other species of mammals. Does it not seem a little unfair not to distinguish between man and lower forms of life? What shall we say of the intelligence, not to say religion, of those who are so particular to distinguish between fishes and reptiles and birds but put a man with an immortal soul in the same circle with the wolf, the hyena, and the skunk? What must be the impression made upon children by such a degradation of man?

In the preface of this book, the author explains that it is for children and adds that "the boy or girl of average ability upon admission to the secondary school is not a thinking individual." Whatever may be said in favor of teaching evolution to adults, it surely is not proper to teach it to children who are not yet able to think.

The evolutionist does not undertake to tell us how protozoa, moved by interior and resident forces, sent life up through all the various species, and cannot prove that there was actually any such compelling power at all. And yet the schoolchildren are asked to accept their guesses and build a philosophy of life upon them. If it were not so serious a matter, one might be tempted to speculate upon the various degrees of relationship that, according to evolutionists, exist between man and other forms of life. It might require some very nice calculation to determine at what degree of relationship the killing of a relative ceases to be murder and the eating of one's kin ceases to be cannibalism.

Evolution Casts Doubt upon Creation Itself

But it is not a laughing matter when one considers that evolution not only offers no suggestions as to a creator but tends to put the creative act so far away as to cast doubt upon creation itself. And while it is shaking faith in God as a beginning, it is also creating doubt as to a heaven at the end of life. Evolutionists do not feel that it is incumbent upon them to show how life began or at what point in their long-drawn-out scheme of changing species man became endowed with hope and promise of immortal life. God may be a matter of indifference to the evolutionists, and a life beyond may have no charm for them, but the mass of mankind will continue to worship their Creator and continue to find comfort in the promise of their Savior that he has gone to prepare a place for them. Christ has made of death a narrow, starlit strip between the companionship of yesterday and the reunion of tomorrow; evolution strikes out the stars and deepens the gloom that enshrouds the tomb.

If the results of evolution were unimportant, one might require less proof in support of the hypothesis, but before accepting a new philosophy of life, built upon a materialistic foundation, we have reason to demand something more than guesses; "we may well suppose" is not a sufficient substitute for "thus saith the Lord."

Darwin's Family Tree Pointed Out by Own Words

If, your honor, and you, gentlemen of the jury, would have an understanding of the sentiment that lies back of the statute against the teaching of evolution, please consider the fact that I shall now present to you. First, as to the animals to which evolutionists would have us trace our ancestry. The following is Darwin's family tree, as you will find it set forth on pages 180–81 of his *Descent of Man*:

> The most ancient progenitors in the kingdom of vertebrata, at which we are able to obtain an obscure glance, apparently consisted of a group of marine animals, resembling the larvae of existing ascidians. These animals probably gave rise to a group of fishes, as lowly organized as the lancelot; and from these the ganoids, and other fishes like the lepidosiren, must have been developed. From such fish a very small advance would carry us on to the amphibians. We have seen that birds and reptiles were once intimately connected together; and the monotremata now connect mammals with reptiles in a slight degree. But no one can at present say by what line of descent the three higher and related classes, namely, mammals, birds, and reptiles, were derived from the two lower vertebrate classes, namely amphibians and fishes. In the class of mammals, the steps are not difficult to conceive which led from the ancient monotremata to the ancient marsupials, and from these to the early progenitors of the placental mammals. We may thus ascend to the lemuridae; and the interval is not very wide from these to the simiadae. The simiadae then branched off into two great stems, the new world and old world monkeys; and from the latter, at a remote period, man, the wonder and glory of the universe, proceeded. Thus we have given to man a pedigree of prodigious length, but not, it may be said, of noble quality.
> (Ed. 1874, Hurst.)

Note the words implying uncertainty: "obscure glance," "apparently," "resembling," "must have been," "slight degree," and "conceive."

Darwin, on page 171 of the same book, tries to locate his first man—that is, the first name to come down out of the trees—in Africa. After leaving man in company with gorillas and chimpanzees, he says, "But it is useless to speculate on this subject." If he had only thought of this earlier, the world might have been spared much of the speculation that his brute hypothesis has excited.

On page 79 Darwin gives some fanciful reasons for believing that man is more likely to have descended from the chimpanzee than from the gorilla. His speculations are an excellent illustration of the effect that the evolutionary hypothesis has in cultivating the imagination. Professor J. Arthur Thomson says that the "idea of evolution is the most potent thought economizing formula the world has yet known." It is more than that; it dispenses with thinking entirely and relies on the imagination.

On page 141 Darwin attempts to trace the mind of man back to the mind of lower animals. On pages 113 and 114 he endeavors to trace man's moral nature back to the animals. It is all animal, animal, animal with never a thought of God or of religion.

Our first indictment against evolution is that it disputes the truth of the Bible account of man's creation and shakes faith in the Bible as the Word of God. This indictment we prove by comparing the processes described as evolutionary with the text of Genesis. It not only contradicts the Mosaic record as to the beginning of human life, but it disputes the Bible doctrine of reproduction according to kind—the greatest scientific principle known.

Our second indictment is that the evolutionary hypothesis, carried to its logical conclusion, disputes every vital truth of the Bible. Its tendency, natural, if not inevitable, is to lead those who really accept it, first to agnosticism and then to atheism. Evolutionists attack the truth of the Bible, not openly at first, but by using weasel-words like "poetical," "symbolical," and "allegorical" to suck the meaning out of the inspired record of man's creation.

We call as our first witness Charles Darwin. He began life as a Christian. On page 39, Vol. I of the *Life and Letters of Charles Darwin,* by his son, Francis Darwin, he says speaking of the period from 1828 to 1831, "I did not then in the least doubt the strict and literal truth of every word of the Bible." On page 412 of Vol. II of the same publication, he says, "When I was collecting facts for *The Origin,* my belief in what is called a personal God was as firm as that of Dr. Pusey himself." It may be a surprise to your honor and to you, gentlemen of the jury, as it was to me, to learn that Darwin spent three years at Cambridge studying for the ministry.

This was Darwin as a young man, before he came under the influence of the doctrine that man came from a lower order of animals. The change wrought in his religious views will be found in a letter written to a German youth in 1879, and printed on page 277 of Vol. I of the *Life and Letters* above referred to. The letter begins: "I am much engaged, an old man, and out of health, and I cannot spare time to answer your questions fully—nor indeed can they be answered. Science has nothing to do with Christ, except insofar as the habit of scientific research makes a man cautious in admitting evidence. For myself, I do not believe that there ever has been any revelation. As for a future life, every man must judge for himself between conflicting vague probabilities."

Note that "science has nothing to do with Christ, except insofar as the habit of scientific research makes a man cautious in admitting evidence." Stated plainly, that simply means that "the habit of scientific research" makes one cautious in accepting the only evidence that we have of Christ's existence, mission, teaching, crucifixion, and resurrection, namely the evidence found in the Bible. To make this interpretation of his words the only possible one, he adds, "For myself, I do not believe that there ever has been any revelation." In rejecting the Bible as a revelation from God, he rejects the Bible's conception of God, and he rejects also the supernatural Christ of whom the Bible, and the Bible alone, tells. And, it will be observed, he refuses to express any opinion to a future.

Now let us follow with his son's exposition of his father's views as they are given in extracts from a biography written in 1876. Here is Darwin's language as quoted by his son:

> During these two years (October 1838 to January 1839) I was led to think much about religion. Whilst on board the *Beagle,* I was quite orthodox, and I remember being heartily laughed at by several of the officers (though themselves orthodox) for quoting the Bible as an unanswerable authority on some point of morality. When thus reflecting, I felt compelled to look for a first cause, having an intelligent mind in

some degree analogous to man; and I deserved to be called an atheist. This conclusion was strong in my mind about the time, as far as I can remember, when I wrote the *Origin of Species*; it is since that time that it has very gradually, with many fluctuations, become weaker. But then arises the doubt, can the mind of man, which has, as I fully believe, been developed from a mind as low as that possessed by the lowest animals, be trusted when it draws such grand conclusions?

I cannot pretend to throw the least light on such abstruse problems. The mystery of the beginning of all things is insoluble by us; and I for one must be content to remain an agnostic.

Darwin Used Bible as Early Arguments

When Darwin entered upon his scientific career, he was "quite orthodox and quoted the Bible as an unanswerable authority on some point of morality." Even when he wrote *The Origin of Species,* the thought of "a first cause, having an intelligent mind in some degree analogous to man" was strong in mind. It was after that time that "very gradually, with many fluctuations," his belief in God became weaker. He traces this decline for us and concludes by telling us that he cannot pretend to throw the least light on such abstruse problems—the religious problems above referred to. Then comes the flat statement that he "must be content to remain an agnostic"; and to make clear what he means by the word *agnostic,* he says that "the mystery of the beginning of all things is insoluble by us"—not by him alone, but by everybody. Here we have the effect of evolution upon its most distinguished exponent; it led him from an orthodox Christian, believing every word of the Bible and in a personal God, down and down and down to helpless and hopeless agnosticism.

But there is one sentence upon which I reserve comment—it throws light upon his downward pathway. "Then arises the doubt, can the mind of man which has, as I fully believe, been developed from a mind as low as that possessed by the lowest animals, be trusted when it draws such grand conclusions?"

Here is the explanation: he drags man down to the brute level, and then, judging man by brute standards, he questions whether man's mind can be trusted to deal with God and immortality.

How can any teacher tell his students that evolution does not tend to destroy his religious faith? How can an honest teacher conceal from his students the effect of evolution upon Darwin himself? And is it not stranger still that preachers who advocate evolution never speak of Darwin's loss of faith, due to his belief in evolution? The parents of Tennessee have reason enough to fear the effect of evolution on the minds of their children. Belief in evolution cannot bring to those who hold such a belief any compensation for the loss of faith in God, trust in the Bible, and belief in the supernatural character of Christ. It is belief in evolution that has caused so many scientists and so many Christians to reject the miracles of the Bible, and then give up, one after another, every vital truth of Christianity. They finally cease to pray and sunder the tie that binds them to their Heavenly Father.

Miracle Should Not Become Stumbling Block

The miracle should not be a stumbling block to any one. It raises but three questions: First, could God perform a miracle? Yes, the God who created the universe can do anything he wants to with it. He can temporarily suspend any law that he has made, or he may employ higher laws that we do not understand.

Second, would God perform a miracle? To answer that question in the negative one would have to know more about God's plans and purposes than a finite mind can know, and yet some are so wedded to evolution that they deny that God would perform a miracle merely because a miracle is inconsistent with evolution.

If we believe that God can perform a miracle and might desire to do so, we are prepared to consider with open mind the third question, namely, Did God perform the miracles recorded in the Bible? The same evidence that establishes the authority of the Bible establishes the truth of the record of miracles performed.

Now let me read to you the honorable court and to you, gentlemen of the jury, one of the most pathetic confessions that has come to my notice. George John Romanes, a distinguished biologist, sometimes called the successor of Darwin, was prominent enough to be given extended space in both the *Encyclopedia Britannica* and *Encyclopedia Americana.* Like Darwin, he was reared in the orthodox faith, and like Darwin, was led away from it by evolution (see "Thoughts on Religion," page 180). For twenty-five years he could not pray. Soon after he became an agnostic, he wrote a book entitled, *A Candid Examination of Theism,* publishing it under the assumed name, Physicus. In this book (see page 29, *Thoughts on Religion*), he says:

> And forasmuch as I am far from being able to agree with those who affirm that the twilight doctrine of the "new faith" is a desirable substitute for the waning splendor of "the old," I am not ashamed to confess that with this virtual negation of God the universe to me has lost its soul of loveliness; and although from henceforth the precept to "work while it is day" will doubtless but gain an intensified force from the terribly intensified meaning of the words that "the night cometh when no man can work," yet when at times I think, as think at times I must, of the appalling contrast between the hallowed glory of that creed which once was mine, and the lonely mystery existence as now I find it—at such times I shall ever feel it impossible to avoid the sharpest pang of which my nature is susceptible.

Do these evolutionists stop to think of the crime they commit when they take faith out of the hearts of men and women and lead them out into a starless night? What pleasure can they find in robbing a human being of "the hallowed glory of that creed" that Romanes once cherished, and in substituting "the lonely mystery of existence" as he found it? Can the fathers and mothers of Tennessee be blamed for trying to protect their children from such a tragedy?

If anyone had been led to complain of the severity of the punishment that hangs over the defendant, let him compare this crime and its mild punishment with the crimes for which a greater punishment is prescribed. What is the taking of a few dollars from one in a day or night in comparison with the crime of leading one away from God and away from Christ?

Shakespeare regards the robbing one of his good name as much more grave than the stealing of his purse. But we have a higher authority than Shakespeare to invoke in this connection. He who spake as never man spake, thus describes the crimes that are committed against the young. "It is impossible but that offences will come; but woe unto him through whom they come. It were better for him that a millstone were hanged about his neck, and he cast into the sea, than that he should offend one of these little ones."

Christ did not overdraw the picture. Who is able to set a price upon the life of a child—a child into whom a mother has poured her life and for whom a father has labored? What may a noble life mean to the child itself, to the parents, and to the world?

And it must be remembered that we can measure the effect on only that part of life which is spent on Earth; we have no way of calculating the effect on that infinite circle of life of which existence here is but a small arc. The soul is immortal, and religion deals with the soul; the logical effect of the evolutionary hypothesis is to undermine religion and thus affect the soul. I recently received a list of questions that were to be discussed in a prominent eastern school for women. The second question in the list read, "Is religion an obsolescent function that should be allowed to atrophy quietly, without arousing the passionate prejudice of outworn superstition?" The real attack of evolution, it will be seen, is not upon orthodox Christianity, or even upon Christianity, but upon religion—the most basic fact in man's existence and the most practical thing in life.

But I have some more evidences of the effect of evolution upon the life of those who accept it and try to harmonize their thought with it.

Over Half of Scientists Deny Existence of God

James H. Leuba, a professor of psychology at Bryn Mawr College, Pennsylvania, published a few years ago a book entitled *Belief in God and Immortality*. In this book he relates how he secured the opinions of scientists as to the existence of a personal God and a personal immortality. He used a volume entitled *American Men of Science*, which, he says, included the names of "practically every American who may properly be called a scientist." There were fifty-five hundred names in the book. He selected one thousand names as representative of the fifty-five hundred and addressed them personally. Most of them, he said, were teachers in schools of higher learning. The names were kept confidential. Upon the answers received, he asserts that over half of them doubt or deny the existence of a personal God and a personal immortality, and he asserts that unbelief increases in proportions to prominence, the percentage of unbelief being greatest among the most prominent. Among biologists, believers in a personal God numbered less that 31 percent, while believers in a personal immortality numbered on 37 percent.

He also questioned the students in nine colleges of high rank, and from one thousand answers received, 97 percent of which were from students between eighteen and twenty, he found that unbelief increased from 15 percent in the freshman class up to 40 to 45 percent among the men who graduated. On page 280 of this book, we read, "The students' statistics show that young people enter college, possessed of the beliefs still accepted, more or less perfunctorily, in the average home of the land, and gradually abandon the cardinal Christian beliefs." This change from belief to unbelief he attributes to the influence of the persons "of high culture under whom they studied."

The people of Tennessee have been patient enough; they have acted none too soon. How can they expect to protect society, and even the church, from the deadening influence of agnosticism and atheism if they permit the teachers employed by taxation to poison the minds of the youth with this destructive doctrine? And remember that the law has not heretofore required the writing of the word *poison* on poisonous doctrines. The bodies of our people are so valuable that druggists and physicians must be careful to properly label all poisons; why not be as careful to protect the spiritual life of our people from the poisons that kill the soul?

There is a test that is sometimes used to ascertain whether one suspected of mental infirmity is really insane. He is put into a tank of water and told to dip the tank dry while a stream of water flows into the tank. If he has not sense enough to turn off the stream, he is adjudged insane. Can parents justify themselves if, knowing the effect of belief in evolution, they permit irreligious teachers to inject skepticism and infidelity into the minds of their children?

Do bad doctrines corrupt the morals of students? We have a case in point. Mr. Darrow, one of the most distinguished criminal lawyers in our land, was engaged about a year ago in defending two rich men's sons who were on trial for as dastardly a murder as was ever committed. The older one, "Babe" Leopold, was a brilliant student, nineteen years old. He was an evolutionist and an atheist. He was also a follower of Nietzsche, whose books he had devoured and whose philosophy he had adopted. Mr. Darrow made a plea for him, based upon the influence that Nietzsche's philosophy had exerted upon the boy's mind. Here are extracts from his speech:

> Babe took to philosophy. . . . He grew up in this way; he became enamoured of the philosophy of Nietzsche. Your honor, I have read almost everything that Nietzsche ever wrote. A man of wonderful intellect; the most original philosopher of the last century. A man who made a deeper imprint on philosophy than any other man within a hundred years, whether right or wrong. More books have been written about him than probably all the rest of the philosophers in a hundred years. More college professors have talked about him. In a way, he has reached more people, and still he has been a philosopher of what we might call the intellectual cult.
>
> He wrote one book called *Beyond the Good and Evil,* which was a criticism of all moral precepts, as we understand

them, and a treatise that the intelligent man was beyond good and evil, that the laws for good and the laws for evil did not apply to anybody who approached the superman. He wrote on the will to power.

I have just made a few short extracts from Nietzsche that show the things that he (Leopold) has read, and these are short and almost taken at random. It is not how this would affect you. It is not how it would affect me. The question is how it would affect the impressionable, visionary, dreamy mind of a boy—a boy who should never have seen it—too early for him.

Mr. Bryan Quotes from Nietzsche's Books

Quotations from Nietzsche:

> Why so soft, oh, my brethren? Why so soft, so unresisting and yielding? Why is there so much disavowal and abnegation in your hearts? Why is there so little fate in your looks? For all creators are hard and it must seem blessedness unto you to press your hand upon millenniums and upon wax. This new table, oh, my brethren, I put over you; become hard. To be obsessed by moral consideration presupposes a very low grade of intellect. We should substitute for morality the will to our own end, and consequently to the means to accomplish that. A great man, a man whom nature has built up and invented in a grand style, is colder, harder, less cautious, and more free from the fear of public opinion. He does not possess the virtues which are compatible with the respectability, with being respected, nor any of those things which are counted among the virtues of the herd.

Mr. Darrow says that the superman, a creation of Nietzsche, has permeated every college and university in the civilized world.

> There is not any university in the world where the professor is not familiar with Nietzsche, not one. . . . Some believe

> it and some do not believe it. Some read it as I do and take it as a theory, a dream, a vision, mixed with good and bad, but not in any way related to human life. Some take it seriously. . . . There is not a university in the world of any high standing where the professors do not tell you about Nietzsche and discuss him, or where the books are not there.
>
> If this boy is to blame for this, where did he get it? Is there any blame attached because somebody took Nietzsche's philosophy seriously and fashioned his life upon it? And there is no question in this case but what that is true. Then who is to blame? The university would be more to blame than he is; the scholars of the world would be more to blame than he is. The publishers of the world . . . are more to blame than he is. Your honor, it is hardly fair to hang a nineteen-year-old boy for the philosophy that was taught him at the university. It does not meet my ideas of justice and fairness to visit upon his head the philosophy that has been taught by university men for twenty-five years.

Transformed into Murderer by Philosophy of Atheist

In fairness to Mr. Darrow, I think I ought to quote two more paragraphs. After this bold attempt to excuse the student on the ground that he was transformed from a well-meaning youth into a murderer by the philosophy of an atheist, and on the further ground that this philosophy was in the libraries of all the colleges and discussed by the professors—some adopting the philosophy and some rejecting it—on these two grounds he denies that the boy should be held responsible for the taking of human life. He charges that the scholars in the universities were more responsible than the boy because they furnished such books to the students, and then he proceeds to exonerate the universities and scholars, leaving nobody responsible. Here is Mr. Darrow's language:

> Now I do not want to be misunderstood about this. Even for the sake of saving the lives of my clients, I do not want to

> be dishonest and tell the court something that I do not honestly think in this case. I do not think that the universities are to blame. I do not think they should be held responsible. I do think, however, that they are too large, and that they should keep a closer watch, if possible, upon the individual.
>
> But you cannot destroy thought because, forsooth, some brain may be deranged by thought. It is the duty of the university, as I conceive it, to be the greatest storehouse of the wisdom of the ages, and to have its students come there and learn and choose. I have no doubt but what it has meant to the death of many; but that we cannot help.

This is a damnable philosophy, and yet it is the flower that blooms on the stalk of evolution. Mr. Darrow thinks the universities are in duty bound to feed out this poisonous stuff to their students, and when the students become stupefied by it and commit murder, neither they nor the universities are to blame. I am sure, your honor and gentlemen of the jury, that you agree with me when I protest against the adoption of any such philosophy in the state of Tennessee. A criminal is not relieved from responsibility merely because he found Nietzsche's philosophy in a library which ought not contain it. Neither is the university guiltless if it permits such corrupting nourishment to be fed to the souls that are entrusted to its care. But, go a step farther, would the state be blameless if it permitted the universities under its control to be turned into training schools for murderers? When you get back to the root of this question, you will find that the legislature not only had a right to protect the students from the evolutionary hypothesis but was in duty bound to do so.

While on this subject, let me call your attention to another proposition embodied in Mr. Darrow's speech. He said that Dickey Loeb, the younger boy, had read trashy novels, of the blood and thunder sort. He even went so far as to commend an Illinois statute which forbids minors reading stories of crime. Here is what Mr. Darrow said: "We have a statute in this state, passed only last year, if I recall it, which forbids minors reading story of crime. Why? There is only one reason;

because the legislature in its wisdom thought it would have a tendency to produce these thoughts and this life in the boys who read them."

If Illinois can protect her boys, why cannot this state protect the boys of Tennessee? Are the boys of Illinois any more precious than yours?

Quotes Darrow's Plea for Richard Loeb's Life

But to return to philosophy of an evolutionist. Mr. Darrow said: "I say to you seriously that the parents of Dickey Loeb are more responsible than he, and yet few boys had better parents." Again, he says, "I know that one of two things happened to this boy; that this terrible crime was inherent in his organism, and came from some ancestor, or that it came through his education and his training after he was born." He thinks the boy was not responsible for anything; his guilt was due, according to his philosophy, either to heredity or to environment.

But let me complete Mr. Darrow's philosophy based on evolution. He says: "I do not know what remote ancestor may have sent down the seed that corrupted him, and I do not know through how many ancestors it may have passed until it reached Dickey Loeb. All I know is, it is true, and there is not a biologist in the world who will not say I am right."

Psychologists who build upon the evolutionary hypothesis teach that man is nothing but a bundle of characteristics inherited from brute ancestors. That is the philosophy which Mr. Darrow applied in this celebrated criminal case. "Some remote ancestor"—he does not know how remote—"sent down the seed that corrupted him." You cannot punish the ancestor—he is not only dead but, according to the evolutionists, he was a brute and may have lived a million years ago. And he says that all the biologists agree with him. No wonder so small a percent of the biologists, according to Leuba, believe in a personal God.

This is the quintessence of evolution, distilled for us by one who follows that doctrine to its logical conclusion. Analyze this dogma of darkness and death. Evolutionists say that back in the twilight of life a beast, name and nature unknown, planted a murderous seed and that the impulse that originated in the seed throbs forever in the blood of the brute's descendents, inspiring killings innumerable, for which the murderers are not responsible because coerced by a fate fixed by the laws of heredity! It is an insult to reason and shocks the heart. That doctrine is as deadly as leprosy; it may aid a lawyer in a criminal case, but it would, if generally adopted, destroy all sense of responsibility and menace the morals of the world. A brute, they say, can predestine a man to crime, and yet they deny that God incarnate in the flesh can release a human being from this bondage or save him from ancestral sins. No more repulsive doctrine was ever proclaimed by any man; if all the biologists of the world teach this doctrine—as Mr. Darrow says they do—then may heaven defend the youth of our land from their impious babblings.

Minds Are Diverted to Trifling Speculation

Our third indictment against evolution is that it diverts attention from pressing problems of great importance to trifling speculation. While one evolutionist is trying to imagine what happened in the dim past, another is trying to pry open the door of the distant future. One recently grew eloquent over ancient worms, and another predicted that seventy-five thousand years hence everyone will be bald and toothless. Both those who endeavor to clothe our remote ancestors with hair and those who endeavor to remove the hair from the heads of our remote descendants ignore the present with its imperative demands. The science of "How to Live" is the most important of all the sciences. It is desirable to know the physical sciences, but it is necessary to know how to live. Christians desire that their children shall be taught all the sciences, but they do not want them to lose sight of the Rock of Ages while they study the age of rocks; neither do they desire them to become so absorbed in measuring the distance between the stars that they will forget him who holds the stars in his hand.

While not more than 2 percent of our population are college graduates, these, because of enlarged powers, need a "heavenly vision" even more than those less learned, both for their own restraint and to assure society that their enlarged powers will be used for the benefit of society and not against the public welfare.

Evolution is deadening the spiritual life of a multitude of students. Christians do not desire less education, but they desire that religion shall be entwined with learning so that our boys and girls will return from college with their hearts aflame with love of God and love of fellowmen, and prepared to lead in the altruistic work that the world so sorely needs. The cry in the business world, in the industrial world, in the professional world, in the political world—even in the religious world—is for consecrated talents; for ability plus a passion for service.

Our fourth indictment against the evolutionary hypothesis is that, by paralyzing the hope of reform, it discourages those who labor for the improvement of man's condition. Every upward-looking man or woman seeks to lift the level upon which mankind stands, and they trust that they will see beneficent changes during the brief span of their own lives. Evolution chills their enthusiasm by substituting aeons for years. It obscures all beginnings in the mists of endless ages. It is represented as a cold and heartless process, beginning with time and ending in eternity, and acting so slowly that even the rocks cannot preserve a record of the imaginary changes through which it is credited with having carried an original germ of life that appeared sometime from somewhere. Its only program for man is scientific breeding, a system under which a few supposedly superior intellects, self-appointed, would direct the mating and the movements of the mass of mankind—an impossible system! Evolution, disputing the miracle, and ignoring the spiritual in life, has no place for the regeneration of the individual. It recognizes no cry of repentance and scoffs at the doctrine that one can be born again.

Prodigal Son Story Contradicts Evolution

It is thus the intolerant and unrelenting enemy of the only process that can redeem society through the redemption of the individual. An evolutionist would never write such a story as the prodigal son; it contradicts the whole theory of evolution. The two sons inherited from the same parents and, through their parents, from the same ancestors, proximate and remote. And these sons were reared at the same fireside and were surrounded by the same environment during all the days of their youth; and yet they were different. If Mr. Darrow is correct in the theory applied to Loeb (namely, that his crime was due either to inheritance or to environment), how will he explain the difference between the elder brother and the wayward son? The evolutionist may understand from observation, if not by experience, even though he cannot explain, why one of these boys was guilty of every immorality, squandered the money that the father had laboriously earned, and brought disgrace upon the family name; but his theory does not explain why a wicked young man underwent a change of heart, confessed his sin, and begged for forgiveness. And because the evolutionists cannot understand this fact, one of the most important in the human life, he cannot understand the infinite love of the heavenly Father, who stands ready to welcome home any repentant sinner, no matter how far he has wandered, how often he has fallen, or how deep he has sunk in sin.

Your honor has quoted from a wonderful poem written by a great Tennessee poet, Walter Malone. I venture to quote another stanza which puts into exquisite language the new opportunity which a merciful God gives to everyone who will turn from sin to righteousness.

> Though deep in mire, wring not your hands and weep;
> I lend my arm to all who say, "I can."
> No shame-faced outcast ever sank so deep
> But he might rise and be again a man.

There are no lines like these in all that evolutionists have ever written. Darwin says that science has nothing to do with the Christ who taught the spirit embodied in the words of Walter Malone, and yet this spirit is the only hope of human progress. A heart can be changed in the twinkling of an eye and a change in the life follows a change in the heart. If one heart can be changed, it is possible that many hearts can be changed, and if many hearts can be changed, it is possible that all hearts can be changed—that a world can be born in a day. It is this fact that inspires all who labor for man's betterment. It is because Christians believe in individual regeneration and in the regeneration of society through the regeneration of individuals that they pray, "Thy kingdom come, Thy will be done in earth as it is in heaven." Evolution makes a mockery of the Lord's Prayer!

Evolution Only Defers Hope of All Mankind

To interpret the words to mean that the improvement desired must come slowly through unfolding ages—a process with which each generation could have little to do—is to defer hope, and hope deferred maketh the heart sick.

Our fifth indictment of the evolutionary hypothesis is that, if taken seriously and made the basis of a philosophy of life, it would eliminate love and carry man back to a struggle of tooth and claw. The Christians who have allowed themselves to be deceived into believing that evolution is a beneficent, or even a rational process, have been associating with those who either do not understand its implications or dare not avow their knowledge of these implications. Let me give you some authority on this subject. I will begin with Darwin, the high priest of evolution, to whom all evolutionists bow.

On pages 149 and 150, in *The Descent of Man,* already referred to, he says:

> With savages, the weak in body or mind are soon eliminated; and those that survive commonly exhibit a vigorous state of health. We civilized men, on the other hand, do our utmost to check the process of elimination; we build asylums for the imbecile, the maimed, and the sick; we institute poor laws; and our medical men exert their utmost skill to save the life of everyone to the last moment. There is reason to believe that vaccination has preserved thousands who, from a weak constitution, would formerly have succumbed to small-pox. Thus the weak members of civilized society propagate their kind. No one who has attended to the breeding of domestic animals will doubt that this must be highly injurious to the race of man. It is surprising how soon a want of care, or care wrongly directed, leads to the degeneration of a

> domestic race; but, excepting in the case of man himself, hardly anyone is so ignorant as to allow his worst animals to breed.
>
> The aid which we feel impelled to give to the helpless is mainly an incidental r
>
> esult of the instinct of sympathy, which was originally acquired as part of the social instincts, but subsequently rendered in the manner previously indicated more tender and more widely diffused. Nor could we check our sympathy, even at the urging of hard reason, without deterioration in the noblest part of our nature. . . . We must, therefore, bear the undoubtedly bad effects of the weak surviving and propagating their kind.

Barbarous Sentiment Expressed by Darwin

Darwin reveals the barbarous sentiment that runs through evolution and dwarfs the moral nature of those who become obsessed with it. Let us analyze the quotation just given. Darwin speaks with approval of the savage custom of eliminating the weak so that only the strong will survive and complains that "we civilized men do our utmost to check the process of elimination." How inhuman such a doctrine as this! He thinks it injurious to "build asylums for the imbecile, the maimed, and the sick," or to care for the poor. Even the medical men come in for criticism because they "exert their utmost skill to save the life of everyone to the last moment." And then note his hostility to vaccination, because it has "preserved thousands who, from a weak constitution would, but for vaccination, have succumbed to smallpox!" All of the sympathetic activities of civilized society are condemned because they enable "the weak members to propagate their kind." Then he drags mankind down to the level of the brute and compares the freedom given to man unfavorably with the restraint that we put on barnyard beasts.

The second paragraph of the above quotation shows that his kindly heart rebelled against the cruelty of his own doctrine. He says that we "feel impelled to give to the helpless," although he traces it to a sympathy which he thinks is developed by evolution; he even admits that we could not check this sympathy "even at the urging of hard reason, without deterioration of the noblest part of our nature." "We must therefore bear" what he regards as "the undoubtedly bad effects of the weak surviving and propagating their kind." Could any doctrine be more destructive of civilization? And what a commentary on evolution! He wants us to believe that evolution develops a human sympathy that finally becomes so tender that it repudiates the law that created it and thus invites a return to a level where the extinguishing of pity and sympathy will permit the brutal instincts to do their progressive (?) work.

Darrow Says Nietzsche Was Gloriously Wrong

Let no one think that this acceptance of barbarism as the basic principle of evolution died with Darwin. Within three years a book has appeared whose author is even more frankly brutal than Darwin. The book is entitled *The New Decalogue of Science* and has attracted wide attention. One of our most reputable magazines has recently printed an article by him defining the religion of a scientist. In his preface he acknowledges indebtedness to twenty-one prominent scientists and educators, nearly all of them doctors and professors. One of them, who has recently been elevated to the head of a great state university, read the manuscript over twice and made many invaluable suggestions. The author describes Nietzsche who, according to Mr. Darrow, made a murderer out of Babe Leopold, as "the bravest soul since Jesus." He admits that Nietzsche was "gloriously wrong," not "certainly," but "perhaps," "in many details of technical knowledge," but he affirms that Nietzsche was "gloriously right in his fearless questioning of the universe and of his own soul."

In another place, the author says, "Most of our morals today are jungle products," and then he affirms that "it would be safer, biologically, if they were more so now." After these two samples of his views, you will not be surprised when I read you the following (see page 34): "Evolution is a bloody business, but civilization tries to make it a pink tea. Barbarism is the only process by which man has ever organically progressed, and civilization is the only process by which he has ever organically declined. Civilization is the most dangerous enterprise upon which man ever set out. For when you take man out of the bloody, brutal, but beneficent hand of natural selection, you place him at once in the soft, perfumed daintily gloved, but far more dangerous hand of artificial selection. And, unless you call science to your aid and make this artificial selection as efficient as the rude methods of nature, you bungle the whole task."

This aspect of evolution may amaze some of the ministers who have not been admitted to the inner circle of the iconoclasts whose theories menace all the ideas of civilized society. Do these ministers know that "evolution is a bloody business"? Do they know that "barbarism is the only process by which man has ever organically progressed"? And that "civilization is the only process by which he has ever organically declined"? Do they know that "the bloody, brutal hand of natural selection" is "beneficent"? And that the "artificial selection" found in civilization is "dangerous"? What shall we think of the distinguished educators and scientists who read the manuscript before publication and did not protest against this pagan doctrine?

To show that this is a worldwide matter, I now quote from a book issued from the press in 1918, seven years ago. The title of the book is *The Science of Power,* and its author, Benjamin Kidd, being an Englishman, could not have any national prejudice against Darwin. On pages 46 and 47, we find Kidd's interpretation of evolution:

> Darwin's presentation of the evolution of the world as the product of natural selection in never-ceasing war—as a product, that is to say, of a struggle in which the individual efficient in the fight for his own interests was always the winning type—touched the profoundest depths of the psychology of the West. The idea seemed to present the whole order of progress in the world as the result of a purely mechanical and materialistic process resting on force. In so doing it was a conception which reached the springs of that heredity born

of the unmeasured ages of conquest out of which the Western mind has come. Within half a century the origin of species had become the Bible of the doctrine of the omnipotence of force.

Kidd goes so far as to charge that "Nietzsche's teaching represented the interpretation of the popular Darwinism delivered with the fury and intensity of genius." And Nietzsche, be it remembered, denounced Christianity as the "doctrine of the degenerate," and democracy as "the refuge of weaklings."

Kidd says that Nietzsche gave Germany the doctrine of Darwin's efficient animal in the voice of his superman, and that Bernhardi and the military textbooks in due time gave Germany the doctrine of the superman translated into the national policy of the superstate aiming at world power (p. 67).

And what else but the spirit of evolution can account for the popularity of the selfish doctrine, "Each one for himself, and the devil take the hindmost," that threatens the very existence of the doctrine of brotherhood.

In 1900—twenty-five years ago—while an international peace congress was in session in Paris, the following editorial appeared in *L'Univers:* "The spirit of peace has fled the earth because evolution has taken possession of it. The plea for peace in the past years has been inspired by faith in the divine nature and the divine origin of man; men were then looked upon as children of one Father, and war, therefore, was fratricide. But now that men are looked upon as children of apes, what matters it whether they are slaughtered or not?"

When there is poison in the blood, no one knows on what part of the body it will break out, but we can be sure that it will continue to break out until the blood is purified. One of the leading universities of the South (I love the state too well to mention its name) publishes a monthly magazine entitled *Journal of Social Forces.* In the January issue of this year, a contributor has a lengthy article on "Sociology and Ethics," in the course of which he says: "No attempt will be made to take up the matter of good or evil of sexual intercourse among humans aside from the matter of conscious procreation, but as an historian, it might be worth while to ask the exponents of the impurity complex to explain the fact that, without exception, the great periods of cultural efflorescence have been those characterized by a large amount of freedom in sex-relations, and that those of the greatest cultural degradation and decline have been accompanied with greater sex repression and purity."

No one charges or suspects that all or any large percentage of the advocates of evolution sympathize with the loathsome application evolution to social life, but it is worthwhile to inquire why those in charge of a great institution of learning allow such filth to be poured out for the stirring of the passions of its students.

Just one more quotation: The *Southeastern Christian Advocate* of June 25, 1925, quotes five eminent college men of Great Britain as joining in an answer to the question, "Will civilization survive?" Their reply is that: "The greatest danger menacing our civilization is the abuse of the achievements of science. Mastery over the forces of nature has endowed the twentieth-century man with a power which he is not fit to exercise. Unless the development of morality catches up with the development of technique, humanity is bound to destroy itself."

Can any Christian remain indifferent? Science needs religion to direct its energies and to inspire with lofty purpose those who employ the forces that are unloosened by science. Evolution is at war with religion because religion is supernatural; it is, therefore, the relentless foe of Christianity, which is a revealed religion.

Let us then hear the conclusion of the whole matter. Science is a magnificent material force, but it is not a teacher of morals. It can perfect machinery, but it adds no moral restraints to protect society from the misuse of the machine. It can also build gigantic intellectual ships, but it constructs no moral rudders for the control of storm-tossed human vessels. It not only fails to supply the spiritual element needed but some of its unproven hypotheses rob the ship of its compass and thus endanger its cargo.

Science Has Made War More Terrible Than Ever

In war, science has proven itself an evil genius; it has made war more terrible than it ever was before. Man used to be content to slaughter his fellowmen on a single plane—the Earth's surface. Science has taught him to go down into the water and shoot up from below and go up into the clouds and shoot down from above, thus making the battlefield three times as bloody as it was before; but science does not teach brotherly love. Science has made war so hellish that civilization was about to commit suicide; and now we are told that newly discovered instruments of destruction will make the cruelties of the late war seem trivial in comparison with the cruelties of wars that may come in the future. If civilization is to be saved from the wreckage threatened by intelligence not consecrated by love, it must be saved by the moral code of the meek and lowly Nazarene. His teachings, and his teachings, alone, can solve the problems that vex the heart and perplex the world.

The world needs a Savior more than it ever did before, and there is only one Name under heaven given among men whereby we must be saved. It is this Name that evolution degrades, for, carried to its logical conclusion, it robs Christ of the glory of a virgin birth, of the majesty of his deity and mission, and of the triumph of his resurrection. It also disputes the doctrine of the atonement.

It is for the jury to determine whether this attack upon the Christian religion shall be permitted in the public schools of Tennessee by teachers employed by the state and paid out of the public treasury. This case is no longer local, the defendant ceases to play an important part. The case has assumed the proportions of a battle-royal between unbelief that attempts to speak through so-called science and the defenders of the Christian faith, speaking through the legislators of Tennessee. It is again a choice between God and Baal; it is also a renewal of the issue in Pilate's court. In that historic trial—the greatest in history—force, impersonated by Pilate, occupied the throne. Behind it was the Roman government, mistress of the world, and behind the Roman government were the legions of Rome. Before Pilate, stood Christ, the Apostle of Love. Force triumphed; and they nailed him to the tree and those who stood around mocked and jeered and said, "He is dead." But from that day the power of Caesar waned and the power of Christ increased. In a few centuries the Roman government was gone and its legions forgotten; while the crucified Lord has become the greatest fact in history and the growing figure of all time.

Again force and love meet face-to-face, and the question, "What shall I do with Jesus?" must be answered. A bloody, brutal doctrine—evolution—demands, as the rabble did nineteen hundred years ago, that he be crucified. That cannot be the answer of this jury representing a Christian state and sworn to uphold the laws of Tennessee. Your answer will be heard throughout the world; it is eagerly awaited by a praying multitude. If the law is nullified, there will be rejoicing wherever God is repudiated, the Savior scoffed at, and the Bible ridiculed. Every unbeliever of every kind and degree will be happy. If, on the other hand, the law is upheld and the religion of the schoolchildren protected, millions of Christians will call you blessed and, with hearts full of gratitude to God will sing again that grand old song of triumph:

> "Faith of our fathers, living still,
> In spite of dungeon, fire and sword;
> O how our hearts beat high with joy
> Whene'er we hear that glorious word—
> Faith of our fathers—holy faith;
> We will be true to thee till death!"

Chapter Notes

THESE KEY SOURCES include both background information and essential details for many stages of the Scopes story.

Impact: The Scopes Trial, William Jennings Bryan, and Issues That Keep Revolving, a wide-ranging and extremely valuable collection of essays and historical accounts edited by Richard M. Cornelius and Tom Davis (Dayton, Tenn.: Bryan College, 2000).

Summer for the Gods, the Pulitzer Prize-winning story of the Scopes trial by Edward J. Larson (Cambridge: Harvard University Press, 1997).

Center of the Storm, John T. Scopes's autobiographical memoir by Scopes and James Presley (New York: Holt Rinehart and Winston, 1967). Unless otherwise noted, quotes attributed to Scopes are from this source.

Six Days or Forever? a free-wheeling but noteworthy account of the trial by Ray Ginger (London: Oxford University Press, 1958).

World's Most Famous Court Trial, containing the full trial transcript plus written statements entered into the record and William Jennings Bryan's expansive closing argument, which he planned to publish after being denied the chance to deliver it in court (privately printed in Cincinnati by Hilleary & Metzger, 1925; reprinted 1990 by Bryan College, Dayton, Tennessee) Unless otherwise noted, all quotations of trial proceedings are from this source.

Unless noted otherwise, newspaper accounts are from International News Service and United Press reports, particularly July 12–28, 1925, when many newspapers carried several front-page stories each day about the trial. Quotations are as published in the *Nashville Banner*.

Equally important were the following interviews, described more fully in the acknowledgments:

Phillip E. Johnson, professor emeritus of Law, University of California at Berkeley, interviewed in Berkeley.

Richard M. Cornelius, professor of English and director of the Scopes Museum, Bryan College, Dayton, Tennessee, interviewed in Dayton.

Kurt P. Wise, associate professor of science and director of the Center for Origins Research and Education, Bryan College, Dayton, Tennessee, interviewed in Dayton.

Thomas Stewart Jr., son of the district attorney and lead prose-cutor, interviewed in Nashville.

Eloise Reed, a Dayton resident present for both of Bryan's appearances at the Southern Methodist Church and for Darrow's examination of Bryan on the witness stand, interviewed in Dayton.

Chapter 1. Desperate Dayton

3. Details of the explosions are from wire service reports as carried in the *Nashville Banner*, particularly "An Appalling Catastrophe" (12/21/1895, 1), and local reporting from the *Chattanooga News.* Background on the Dayton Coal and Iron Company comes from an author interview with Eloise Reed, whose father worked for the company, and *A History of Rhea County,* Bettye J. Broyles, compiler (Rhea County [Tennessee] Historical and Genealogical Society, 1991).

7. Details about mine locations were collected on author visits to the site.

8. Information about Rappelyea comes from *Six Days or Forever? Center of the Storm*, and interviews with Richard Cornelius and Mr. Thomas Stewart Jr.

Chapter 2. A City's Opportunity

10. ACLU history and biographical information on Roger Nash Baldwin from *Roger Nash Baldwin and the American Civil Liberties Union,* by Robert C. Cottrell (New York: Columbia University Press, 2000).

12. The account of Rappleyea seeing the ACLU notice, the drug store meeting, and the process that eventually led to the trial is assembled from those in *Summer for the Gods, Six Days or Forever? Center of the Storm,* Cornelius's essay "World's Most Famous Court Trial" in *Impact,* and the author interview with Mr. Stewart.

13. Details of Scopes's tennis game from an interview with Eloise Reed, whose brother was one of the foursome on the court.

14. Hunter, George William, *A Civic Biology* (New York: American Book Company, 1914); originally published 1909; the 1914 edition was in use the year Scopes taught in Dayton.

Chapter 3. An Orator's Opportunity

17. The principle source of background leading up to the trial is *Summer for the Gods,* with additional details from *Six Days or Forever? Center of the Storm,* and *Trials of the Monkey, an Accidental Memoir,* by Matthew Chapman, great-great grandson of Charles Darwin (New York: Picador USA, 2001).

18. Unless otherwise noted, Bryan speeches are quoted from *Selected Orations of William Jennings Bryan,* ed. R. M. Cornelius (Dayton, Tenn.: Bryan College, 2000).

Chapter 4. Anticipation

27. The story of Scopes coaching his students has appeared in *Six Days or Forever?* and elsewhere. Eloise Reed confirmed in an author interview that the boys were coached.

28. Scopes trips to NYC are described in numerous sources including *Center of the Storm, Summer for the Gods,* and *Roger Nash Baldwin.* The obvious difference in perspective between the two books produces different accounts of events. Additional information from *Roger Baldwin: Founder of the American Civil Liberties Union:*

A Portrait (Boston: Houghton Mifflin, 1976) and "The Reminiscences of Roger Nash Baldwin" from the Columbia University Oral History Collection, quoted by Cottrell.

31. "Man, 109, Holds Evolution Bunk," *Nashville Banner,* July 5, 1925, 9.

33. The claim that Scopes was afraid and went home to hide comes from an author interview with Thomas Stewart Jr.

Chapter 5. The Circus Begins

40. Unless otherwise noted, all H. L. Mencken quotations are from *The Impossible H. L. Mencken*, Marion Elizabeth Rodgers, ed. (New York: Doubleday, 1991).

43. Lawerence, Jerome, and Robert E. Lee, I*nherit the Wind.* New York: Bantam Books, 1955.

Chapter 7. Face-off

53. *New York Times* page-one article, "Darrow Scores Ignorance and Bigotry Seeking to Quash Scopes Indictment," July 14, 1925.

53. "Darrow v. Bryan," by Joseph Wood Crutch in *Nation*, July 29, 1925. Additional details in *Summer for the Gods.*

57. Judge Raulston's anger at news of his ruling on the motion to quash and account of the aftermath from an author interview with Mr. Stewart and *Center of the Storm.*

Chapter 8. In the Beginning

67. One of the best and most succinct sources of this background material is *The Creationists: The Evolution of Scientific Creationism*, by Ronald L. Numbers (New York: Alfred A. Knopf, 1992), from which the quotations here are taken.

Chapter 9. The Stakes

73. Cornelius G. Hunter, *Darwin's God: Evolution and the Problem of Evil.* Grand Rapids: Brazos Press, 2001.

Chapter 10. Back to the Trial

83. Material in this chapter is chiefly from the trial transcript, with further details from wire service reports as noted and *Center of the Storm.*

84. Weather information from "Hottest Weather in Years Reported," *Nashville Banner*, July 15, 1925, 3.

Chapter 11. Sparring Over Experts

92. This chapter is based on the trial transcript.

Chapter 12. Malone Tops Bryan

101. Material in this chapter is chiefly from the trial transcript.

103. "Eventful Hour of Scopes Trial," *Nashville Banner*, July 17, 1925, 1

106. "Bryan Defends Tennessee and Its Law," *New York Times*, July 17, 1925, 1

108. Raymond Clapper's newspaper dispatches appeared throughout the trial. This quotation is from the *Nashville Banner* of July 17, 1925.

109. Richard Cornelius declares that while Malone's presentation in court was wildly successful, its logic was not as compelling as it seemed.

Chapter 13. Heating Up

110. The chief source of information here is the trial transcript.

113. The rumor about running Mencken out of town appears in several sources, and was repeated by Mr. Stewart and Mrs. Reed in author interviews.

114. The description of Bryan's proposed trip to the Holy Land is from a brochure at the Bryan College archives.

Chapter 14. The Evolution War

120. *The Creationists* is a general reference for this historical background, see ch. 5 citation.

128. "How the Scopes Trial Changed Biology Textbooks," by Randy Moore, collected in *Impact.*

Chapter 15. Inherit the Wind

131. *Inherit the Wind*, see ch. 5 citation.

135. "A New Image of Bryan," *Life*, September 26, 1960, 77.

135. "New Films: The Monkey Trial," *Newsweek*, October 17, 1960, 114.

135. "The Current Cinema," *The New Yorker*, October 22, 1960.

136. Account of the Dayton premiere is from the author interview with Mrs. Reed.

136. Account of Tom Stewart's portrayal in the movie is from the author interview with his son.

137. "The Truth About *Inherit the Wind*" by Carol Iannone first appeared in *First Things*, February 1997; reprinted in *Impact.*

Chapter 16. Establishing Atheism

139. Darwin Centennial information and quotations from "Huxley at Chicago," *The Christian Century*, December 9, 1959, 1429 ff. and "Science v. Theology," *Time*, August 1, 1960, 45; additional information and insights from author interview with Phillip Johnson.

140. "The New Divinity," from *Essays of a Humanist* by Julian Huxley (New York: Harper & Row, 1964).

142. Historical background from *The Creationists.*

143. John C. Whitcomb Jr. and Henry M. Morris, *The Genesis Flood* (Philadelphia: Presbyterian and Reformed Publishing, 1961).

143. There are a vast number of press accounts and essays from the summer of 1963 on the issue of the Supreme Court ban on prayer in public schools. Among the most helpful to the authors were "ABC's on Prayers in School," *U.S. News & World Report*, July 1, 1963; and "Church and State," Newsweek, July 1, 1963.

144. "School Prayer's Bad Day in Court," *U.S. News & World Report*, June 17, 1985.

145. Dawkins, Richard, *The Blind Watchmaker: Why the evidence of evolution reveals a universe without design*. New York: W. W. Norton & Company, 1986.

Chapter 17. The Main Event

147. Chronology and secondary quotations about the weekend strategy session at the mansion are from the author interview with
Mr. Stewart and *Summer for the Gods.*

147. "Added Thrill Given Dayton," *Nashville Banner*, July 21, 1925. Here as in many papers around the country, news of Monday afternoon's surprise face-off between Bryan and Darrow was in the same Tuesday afternoon editions as the announcement of the guilty verdict, which had come down Tuesday morning. Thus, at least in the Tennessee capital, news of the Bryan-Darrow confrontation, arguably the most famous residual aspect of the trial, was shunted to page 2, overshadowed by the page-one story, "Jury Finds John T. Scopes Guilty," and its sidebars.

152. Audience reaction from author interview with Mrs. Reed, who attended the trial that day.

154. Richard Cornelius points out that one important reason Bryan didn't have a chance to shine as as brightly as he might have was that "he couldn't score points when only Darrow got to serve." The fact that Bryan was the witness forced him into a defensive posture.

157. Documents assessing the fine and costs are reproduced in *World's Most Famous Court Trial.*

Chapter 19. The Week After

167. "Darrow Quizzes Bryan," *Commercial Appeal*, July 21, 1925.

168. Darrow's "yap schoolteacher" comment appears in "World's Most Famous Court Trial," by R. M. Cornelius, in *Impact.*

170. The story of Bryan's visit to Winchester from author interview with Mr. Stewart.

173. Some accounts have visitors going inside the house to pay their last respects, but the contemporary wire stories report him lying in state on the front lawn. See "W. J. Bryan's Body to Lie in State," *Nashville Banner*, July 27, 1925, 1.

Chapter 20. Wrapping Up the Trial

174. Tom Stewart Jr. believed his father realized the judge was making a mistake but let it go knowing it would reverse the conviction. The trial transcript records a conversation between Stewart and Judge Raulston about the fine. Other Mencken and Darrow sources.

Chapter 21. Fighting the Religion of Evolution

182. Nancy Pearcey, *Total Truth* (Wheaton, Ill.: Crossway, 2004).

182. Dennett, Daniel, *Darwin's Dangerous Idea* (New York: Simon & Schuster, 1994).

183. General background from author interview with Phillip Johnson. Quotations of Johnson are from this interview unless otherwise noted.

184. Dawkins, Richard, *The Blind Watchmaker*, see ch. 16 notation.

187. Phillip E. Johnson, *Darwin on Trial.* Washington, D.C.: Regnery Gateway, 1991.

Chapter 22. Explaining Intelligent Design

192. Elaboration of Johnson's position is chiefly from author interviews supplemented by, and with secondary quotations from, *Darwin on Trial.*

193. George E. Webb, *The Evolution Controversy in America.* Lexington: University Press of Kentucky, 1994.

193. Richard Dawkins, *Unweaving the Rainbow: Science, Delusion and the Appetite for Wonder.* Boston: Houghton Mifflin Company, 1998.

194. Michael J. Behe, *Darwin's Black Box: The Biomechanical Challenge to Evolution.* New York: Free Press, 1996.

195. William A. Dembski, *Intelligent Design: The Bridge Between Science and Theology.* Dowers Grove, Ill.: InterVarsity Press, 1999.

202. The whole creation/evolution/intelligent design debate has been exhaustively documented on the Internet. Enter the name of any participant into a search engine and it will produce many listings and links offering both historical background and the latest news on the controversy. An excellent place to start is with the voluminous writings of Phillip E. Johnson on the Access Research Network at www.acr.org/documents/johnson. For historical background start with the Bryan College Web site at www.bryan.edu.

Chapter 23. Kansas, Ohio, Georgia, Tennessee

204. Kenneth R. Miller, *Finding Darwin's God: A Scientist's Search for Common Ground Between God and Evolution.* New York: HarperCollins, 1999.

211. Background and quotations (unless otherwise noted) from author interview with Kurt Wise.

212. Kurt P. Wise, *Faith, Form, and Time: What the Bible Teaches and Science Confirms about Creation and the Age of the Universe.* Nashville: Broadman & Holman, 2002.

213. Author interview with Phillip Johnson

Chapter 24. The Wedge

214. Phillip E. Johnson, *The Wedge of Truth: Splitting the Foundations of Naturalism.* Dowers Grove, Ill.: InterVarsity Press, 2000.

220. Author interview with Johnson.

220. *World* magazine, April 3, 2004.

Chapter 26. Surmounting Stereotypes

241. Richard Land with John Perry, *For Faith & Family: Changing America by Strengthening the Family.* Nashville: Broadman & Holman, 2002.

Acknowledgments

THIS BOOK IS the work of many hands. Thanks to David Shepherd, publisher at Broadman & Holman, for the original concept and for keeping it aloft through long years of discussion and development. Thanks also to executive editor Leonard G. Goss at B&H who first brought the authors together, cheered them on tirelessly, and steered the project confidently to its conclusion. John Landers has done his customarily masterful job of keeping us all on task and on time.

Our thanks and prayers are with Phillip Johnson, who so graciously spent an afternoon in his home answering questions about Intelligent Design while still recovering from a stroke, and who has since suffered a second.

Special thanks to Richard Cornelius of Bryan College, a living library of knowledge on the Scopes trial who has written widely on the subject, who generously shared his insights over several meetings and critiqued our manuscript; and to Kurt Wise of Bryan, whose views on both science and Christianity were an enlightening addition. Tom Davis offered valuable help in securing historical photos. Ira Flatow kindly allowed us to reprint the transcript of his *Science Friday* Scopes anniversary broadcast.

Two remarkable people brought us history in the flesh. Thomas Stewart Jr. vividly recalled his memories of Dayton, the trial, Bryan's enormous appetite, and other things only an eleven-year-old boy would remember. (Tom Jr. is worth a book of his own: he was the captain Patton sent to rescue the famous Lipizzaner horses of Vienna at the end of World War II, portrayed in the Disney film *Miracle of the White Stallions.)* Eloise Purser Reed, one of the last living witnesses to the trial and surely one of the most elegant and hospitable nonagenarians anywhere, painted a rich portrait of life in Dayton in 1925 as well as of the trial itself.

We have made every effort in the text and chapter notes to attribute ideas and quotations to their rightful owners. If we have erred or omitted it is out of ignorance and not malice.

Bibliography

"ABC's on Prayer in School," *U.S. News & World Report*, July 1, 1963, 41.

"Added Thrill Given Dayton," *Nashville Banner*, July 21, 1925, 2.

"An Appalling Catastrophe," *Nashville Banner*, December 21, 1895, 1.

"Away with a Manger," *New Republic*, October 31, 1983, 4.

"Balancing Act," *Newsweek*, July 1, 1963.

Behe, Michael J. *Darwin's Black Box: The Biomechanical Challenge to Evolution.* New York: Free Press, 1996.

"The Bible—Better in School Than in Court," *Life*, April 13, 1963.

Broyles, Bettye J., compiler. *A History of Rhea County.* Dayton, Tenn.: Rhea County [Tennessee] Historical and Genealogical Society, 1991.

"Bryan Defends Tennessee and Its Law," *New York Times*, July 17, 1925, 1.

Chapman, Matthew. *Trials of the Monkey: An Accidental Memoir.* New York: Picador USA, 2001.

"Church and State," *Newsweek*, July 1, 1963.

Cornelius, R. M., ed. *Selected Orations of William Jennings Bryan.* Dayton, Tenn.: Bryan College, 2000.

Cornelius, R. M. "Their Stage Drew All the World: A New Look at the Scopes Evolution Trial," reprinted from *Tennessee Historical Quarterly*, Summer 1981.

———. *Understanding William Jennings Bryan and the Scopes Trial: A Study Guide.* Dayton, Tenn.: Bryan College, 2001.

———. *William Jennings Bryan, the Scopes Trial, and Inherit the Wind.* Dayton, Tenn.: Bryan College, 2003.

Cornelius, Richard M., and Tom Davis, ed. *Impact: The Scopes Trial, William Jennings Bryan, and Issues That Keep Revolving.* Dayton, Tenn.: Bryan College, 2000. Essays include "State of Tennessee v. John Scopes," Donald F. Paine; "World's Most Famous Court Trial," Richard M. Cornelius; "The Scopes Trial and the Evolving Concept of Freedom," Edward J. Larson; "How the Scopes Trial Changed Biology Textbooks," Randy Moore; "The Truth About *Inherit the Wind*," Carol Iannone; "The Local Scoop on Scopes," Wayne Haston; "The Science Played Again," Kurt P. Wise; "Clarence Darrow: Legendary Lawyer of American History," Elmer Gertz; "William Jennings Bryan's Last Campaign," Stephen Jay Gould.

Cottrell, Robert C. *Roger Nash Baldwin and the American Civil Liberties Union.* New York: Columbia University Press, 2000.
"Creation Case Argued Before Supreme Court," *Science*, January 1987, 22ff.
"The Creation-Science Case: Is It Science or Religion?" *Christianity Today*, January 16, 1987.
Crutch, Joseph Wood, "Darrow v. Bryan," *Nation,* July 29, 1925.
"The Current Cinema," *New Yorker*, October 22, 1960.
"Darrow Scores Ignorance and Bigotry Seeking to Quash Scopes Indict-ment," *New York Times,* July 14, 1925, 1.
"Darrow Quizzes Bryan," *Commercial Appeal,* July 21, 1925.
Dawkins, Richard. *The Blind Watchmaker*. New York: Norton, 1986.
———. *Unweaving the Rainbow: Science, Delusion, and the Appetite for Wonder.* Boston: Houghton Mifflin, 1998.
Deloria, Vine, Jr. *Evolution, Creationism, and Other Modern Myths: A Critical Inquiry*. Golden, Colo.: Fulcrum, 2002.
Dembski, William A. *Intelligent Design: The Bridge Between Science and Theology.* Dowers Grove, Ill.: InterVarsity Press, 1999.
Dembski, William A. and James M. Kushiner, ed. *Signs of Intelligence: Understanding Intelligent Design*. Grand Rapids: Brazos Press, 2000.
Demmett, Daniel. *Darwin's Dangerous Idea*. New York: Simon & Schuster, 1994.
Denton, Michael. *Evolution: A Theory in Crisis*. Bethesda, Md.: Alder & Alder, 1986.
"Eventful Hour of Scopes Trial," *Nashville Banner,* July 17, 1925, 1.
Ginger, Ray. *Six Days or Forever? Tennessee v. John Thomas Scopes*. London: Oxford University Press, 1958.
"High Court: The Day God and Darwin Collided," *U.S. News & World Report*, June 29, 1987, 12.
"Hottest Weather in Years Reported," *Nashville Banner,* July 15, 1925, 3.
Hunter, Cornelius G. *Darwin's God: Evolution and the Problem of Evil*. Grand Rapids: Brazos Press, 2001.
Hunter, George William. *A Civic Biology*. New York: American Book Company, 1914.
"Huxley at Chicago," *Christian Century,* December 9, 1959, 1429 ff.
Huxley, Julian. "The New Divinity," from *Essays of a Humanist* (Chatto & Windus, 1964) www.update.uu.se/fbendz/library/jh_divin.htm.
Johnson, Phillip E. *Darwin on Trial*. Washington, D.C.: Regnery Gateway, 1991.
———. *The Wedge of Truth: Splitting the Foundations of Naturalism*. Downers Grove, Ill.: InterVarsity Press, 2000.
Kernan, Alvin. *In Plato's Cave*. New Haven: Yale University Press, 1999.
Land, Richard, with John Perry. *Changing America by Strengthening the Family.* Nashville: Broadman & Holman, 2002.
Larson, Edward J. *Summer for the Gods: The Scopes Trial and America's Continuing Debate over Science and Religion*. Cambridge: Harvard University Press, 1997.
Lawrence, Jerome, and Robert E. Lee, *Inherit the Wind*. New York: Bantam Books, 1955.
"Man, 109, Holds Evolution Bunk," *Nashville Banner,* July 5, 1925, 9.
Meland, Bernard Eugene. "Huxley at Chicago," *Christian Century*, December 9, 1959.
Mencken, H. L. *A Second Mencken Chrestomathy*. New York: Alfred A. Knopf, 1994.

Miller, Kenneth R. *Finding Darwin's God: A Scientist's Search for Common Ground Between God and Evolution*. New York: HarperCollins, 1999.

Morgan, W. C. "The Dayton Coal and Iron Company Limited," from *A History of Rhea County*, Bettye J. Broyles, compiler. Rhea County Historical and Genealogical Society, 1991.

Murray, Madalyn, letter published in *Life*, April 13, 1963.

"New Films: The Monkey Trial," *Newsweek*, October 17, 1960, 114.

"A New Image of Bryan," *Life*, September 26, 1960, 77.

"New-Time Religion?" *Time*, December 7, 1959, 88.

"Nobel Scientists File Brief Against Creationism," *Newsweek*,

Numbers, Ronald L. *The Creationists: The Evolution of Scientific Creationism*. New York: Alfred A. Knopf, 1992.

Pearcey, Nancy. *Total Truth*. Wheaton, Ill.: Crossway, 2004.

Pearcey, Nancy R., and Charles B. Thaxton. *The Soul of Science: Christian Faith and Natural Philosophy*. Wheaton: Crossway Books, 1994.

"Prayer in the Schools," *Newsweek*, June 17, 1985, 28.

Reeves, Albert W., *Rock of Ages or Age of Rocks*. Unpublished manuscript, 1999.

Rodgers, Marion Elizabeth, ed. *The Impossible H. L. Mencken*. New York: Doubleday, 1991.

"School Prayer's Bad Day in Court," *U.S. News & World Report*, June 17, 1985, 9.

"Science v. Theology, 1960," *Time*, August 1, 1960, 45.

Scopes, John T., and James Presley. *Center of the Storm: Memoirs of John T. Scopes*. New York: Holt Rinehart and Winston, 1967.

"Scopes 75th Anniversary Broadcast," *Science Friday*, National Public Radio, July 21, 2000.

Shideler, Emerson W. "Can Science and Theology Converse?" *Christian Century*, February 24, 1960.

Sissel, H. B., *Rev.* "The Fight Against School Prayer."

Staub, Dick. "The Dick Staub Interview: Phillip Johnson," *Christianty Today*, December 2, 2002.

"Supreme Court Abolishes Louisiana Creationism Law," *Publishers Weekly*, July 3, 1987.

"Supreme Court Questions Creationism Theory," *Publishers Weekly*, December 26, 1986.

"The View from 2025: How Design Beat Darwin," *World*, April 3, 2004.

"W. J. Bryan's Body to Lie in State," *Nashville Banner*, July 27, 1925, 1.

Webb, George E. *The Evolution Controversy in America*. Lexington, Ky.: University Press of Kentucky, 1994.

Whitcomb, John C., Jr., and Henry M. Morris. *The Genesis Flood*. Philadelphia: Presbyterian and Reformed Publishing, 1961.

Wise, Kurt P. *Faith, Form, and Time: What the Bible Teaches and Science Confirms about Creation and the Age of the Universe*. Nashville: Broadman & Holman, 2002.

World's Most Famous Court Trial: Tennessee Evolution Case. Cincinnati: Hilleary & Metzger, 1925; reprint, Dayton, Tenn.: Bryan College, 1990.

Index